Amish

Cooking

PATHWAY PUBLISHING CORPORATION

Aylmer, Ontario   LaGrange, Indiana

Foreword

The recipes in this book are taken from our cookbook "FAVORITE AMISH FAMILY RECIPES" and from the recipe pages of FAMILY LIFE magazine. These recipes come from many different places, mothers have tested them in family kitchens and submitted them as their family favorites. We wish we could use all the recipes we have received, but space does not permit us to do this. We have tried to select the most simple, nourishing, and time-saving recipes. Even so, many excellent recipes must go unprinted.

Since we are living in times when the dollar doesn't seem to go very far, we have tried to select recipes which are practical and economical. In this book you will find various kinds of mixes—cake, biscuit, pancake mixes— breakfast cereals, crackers, pretzels, soaps, lotions and shampoos. Most of these recipes are better and more economical than the store-bought ones. There is also a section of canning, meat preserving, and practical household hints.

Throughout the nine years since FAMILY LIFE was first published, mothers have clasped their hands across the many miles with other mothers in a common effort to help each other by submitting recipes, household hints, suggestions in cooking and housekeeping and words of encouragement in general. Most of these letters said, "Please don't print my name if you use this material." We think it would be nice if we could use these names under the items they sent in, but it would be impossible to get them now and to get permission to use them. So we have decided to omit all names, but our appreciation goes out to our many friends in the homes where these recipes have come from. Our wish is that they may all be benefitted by this cookbook which they have helped to make possible.   -Aunt Becky

BLESS THIS HOME

Bless this home, O Lord, we pray
Guard it safely night and day,
Bless the family living here
Bind them close with love and cheer.

Bless the food which is prepared
And each guest with whom it's shared.
Bless the children through the years
Guide them in their joys and tears.

Bless the mother — tender, kind
And the father by her side
Bless their pure and faithful love
Making home like heaven above.

Bless this Home, O Lord, we pray
Where we live and walk and play;
Bless us all that ever we
May live, O gracious Lord, with Thee.
                    Adapted by Ella May Miller

"Enable us to use Thy manifold blessings with modera-
tion. Grant our hearts wisdom to avoid excess in eating
and drinking and in the cares of this life. Teach us to put
our trust in Thee and to await Thy helping hand."
                    A Devoted Christian's Prayerbook

Table of Contents

Home Hints

Poems and Inspirations

I DON'T THINK THERE'S ANOTHER SECTION IN THIS cookbook that will be as interesting to the average mother as the bread section; bread is the most important item on the family table. At one time it seemed to have lost its honored title as the "staff of life" because of the refined ingredients that went into it. But in the past few years many mothers have been conscious of giving their family the very best in nutrition and have turned again to the use of whole wheat flours.

When Mother's children were small she knew very little of vitamins, minerals, or of watching calories. Her first concern was to have food on the table, even if at times it consisted of meager fare compared to some of today's meals.

During the cold days she would carry the dough tray into the living room and set it close by the side of the jacketless wood stove. Inside the tray was the usual jar of sourdough and standing on the floor nearby was the large sack of Redwing flour.

At that time many mothers did their baking in outdoor bake ovens. These were built of brick but were usually nicely white-washed with lime water on the outside. The ovens were approximately 8 feet long, 4 1/2 feet high and 4 feet wide. Fire was made on the inside shelf; then after the oven was heated the ashes were raked forward to an opening inside the small iron door where they fell to the bottom of the oven. A feather was held inside the oven to test the heat. If the feather singed too soon, the oven was too hot. A large amount of bread, pies, and cookies were baked in the oven at the same time. After they were taken out, dinner was put in.

A few of these ovens still exist in the Amish communities and some are still in good condition.

BREADS

DOUGHNUTS

ROLLS

MUFFINS

BUNS

GENERAL BREADMAKING
DIRECTIONS

After mixing ingredients as directed in recipe, grease hands and knead dough vigorously about five to ten minutes, or until dough squeaks. You may wish to turn dough out on floured table top for kneading. Place dough in greased bowl and grease top of dough. Cover and set in warm place, out of draft, and let rise till double. Knead lightly. Again grease bowl and top of dough and let rise until double. Repeat this procedure until dough has risen two or three times (whatever the recipe calls for).

Divide into given portions and form into loaves. Bang each loaf hard with the palm of the hand to get rid of air bubbles. Place into greased loaf pan with smooth side up. Brush grease over top of each loaf and prick deeply with fork to release air bubbles. Let rise until double in size. Bake as directed. Grease top of loaf again immediately after removing from oven. Remove from pans and cool on racks.

Sealing bread in plastic bags before it is completely cooled off will keep crust nice and soft.

TABLE OF EQUIVALENT MEASURES

1 stick (1/4 lb.) butter or margarine = 1/2 cup
1 square chocolate = 3 tablespoons cocoa
2 large eggs = 3 small eggs
1 cup macaroni = 2 1/4 cups cooked
1 cup buttermilk = 1 or 2 tablespoons vinegar with sweet milk
    to fill cup (let stand 5 minutes)
1 tablespoon quick-cooking tapioca = 1 tablespoon cornstarch or
    1 1/3 to 1 1/2 tablespoons flour
1 package active dry yeast = 1 tablespoon
1 package plain gelatin = 1 tablespoon
1 lb. granulated sugar = 2 cups
1 lb. brown sugar = 2 1/4 to 2 1/2 cups (packed)
1 lb. confectioners sugar = 4 to 4 1/2 cups (sifted)
1 lb. all-purpose flour = 4 cups
1 lb. butter = 2 cups

AYLMER BREAD

For each loaf use:
1 cup very warm water
1 tsp. melted lard or cooking oil
1 tsp. salt (scant)
1 tbsp. sugar
1 tsp. dry yeast
3 cups flour
(milk may be used as part of liquid, if desired)

Combine first five ingredients in order given. Let stand until yeast dissolves. Stir in half of flour, beat until smooth. Add remaining flour. Work dough on greased board or in bowl. Knead vigorously with both hands 5 to 10 minutes, or until the dough squeaks. Grease hands lightly if dough wants to stick while working. Cover. Set in warm place (out of draft) to rise until double. Knead lightly. Let rise again until double. Knead. Let rise again, punch down and divide into loaves. Brush grease over each loaf and prick deeply with fork. This is to release air bubbles. Let rise double size. Bake 30 minutes, or until done. 400° for 15 minutes, 350° remaining 15 minutes.

Grease top of loaf when removing from oven. Take out of pans and cool on racks.

For 8 loaves, use two rounded tbsp. yeast.

POTATO BREAD

1 medium sized potato
2 tbsp. butter
3 tsp. salt
1 cup warm water

1 quart water
2 pkgs. dry yeast
11 to 12 cups sifted flour
1/2 cup sugar

Cook the diced, peeled potato in the quart of water until tender. Drain the potato, reserving water. Mash potato until no lumps remain and add to the water. Stir in the butter and salt. Cool until lukewarm. Dissolve the yeast in the 1 cup warm water. Let stand 5 to 10 minutes. Add 6 cups flour gradually to the potato water, beating until smooth. Mix in the yeast. Beat thoroughly. Cover and let rise in a warm place about 2 hours. Then work in enough of remaining flour to make a soft dough. On a floured surface knead dough until smooth and satiny. Put dough into a greased bowl. Grease top of dough. Cover, then let rise until double, or about 1 1/2 hours. Punch down dough and divide into three portions. Form each portion into a loaf and place in a greased pan.

Cover, let rise until doubled, 30 to 40 minutes. Bake at 375° for 40 minutes. Let cool.

*FOR RAISIN BREAD add 1 lb. dark seedless raisins, 1/2 teaspoon cloves, and 2 teaspoons cinnamon after all the flour has been worked in. Also add 1/2 cup extra sugar. Frost with confectioner's sugar.

BEST WHOLE WHEAT BREAD

2 cups milk
1/3 cup sugar
1/3 cup shortening, plus 2 tbsp.
1 tbsp. salt
2 cups whole wheat flour

1 cup cold water
1 cup very warm water
3 tbsp. yeast
White flour

Scald milk. Add shortening, sugar and salt, stir till dissolved. Add whole wheat flour and beat rapidly with spoon. Add dissolved yeast and cold water. Mix well, then add enough white flour to make a nice soft dough. Let rise till double, punch down and turn over in greased bowl. Let rise until double again. Then shape into 3 loaves and spank real hard to take out all air bubbles. Cover for 15 minutes. Let rise until double, then bake at 350° for 50 to 60 minutes.

WHOLE WHEAT BREAD

1 cake yeast
1/4 cup lukewarm water
2 tbsp. sugar
1 tbsp. salt

3 1/4 cups sifted whole wheat
        flour
2 tbsp. cooking oil
2 cups milk, scalded
2 1/4 cups all-purpose flour

Crumble yeast into lukewarm water; add 1 teaspoon sugar. Stir will; let stand in warm place until foamy. Pour milk into mixing bowl; add remaining sugar and salt. Cool until lukewarm; add yeast. Add 3 cups whole wheat flour; beat thoroughly. Add shortening; stir in enough all purpose flour to make soft dough. Let dough stand 10 minutes. Turn on floured board. Knead 10 minutes, working in remaining whole wheat flour, until dough is soft but not sticky. Place in bowl and let rise. Knead. Shape into loaves. Let rise until double. Bake in hot oven (400°) 10 minutes, then reduce heat to 375°and bake 40 minutes longer. Makes 2 loaves.

BROWN BREAD

1 1/3 cup milk
1 1/4 cup honey
2 tbsp. salt
2/3 cup butter or corn oil

3 cups lukewarm water
2 tbsp. sugar (dissolved in water)
6 tbsp. cake yeast

   Pour water into large bowl, add sugar and yeast and let stand for 10 minutes without stirring.
   Scald milk; add honey, salt and melted butter. Set aside to cool. When cool add to yeast mixture and mix well. Stir in 5-6 cups whole wheat flour. Then add enough white (unbleached) flour to make soft dough. Knead 15 minutes or until smooth and elastic. This makes 6 medium-sized loaves.
(Brown sugar may be substituted for honey.)

HEALTH-CONSCIOUS HOUSEWIFE BREAD

1 qt. buttermilk, whey,
   or sweet milk
2 tbsp. brown sugar
1/2 tsp. salt
2 rounded tbsp. dry yeast

1 tbsp. dark molasses
2 cups stone ground whole
   wheat flour
2 cups rye flour
2 cups unbleached white flour
3/4 cup lard

   Mix all 3 flours in large bowl and have ready to use. Heat liquid to more then lukewarm, not hot. Pour into a large bowl. Then add sugar, molasses and salt. Stir well until dissolved. Melt yeast in 1 cup warm water. Add 1 teaspoon brown or white sugar to yeast. It rises faster. When yeast has dissolved and starts to rise, add to liquid mixture. Stir in enough flour mixture with large spoon to make a stiff batter. Then add 3/4 cup melted lard and beat dough smooth. Let dough rise for 12 minutes. This is very important to make a soft brown bread. After 12 minutes, add more flour to form a bread dough same as for white bread. If this is not enough flour, add more unbleached or white flour to finish. If there is flour left over, you can always store away till next batch. Bread made by this method never gets stiff and hard with age. Never bake bread in a too hot oven. 350° is about right, and bake for 1 hour. Of course oven thermometers vary.

OATMEAL BREAD

4 cups boiling water
1 cup whole wheat flour

4 tbsp. butter or oleo
2 pkgs. dry yeast

2 cups quick oatmeal   2 tbsp. salt
1/2 cup brown sugar   10 cups flour (approx.)

Pour the boiling water over the oatmeal, whole wheat flour, sugar, salt and butter. Cool until lukewarm. Dissolve yeast in 1 cup warm water. Add to batter. Add enough white flour to make elastic dough. Place in bowl and let rise. Punch down. Let rise again until double. Shape into four loaves. Let rise again till about double. Bake at 350° for at least 30 minutes or longer.

HONEY OATMEAL BREAD

2 1/2 cups boiling water   3/4 cup cooking oil
2 cups quick cooking oatmeal   4 beaten eggs
1 cup honey (or part Karo)   2 pkg. dry yeast
2 cups or more whole wheat flour 2 tbsp. salt

Dissolve yeast in 1 cup warm water. Pour boiling water over oatmeal and set aside to cool till lukewarm. Mix all ingredients and beat well, then add yeast, being sure everything is just warm before adding. Work in enough white flour (preferably unbleached) to make a nice spongy dough that is not sticky. Grease top and let rise; knead and let rise again. Bake at 400° for 10 minutes. Lower heat to 350° for 25 to 30 minutes— depending on the size of loaves. A delicious, nourishing bread.

RAISIN OATMEAL BATTER BREAD

1 pkg. active dry yeast   2 cups flour
2 cups warm water   2 cups whole wheat flour
1 1/2 tsp. salt   1 cup rolled oats
3 tablespoons sugar   1/2 cup seedless raisins
2 tbsp. soft shortening

Dissolve yeast in warm water in large mixing bowl. Stir in salt, sugar and shortening, plus 2 cups flour and oats. Beat for 3 minutes, then stir in rest of flour and raisins, mixing till smooth and satiny.

Cover with cloth and let rise in a warm place until double in size. Stir down while counting 15 slowly. Spoon into greased loaf pan. Cover with cloth. Let rise. Bake at 360° for 50 minutes.

DATE AND NUT BREAD

Pour 1 1/2 cups boiling water over 1 cup chopped pitted dates or raisins. Let stand 10 minutes. Add the following and beat well:

1 1/2 cups sugar
2 1/4 cups sifted flour
1/2 tsp. salt
2 tsp. soda
1 tbsp. melted shortening

1 beaten egg
1/2 tsp. baking powder
1/2 tsp. vanilla
1 cup chopped nuts

Bake in greased 10 x 5 x 3 loaf pan at 350° for 1 hour, 15 minutes or until done. You may like it best after it "ages" for a day or two, or from the freezer later on.

ORANGE NUT BREAD

Grated rind of 1 orange
1/2 cup water
1 tsp. salt
1/2 cup sugar
Juice of 1 orange
1 egg, beaten
1 cup sifted flour

Milk
1 cup whole wheat flour
2 tsp. baking powder
1/4 tsp. soda
1/4 cup shortening
1/2 cup chopped nuts

Combine orange rind, water, salt, and sugar and boil 10 minutes. Cool. Add milk to orange juice to make one cup, then add to cooled mixture. Sift flours with baking powder and soda. Cut in shortening until mixture is like meal. Pour liquids into dry ingredients and stir vigorously until well mixed. Add nuts and blend. Bake in loaf pan in moderate oven 50 to 60 minutes.

DELICIOUS PUMPKIN BREAD

1 2/3 cups sifted regular flour
1/4 tsp. baking powder
1 tsp. soda
3/4 tsp. salt
1/2 tsp. cinnamon
1/2 tsp. nutmeg
1 1/3 cup sugar

1/3 cup shortening
1/2 tsp. vanilla
2 eggs
1 cup mashed pumpkin
1/3 cup water
1/2 cup chopped walnuts
      or pecans

Grease a regular loaf pan (9 x 5 x 3 inches).

Sift together the flour, baking powder, soda, salt and spices. Cream shortening, sugar, and vanilla. Add eggs, one at a time, beating thoroughly after each addition. Stir in pumpkin. Stir in dry ingredients alternately with water, beating just until smooth. Do not overbeat. Fold in nuts. Turn batter into prepared pan. Bake at 350° for about 45 to 55 minutes or until done. Turn out on a wire rack and cool. Store in tight container. Slice and serve with butter.

HOMEMADE BREAD

1 1/2 cups lard in quart measure. Fill it 3/4 full with hot water to dissolve fat. Dissolve 2 tablespoons yeast in 1 pint lukewarm water. Add cold water to **lard until it is lukewarm.** In a dish put the following: 2 quarts flour, 4 teaspoons salt, 1 heaping cup brown sugar. Mix everything together, then continue adding flour until right consistency.

SWEET BUNS

3 cups lukewarm water   1 tbsp. lard
1 1/2 cups sugar   1 tbsp. salt
1 cake yeast

Mix all together until yeast is dissolved. Then stir in flour (about 8 cups) to make a fairly stiff dough. Let rise in warm place for 2 hours. Makes about 4 dozen.

CHELSEA BUNS

1 pkg. dry yeast   1/2 cup lukewarm water
1/2 cup cooled mashed potatoes 1 tsp. sugar
1/3 cup melted shortening   1/3 cup sugar
2 well-beaten eggs   1/2 tsp. salt
2 1/2 cups flour (approx.)

Combine potato, water and 1 tsp. sugar. Sprinkle yeast on top. Let stand until light. Add the rest, stirring in enough flour to make make a soft dough. (Not as stiff as bread dough.) Knead until smooth. Let rise until double in bulk.

2 tbsp. soft butter   1/4 cup corn syrup
3/4 cup brown sugar   1/2 tsp. vanilla
1/2 cup chopped nuts

Mix, all but nuts and spread in greased 9 x 13 pan. Sprinkle with nuts. Roll the dough into 9 x 15 rectangle.

1/4 cup soft butter   3/4 cup brown sugar
1 tbsp. cinnamon   1 cup washed raisins

Spread the butter on the dough and sprinkle with sugar, cinnamon and raisins. Roll up like jelly roll and cut into 15 one-inch slices. Place cut side down in pan. Cover. Let rise until buns fill the pan. Bake at 375° for about 40 minutes. Cool for 3 minutes then invert and **remove pan.** (Good when nuts are omitted and raisins are sprinkled in the bottom of pan. Good when both are omitted.)

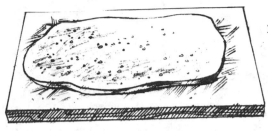

1. Roll a portion of the dough into a rectangle about 1/4 inch thick. Spread lightly with soft butter and sprinkle with sugar and cinnamon.

2. Roll up as you would for jelly roll.

3. To slice, slip a length of regular sewing thread under the roll, placing the thread to make slices about one inch thick.

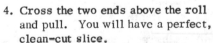

4. Cross the two ends above the roll and pull. You will have a perfect, clean-cut slice.

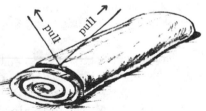

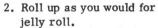

5. Place the slices, cut side down, on a greased cookie sheet or cake pan, about 1/2 inch apart.

PULL BUNS

Pluckets:

1 cup scalded milk
1/3 cup sugar
1/2 tsp. salt
About 3 3/4 cups flour

1 yeast cake dissolved in
  1/4 cup lukewarm water
1/3 cup melted butter
3 eggs, well beaten

Add the sugar, butter and salt to scalded milk. When lukewarm add dissolved yeast, eggs and just enough flour to make a stiff batter. Cover and let rise until mixture doubles in bulk. Knead down and let rise again. Roll small balls, about the size of walnuts, and dip them in melted butter. Then roll each ball in a mixture of 3/4 cup sugar, 1/2 cup ground nut meats and 3 teaspoons cinnamon. Pile balls loosely in an ungreased angel food cake pan and let rise again for 30 minutes. (Do not use pan with removeable bottom). Bake about 40 minutes beginning with 400° and decreasing after 10 minutes, to 350°. Bake until brown. Turn pan upside down and remove immediately. Serve warm. The buns will be stuck together and that's the way you serve them. Everyone plucks his bun right from the central supply. (If you want this for dinner, start it in the morning.)

COFFEE BUNS

Dissolve 1 pkg. dry yeast in 1/4 cup lukewarm water.
Mix like pie crumbs:
  4 cups bread flour
  1 cup shortening
  1/4 cup sugar

Add:
2 eggs
1 cup milk, scalded & cooled
1 tsp. salt
1/2 tsp. lemon extract

Make crumbs, then add remaining ingredients. Let rise in refrigerator overnight. Divide dough in 3 parts. Roll out, spread with melted butter, sprinkle with brown sugar and cinnamon. Slice very thin and then bake at 350 for 15 minutes or until brown. It is not necessary to let them rise again. Top with powdered sugar icing if preferred. Take 1 cup powdered sugar. Dissolve with a very small amount of hot water. Dribble over the hot buns.

RAISIN CINNAMON ROLLS

1/2 cup milk
1 1/2 tsp. salt
1/2 cup lukewarm water

1/2 cup gran. sugar
1/4 cup shortening
2 tsp. sugar

2 tbsp. dry yeast   2 beaten eggs
4 cups flour

   Scald milk, then add sugar, salt, and shortening. Cool to lukewarm. Sprinkle yeast over 1/2 cup lukewarm water in which 2
teaspoons sugar has been added. Let stand 10-15 minutes. Stir
and add to milk. Add the beaten eggs. Work in about 4 cups flour.
Cover and let rise until double in bulk. Divide the dough and roll
each half into 9 x 12 rectangle. Brush with melted butter. Sprinkle
each half with 1/2 of the following mixture: 1 cup brown sugar, 2
tablespoons cinnamon, 2/3 cup raisins.
   Roll up as for jelly roll. Cut in 1-inch slices and place on
greased pans. Cover and let rise until double in bulk. Bake at
350° about 35 minutes. Frost while warm.
Icing: 1 cup icing sugar   1/4 tsp. vanilla
     Enough milk to make a stiff icing.

QUICK YEAST ROLLS

2 tbsp. sugar   1 cake yeast or 1 pkg. granules
2 tbsp. shortening, melted   1 cup lukewarm water
       and cooled   3 1/4 cup sifted bread flour
1 1/2 tsp. salt

   Add sugar, shortening, salt and crumbled yeast to lukewarm
water; add 1 cup of the flour and beat with a rotary beater until
smooth. Mix in remaining flour. Place dough on slightly floured
board. Let rest about 5 minutes. Knead well until smooth then
place in greased bowl. Cover and let rise about 1 hour. Bake in
a hot oven 12 to 15 minutes. Makes 18 medium sized rolls.

BUTTERHORNS

1 cake yeast   1 cup lukewarm water
1/2 cup sugar   1/2 cup melted oleo
3 eggs, beaten   1 tsp. salt
4 1/2 to 5 cups sifted flour

   Blend yeast with 1 tablespoon of the sugar. Add beaten eggs and
rest of sugar. Add the rest of ingredients, then flour. Put in refrigerator overnight. Roll out like pie dough, cut in pie-wedge
shapes and roll up. After rolled up, dip in melted oleo. Let rise
3 hours and bake at 325° for 15 to 20 minutes. If you leave in refrigerator for awhile, punch down each day.

NO-KNEAD ROLLS

Scald 4 cups of milk. **Add 11 tbsp. margarine.** While still hot, mix 2 or 3 pkgs. cake yeast or 2 heaping tablespoons dry yeast and 1/3 cup sugar to 1 cup warm water. When milk has cooled to about 115° or to lukewarm, add 1 1/2 cup sugar, 5 beaten eggs, 2 teaspoons salt, and the yeast and water mixture. Add flour (1 1/2 cups or more for each cup of liquid). It should be soft enough to stir with a spoon. Let rise. Stir down and let rise again. Roll out on floured board. Butter well and sprinkle with cinnamon. Roll together and slice about 1 inch thick. Place on buttered cookie sheets or baking pans. Let rise until light and fluffy then bake in 350° oven for 15 to 20 minutes or until a nice golden brown. Frost when cool.

* The rolls may be dipped in melted margarine and rolled in the following mixture: 1 1/2 cups white sugar, 1 1/2 cups brown sugar, 2 tablespoons cinnamon and 1/2 cup nuts. Place on pans and let rise. Bake as above then remove from pans while still warm.

CORNMEAL ROLLS

1/3 cup corn meal	2 cups milk
1/2 cup sugar	2 eggs, beaten
1 tsp. salt	1 pkg. yeast
1/2 cup melted shortening	1/4 cup lukewarm water
4 cups flour	

Combine cornmeal, sugar, salt, shortening and milk in double boiler; cook until thick, stirring often. Cool to lukewarm; add eggs and yeast dissolved in water. Beat well. Let rise in greased bowl 2 hours. Add flour to form soft dough. Knead lightly; let rise in greased bowl 1 hour. Knead, roll out, cut with biscuit cutter. Brush with fat, crease, fold like Parkerhouse rolls. Place on oiled sheet; let rise 1 hour. Bake at 375° for 15 minutes. **Yields 3 dozen.** This makes a very soft dough. The rolls may be made in different shapes. Use flour generously when handling and shaping them.

WHOLE WHEAT MUFFINS

2 cups whole wheat flour	2 tbsp. sugar
4 tsp. baking powder	1 cup milk
1 tsp. salt	2 tbsp. lard

Mix flour, baking powder, salt and sugar. Stir in milk. Mix in melted shortening and beat well. Bake in muffin pans in a moderate oven. Makes 18 muffins. Chopped figs or dates may be added if desired. Bake at 425° for 20 to 25 minutes.

CORNMEAL MUFFINS

1 cup cornmeal	1 cup milk
1 cup flour	2 eggs
1/4 cup sugar	4 tbsp. melted butter or
1 tsp. salt	other shortening
4 tsp. baking powder	

Sift dry ingredients together. Add milk, eggs, and melted shortening. Stir quickly until dry ingredients are moistened. Bake in muffin tins about 20 minutes at 400°.

BLUEBERRY MUFFINS

2 tbsp. shortening	3 tsp. baking powder
2 tbsp. sugar	1/4 tsp. salt
1 egg	1 cup milk
2 cups flour	

Cream together shortening and sugar; add egg, flour, baking powder and milk. Mix thoroughly, then add 1 1/4 cups floured blueberries. Bake in tins 400° for 20 minutes.

BRAN MUFFINS

2 cups whole wheat flour	1 egg
1/2 cup brown or raw sugar	2 tsp. baking powder
3/4 cup sour milk or cream	1/2 tsp. soda
1/2 cup shortening or veg. oil	

Mix dry ingredients then add beaten egg, then the remaining ingredients. Mix quickly. Pour in muffin tins and bake. For varying tastes add nuts, raisins, dates, or bran from the mill. Can be eaten like shortcake with fruit, or like bread. Bake at 400-425° for 20 to 25 minutes.

BISCUITS SUPREME

2 cups flour	2 tsp. sugar
1/2 tsp. salt	1/2 cup shortening

4 tsp. baking powder	2/3 cup milk
1/2 tsp. cream of tartar	

Sift dry ingredients together. Cut in shortening until mixture resembles coarse crumbs. Add milk all at once and stir just until dough follows fork around bowl. Roll 1/2 inch thick. Cut with biscuit cutter. Place on ungreased cookie sheet. Bake in hot oven (450°) for 10 to 12 minutes.

SOUTHERN BISCUITS

2 cups flour	3 tsp. baking powder
4 tbsp. shortening	1 cup buttermilk
3/4 tsp. salt	1 tsp. soda

Sift flour and all dry ingredients, work shortening into flour. Add liquid to make soft dough. Roll out on a slightly floured board to thickness of 1/2 inch. Cut with biscuit cutter; put in greased pan. Bake in hot oven 425° for 15 minutes.

For cheese biscuits add 1 cup grated cheese to the mixture.

CREAM STICKS

2 pkgs. yeast dissolved in	2/3 cup sugar
1 cup warm water	2 eggs
1 cup scalded milk	1/2 tsp. salt
1/2 cup margarine	1 tsp. vanilla
	6 cups flour

Let dough rise till double in size; knead and form into sticks 3 1/2 x 1 1/2 in. Let rise again. Deep fat fry.
Filling: 3 tbsp. flour, 1 cup milk - cook together.
Cream: 1 cup sugar and 1 cup crisco. Add flour, milk mixture, and 1 tsp. vanilla; cream well; add 2 1/2 cups powdered sugar. Slit open top of cream sticks and fill. Frost with the following:

Frosting: 1/2 cup brown sugar
          4 tbsp. butter
          2 tbsp. milk
Mix and let come to a boil. Cool. Add powdered sugar and vanilla.

IDA MAE DOUGHNUTS

Add 1 1/2 package yeast to 2 cups water and 1 cup scalded milk (lukewarm) to which 1/2 cup sugar has been added. Let stand 15 minutes, then add:

3/4 cup cream

5 eggs, beaten

3/4 cup raisins, if desired

1/2 cup margarine or butter

1 cup sugar

1/2 tsp. salt

About 9 or 10 cups flour — enough to make a moderately stiff dough. Let rise, then roll out. Cut out doughnuts and let rise again.

Add several tablespoons vinegar to lard or cooking oil to keep the grease from soaking into the doughnuts. Heat and deep fry. Makes about 50 medium-sized doughnuts.

YEAST DOUGHNUTS

2 cakes yeast

1 cup scalded milk

1/4 lb. shortening

1 cup lukewarm water

2 tsp. salt

3 eggs

Sift flour (6 cups or more). Pour water over yeast and 1 table-spoon sugar. Stir and let stand. Meanwhile pour scalded milk in a bowl and add salt, 3 tablespoons sugar and then shortening. When lukewarm add water and yeast, and 3 cups flour. Beat until smooth and add beaten eggs and rest of flour. Let rise in a warm place until double. Roll, and then cut out and let rise again. Fry in hot grease. Makes about 75.

NO-FRY DOUGHNUTS

2 pkgs. active dry yeast

1/4 cup warm water

1 1/2 cup lukewarm milk

 (scalded, then cooled)

1/2 cup sugar

1 tsp. salt

1 tsp. nutmeg

1/4 tsp. cinnamon

2 eggs

1/3 cup shortening

4 1/2 cup flour

1/4 cup butter or oleo, melted

cinnamon sugar or sugar

In large mixing bowl, dissolve yeast in warm water. Add milk, sugar, salt, nutmeg, cinnamon, eggs, shortening and 2 cups of flour.

Blend 1/2 minute with egg beater, scraping bowl constantly. Beat hard for 2 minutes, scraping bowl occasionally. Stir in remaining flour until smooth, scraping side of bowl. Cover. Let rise in warm place until double (50 to 60 minutes.) Turn dough onto well-floured cloth-covered board; roll around lightly to coat with flour. (Dough will be soft to handle.) With floured covered rolling pin, gently roll dough about 1/2 in. thick. Cut with floured 2 1/2 inch doughnut cutter. Lift doughnuts carefully with spatula and place 2 in. apart on greased baking sheet. Brush doughnuts with melted butter. Cover; let rise until double about 20 minutes. Heat oven to 425° Bake 8 to 10 minutes or until golden in color. Immediately brush with melted butter and shake on cinnamon sugar or sugar. Makes 1 1/2 to 2 dozen doughnuts.

RUBY'S LONG JOHNS

1 1/2 pkgs. dry yeast
1/4 cup warm water
1/2 cup shortening
1 tsp. salt
2 beaten eggs

1/2 cup boiling water
1/3 cup sugar
1/2 cup milk
5 to 6 cups sifted flour

Dissolve yeast in warm water. Combine boiling water and shortening. Add sugar and salt. Stir until lukewarm. Blend in yeast, milk and eggs. Gradually stir in enough flour for easy handling. Knead until smooth. Place in greased bowl. Turn over to grease top. Cover. Let rise in a warm place until double (about 1 hour). Turn dough on floured surface. Roll to 1/2 inch thickness. Cut in strips, any size. Cover. Let rise to double (about 30 minutes). Deep fry at 375°. Drain on absorbent paper. Dip in thin glaze.

PUFFY STICKS

1 cup boiling water
1/4 cup shortening
1/2 cup sugar
1 tsp. salt

1 cup milk
1 cake yeast
2 eggs
8 cups flour

Pour boiling water on shortening, sugar and salt. Add milk. When lukewarm add yeast cake which has been dissolved in 1/2 cup of lukewarm water. Add beaten eggs and about half the flour. Beat vigorously. Add remaining flour to make a soft dough. Place in greased bowl and cover and keep in ice box until ready to use. Then take part of dough, roll to about 1/4 in. thick. Cut in oblong pieces with a knife and fry in deep fat (400°–425°) and serve. Put rest of dough in ice box to keep for another day.

CREAM PUFFS

1/2 cup butter
1 cup boiling water

1/4 tsp. salt
4 eggs

1 cup sifted all-purpose flour

1. Melt butter in boiling water.
2. Add flour and salt at same time, stir vigorously. Cool, stirring constantly until the mixture forms a ball that doesn't separate.
3. Add eggs one at a time, beating hard after each addition until mixture is smooth.
4. Form cream puffs 2 1/2" in diameter and place 2" apart on greased cookie sheets. Bake at 450° for 15 minutes or 325° for 25 minutes.
5. Remove from sheet and cool on a wire rack.
6. When cream puffs are cold, cut a hole in the side of each. Fill cream puff with sweetened whipped cream or vanilla sauce. Makes 12 puffs.

BREAD HINTS

* Some recipes call for cake yeast and others for dried yeast. This is interchangeable. One package yeast is the same as one cake yeast, If bulk yeast is used, 1 tablespoon yeast is used for one package.

* Adding a little sugar to the liquid used to dissolve the yeast will make it more active.

* All milk used in bread recipes should be scalded then cooled to lukewarm before using.

* For many bread and roll recipes, the steps may be simplified if all the liquid, the sugar, salt and even the shortening is put into a bowl and the yeast sprinkled or crumbled in to dissolve it. When yeast is dissolved or becomes bubbly, add the rest of the ingredients as the various recipes call for.

* Always have flour, when making bread or rolls, at room temperature before mixing. This will help keep the dough at a warm temperature and encourages it to rise.

* Always use All Purpose flour with any recipe that calls for yeast. This flour is made from hard wheat. To many people this is simply known as bread flour. Some common brands are Pillsbury, Gold Medal, and Robin Hood. Use your own desired brand.

*   If your bread loaves get flat instead of nice and round, try making a stiffer dough.

*   For a finer textured bread, try letting dough rise in a place where it's a little cooler.

*   Using milk instead of other liquid usually gives a softer crust which becomes a richer brown when baked.

*   People who bake regularly will not need to grease bread pans before baking if:

>   (a) You do not wash pans between bakings.
>   (b) You work out loaves with greased hands.
>   (c) New or cleaned pans are seasoned by greasing well for a few bakings and set aside without washing.

    Bread will easily slip out of pans, leaving them clean and ready for the next time.

*   For best results with bread, have the water very warm (but not hot)- 115°.
*   Using part milk instead of water, assures a browner crust.
*   For extra flavor in your homemade bread, use cooking oil instead of lard.
*   Bread is better when worked down twice, or oftener.
*   If bread is baked before it rises to double size, it will not crumble so easily.
*   Replace 1/8th of your water with vinegar in your bread recipe if you do not make the dough too stiff. Dough should be sticky and you have to use shortening on your hands to work the dough.
*   Grease the top of your bread when taking it from the oven. This will make the crust softer.

*   You can add whole wheat flour to any bread recipe if you do not make the dough too stiff. Dough should be sticky and you have to use shortening on your hands to work the dough.

SOUPS

I WAS TEN YEARS OLD WHEN I ENTERED MOTHER'S school of cooking. Before going out to milk, she would always explain how everything should be made. In the morning we would at times have tomato gravy with our fried leftover potatoes. "Take one big spoon of flour and pile it real full," she would say. "Add a pinch of salt; then pour only a bit of milk on it at a time so it won't get lumpy..."

I was impressed by Mother's knowledge. Why, she could tell exactly how much flour to use and whether I should use milk or water, sugar or salt, and she didn't even need a recipe book!

In the evening a lid would be taken off the stove and the little black, iron, mush pot would be inserted so as to catch the full heat of the flames. Corn mush, soup, or potatoes were cooked in this little pot. But how we hated to wash that kettle! When we put it into our dishpan, the black soot would float on top of the water. I felt the world made great progress when stainless steel came into being. Even so, I still think food tasted best when made in the lowly iron kettle on a woodstove. Maybe the flavor is enhanced by the memory that goes with it!

Corn mush and soups were the main items on the supper table at that time, and in many Amish homes it still is today. In the evening when Mother is tired from a long day's work, there's nothing quite as simple as making a dish of hot, nourishing soup for supper.

CHILLY DAY STEW

Into a kettle of rapidly boiling water, chop 1 large carrot. While it is cooking, clean and chop 3 onions. Add them to the stew kettle. **Prepare** 1 quart potatoes, peeled and diced. Add this to the mixture; also 2 tablespoons rice and 2 tablespoons macaroni, 1 teaspoon salt and water to cover. Cook slowly until tender. When ready to serve, add 1 pint cream or substitute butter and milk. Let mix thoroughly, but do not boil again. Serve with crackers or hot toast.

OLD-FASHIONED BEAN SOUP AND HAM

1 lb. navy beans	1 medium onion, chopped
3 qt. water	3 carrots, sliced
1 ham bone (or bacon)	1 tbsp. salt
1/2 cup chopped green pepper	1/4 tsp. pepper
1 cup celery, chopped	1 cup tomato juice
2 cups diced potatoes	

Simmer beans in water with the ham bone for 2 hours. Add other ingredients and simmer 2 hours longer or until the beans are tender. (Cut down cooking time of the beans by soaking them first before boiling.)

HAM SOUP

4 cups ham (cubed)	4 medium sized potatoes
3/4 cup onion	3 qts. milk
large handful of noodles	

Combine ham and onions. Cook until ham is soft and brown. Cut potatoes in small cubes. Add a little salt and cook until soft. Cook noodles in salt water until soft; drain. Add to ham. Also add the milk. Bring to a boil. Add salt and pepper. Serve with crackers.

SPLIT PEA SOUP

1 cup dried split peas	3 tbsp. butter
1 ham bone	3 tbsp. flour
3 qts. water	1 tsp. salt
1 tbsp. minced onion	2 cups milk

Soak peas in water overnight. Drain in morning and cover with 3 quarts water. Add ham bone and onion and cook until soft. Melt butter and stir in flour until well blended and smooth. Add salt, pepper and milk and cook, stirring constantly until mixture thickens. Combine with the peas and ham and cook until rather thick.

CREAM OF PEA SOUP

1 qt. peas	3 cups milk
1 cup cubed ham	1 tsp. salt
1/2 cup ham broth	1 tbsp. sugar

Cook peas and put through a strainer; reserving the water in which peas were cooked. Brown and cook ham until tender. Combine all ingredients and the water. Bring to a boil. If desired, add 1/2 cup cream before serving. Serve with crackers.

CORN SOUP

1 1/2 cups creamed corn	1 tbsp. sugar
3 pts. milk	2 eggs, well beaten
1 tsp. salt	2 tbsp. butter

Combine milk, corn, salt and sugar. Boil together for a few minutes. Add the well beaten eggs. (Do not stir.) Boil a little longer; then beat lightly. Add butter. Serve with crackers.

CREAM OF CORN SOUP

2 cups water	1 tbsp. onion, chopped
2 cups canned corn	2 tbsp. butter
1/2 cup celery, chopped	2 tbsp. flour
1/2 cup parsley, chopped	1 tsp. salt
2 cups milk	1/8 tsp. pepper

Add corn, celery and parsley to boiling water. Cover and simmer 20 minutes. Strain. Scald milk and onions and add to strained corn stock. Melt butter and add to flour. Add to combined liquid. Season and heat to boiling point.

ONION TOMATO SOUP

(Saute -- means cook in butter or margarine until tender but not brown)

Saute about **half of a medium-sized onion, cut up and some dried or** fresh celery leaves in **4 tbsp. oleo.**   When onion is tender, stir in about 1/2 cup flour. Stir until flour is slightly browned, then slowly add tomato juice, stirring to smooth the lumps, until about the thickness of gravy. Add some water, sugar and red pepper or paprika and salt. Suit your own taste. Before serving add some cream or milk.

BACON BEAN SOUP

1 lb. bacon ends (cut up in small pieces. Do not fry.)
1 lb. navy beans
1 chopped onion
About 4 quarts of water and salt and pepper to taste.

Boil slowly for about 2 hours. Very good for those cold winter evenings. Bacon ends at the store are inexpensive and have more smoke flavor and meat. Eat with crackers.

DELICIOUS BEAN SOUP

1 lb. (2 cups) navy beans, dried   1 cup finely chopped onion
1 meaty ham bone (1 1/2 lb.)   1 clove garlic
1 cup cubed potato   1 cup cubed carrots
1 cup thinly sliced celery   1 small bay leaf

Cook beans in 2 1/2 quarts of water for 2 minutes. Remove from heat; let stand 1 hour. Add ham bone, minced garlic, and bay leaf to beans. Cover and simmer 2 hours or until almost tender. Add vegetables, salt and pepper to taste; simmer 1 hour more. Remove ham bone and cut off meat. Dice meat and add to beans. Reheat to almost boiling. Remove bay leaf.

AMISH BEAN SOUP

Brown 2 or 3 tablespoons butter in a saucepan. Add 1 cup cooked beans and 1/4 cup water. Bring to the boiling point, then add about 3 quarts milk, salt and pepper to taste; allspice if desired. Boil, then remove from stove. Add about 2 quarts stale, thinly sliced bread, or enough to thicken. Cover and let stand about 1/2 hour before serving. Serve with pickled red beets or pickles.

Variations: Instead of beans use diced potatoes.
* For egg soup add about 6 or 8 diced hardboiled eggs with the bread crumbs, omitting the beans.

YANKEE BEAN SOUP

1 1/4 cups dried navy beans
5 cups water
1/2 tsp. salt
1 tsp. molasses
1/2 cup salt pork, cut in 1/4 inch cubes
1/3 cup onion rings
3 slices bacon, cut in pieces
1/4 cup chopped onion
1/2 cup diced cooked carrots
1/3 cup finely chopped celery leaves
1 tsp. molasses
2 cups milk
salt to taste

Place beans in 3-4 quart sauce pan. Add water. Boil; remove from heat. Let stand 2 hours or overnight. Add 1/2 teaspoon salt, 1 teaspoon molasses, pork and onions. Cover and simmer 2 hours or until beans are tender. Shake pan occasionally to prevent sticking. Cook bacon and chopped onion until bacon is lightly browned. Mash beans slightly. Add bacon and the remaining ingredients. Simmer 10 minutes.

POTATO CREAM SOUP

2 cups raw potatoes, diced	3 1/2 tbsp. flour
2 stalks celery, diced or 2	1 1/2 tsp. salt
tbsp. dried celery leaves	1 tbsp. butter
2 onions, minced	2 cups milk
2 1/2 cups water	1/4 tsp. pepper

Cook potatoes, onion and celery in boiling water. Melt butter in double boiler. Add flour, then milk and seasoning. Cook until mixture is thick and smooth. Rub the potato mixture through a sieve. Add the white sauce. Garnish with parsley to serve.
Variation:
* This soup may also be made with just milk instead of sauce. Serve with crackers.

* 1 cup noodles may be used instead of the potatoes and sauce. Bring milk to a boil and cook until noodles are soft. Combine all ingredients. Let stand a short while before serving.

* Chopped hardboiled eggs may also be added.

CABBAGE CHOWDER

4 cups coarsely shredded	1 tbsp. salt
cabbage	1/2 tsp. sugar
2 cups sliced carrots	1/4 tsp. pepper
3 cups diced potatoes	4 cups scalded milk
3 cups water	2 tbsp. butter

Cook vegetables and seasonings in water until tender. Add the scalded milk and butter. Serve with crackers.

CREAM OF CHICKEN SOUP

Make a medium white sauce. Add a little bit of chopped onion, some peas, diced carrots, cooked, diced potatoes, chopped chicken meat, a pinch of sugar, salt and pepper to taste.

* The above may be used as a casserole. Just add more vegetables, a thicker sauce and top with biscuits. Bake.

QUICK LUNCH

Saute about 1/2 onion, diced, in some margarine until golden. Add: 1 pint sweet corn and 1 pint tomato juice. Add: salt, pepper, and small amount of brown sugar to taste. Bring to a boil then break an egg for each person into the boiling mixture. Cover and cook about 3 to 4 minutes - until eggs are soft boiled. When using more than 6 eggs, double the amount of corn, tomatoes, and onion. Children enjoy dipping bread or toast into the egg yolk then cut up the remaining egg white and eat it with the soup. This is also good with crackers.

RIVVEL SOUP

1 cup flour	1 egg
1/2 tsp. salt	

Mix salt with flour, then toss egg lightly through flour with fork until small crumbs form. Stir into 1 quart of scalding whole milk. Bring to a boil and serve at once.

POTATO RIVVEL SOUP

1 medium sized onion, chopped
5 medium potatoes, diced
salt and pepper

Cook in a little water until the potatoes are soft. To make rivvels take two beaten eggs and 1 teaspoon salt. Add flour and toss and stir until lumpy and sort of dry. Sift excess flour out of rivvels, then dump rivvels into the potato mixture and boil 5 minutes.
Add: 1/2 cup butter, 1/8 tsp. celery seed, 1 to 1 1/2 qt. milk, a pinch of parsley. Heat and serve.

This is good for those cold winter evenings.

FRENCH ONION SOUP

Melt 1/4 cup butter or oleo in large pan. Add 3 large onions, sliced. Fry slowly till soft and golden. Add 1 quart beef broth and 1 quart water and 1 teaspoon worcestershire sauce. Season with salt and pepper. Serves 6 to 8. (Stir onions occasionally while frying.)
Special touch: Just before serving, slice in a couple weiners.
Serve with cheese crackers. For richer soup, add a couple beef bouillon cubes.

WIENER SOUP

1 1/2 qt. milk   1 tsp. salt
1/2 lb. wieners (sliced)   2 tbsp. butter
noodles, a handful

Cook noodles until tender. Heat milk, add wieners, salt and noodles and boil together. Add butter. Serve with crackers.

WINTER VEGETABLE SOUP

1 qt. beef broth or 1 soup bone   1 pt. corn
1 pt. celery   1 pt. green beans
1 pt. carrots   1 cup soup beans
1 pt. cabbage   1 pt. lima beans
1 pt. peas   1 pt. tomatoes
2 tbsp. salt   water

Chop celery, carrots, cabbage, and green beans (medium fine). Combine with the other ingredients. Cook for 2 1/2 to 3 hours. Add 1/2 cup rice 15 minutes before serving.

VEGETABLE SOUP

1 large soup bone or
   ribs of beef
2 cups diced potatoes
2 large onions
1 cup shredded cabbage
1 can tomatoes or
   4 ripe tomatoes
3 large carrots
Parsley leaves

1/2 stalk celery
1/2 can whole corn or
   4 ears of corn
1/2 pt. string beans, cut fine
1 cup limas
1/8 cup rice
1/4 cup barley
1 green & 1 red pepper
water

Cook soup bone or meat until half done. Add raw vegetables and **cook 1/2 hour, then add cooked vegetables and cook until all ingredi**ents are well done. If rice or barley are used, cook separately or put in kettle when meat is placed on stove.

HEARTY HAMBURGER SOUP

2 tbsp. butter
1 cup chopped onion
1 cup sliced carrot
1/2 cup chopped green pepper
1 lb. ground beef
2 cups tomato juice

1 cup diced potatoes
1 1/2 tsp. salt
1 tsp. seasoned salt
1/8 tsp. pepper
1/3 cup flour
4 cups milk

Melt butter in saucepan; brown meat; add onion and cook till transparent. Stir in remaining ingredients except flour and milk. Cover and cook over low heat until vegetables are tender - about 20 to 25 minutes. Combine flour with 1 cup of the milk. Stir into soup mixture. Boil. Add remaining milk and heat, stirring frequently. Do not boil after adding remaining milk. This makes quite a large amount.

This recipe can be adapted to your family's taste. I always substitute celery for the green pepper. Instead of the 4 cups milk I use 1 to 1 1/2 cups skim milk powder and less flour.

SUCCOTASH CHOWDER

1 large onion, chopped
3 tbsp. butter
1 cup fresh or canned corn
1 cup fresh or canned
   lima beans
2 cups potatoes, diced
1 cup water

1 tsp. salt
1/4 tsp. pepper
1 tsp. parsley, chopped
3 cups milk
2 tbsp. flour
1/4 cup water

Saute onion in butter in pressure cooker until slightly browned. Add vegetables, water, salt and pepper. Cover. Set control. After the control jiggles, cook for 2 minutes, reduce pressure instantly. Add milk to vegetables and heat to boiling. Blend flour with water to make a smooth paste. Add to soup and cook one minute, stirring constantly. Garnish servings with chopped parsley.

SALMON SOUP

Brown 2 or 3 tablespoons butter in a saucepan. Add about 3 quarts milk, salt and pepper to taste. When it begins to boil, add 1 can salmon, chopped. Heat and serve with crackers or toasted bread cubes.

OYSTER STEW

3 pt. milk   1 tbsp. salt (scant)
1 pt. water

Bring to a boil. Let boil a few minutes. Add a (10 oz.) can oysters or **amount desired.** Keep over heat for a few minutes but do not boil, then reduce heat and let stand till oysters come to the top. Then use low heat 5 or 10 minutes longer or until oysters disappear from the top. Add 3 tablespoons butter. Serve with crackers.

CHILI SOUP

1 lb. ground beef   1 small can kidney beans
2 tbsp. shortening   and liquid
2 onions, minced   2 tsp. salt
1/2 green pepper   1 tsp. chili powder
1 small can tomatoes or tomato soup

Brown beef in shortening, add onions and diced pepper. Brown lightly. Stir in tomatoes, kidney beans, salt and chili powder. Simmer 1 hour.

VEGETABLE OYSTER SOUP (Salisfy)

Scrape the salisfy clean then slice thin (about 1 or 2 cups, according to family size). Cook in water until tender. Add milk, salt and pepper to taste and a chunk of butter. Bring to the boiling point. Serve over crackers. A few dried parsley or celery leaves may be added.

VEGETABLE AND

CASSEROLE DISHES

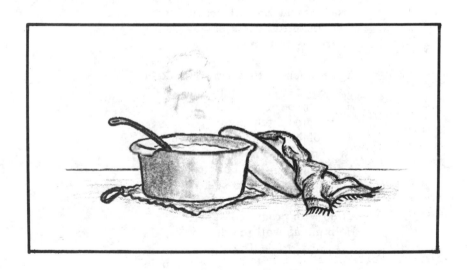

KITCHEN PRAYER

Dear Lord, before I start this day
  of tasks that it will bring
May I refresh my soul right here
  where pots and kettles sing.
This is my "realm" where I perform
  the work I best can do
And here I always seem to feel
  especially near to You.

For you have planned in this small room
  such homely tasks for me
That I can do them easily
  and keep my mind on Thee.
The writings of the Holy Book,
  the lessons they all teach,
I've but to live them day by day
  serenity to reach.

Again when twilight time has come
  give me a short time, too,
Here, through the deepening shadows,
  my tidied kitchen view.
And solace find in simple things
  accomplished here by me--
A flaky pie, a loaf of bread,
  my family's joy to see.
The things that in this little home
  I do with practiced skill,
Help me as well in other ways,
  O Lord, to do Thy will.

                Harriet Elmbald

BAKED BEANS

Soak 2 lbs. beans in water overnight. Cook until almost soft; drain. Add:
1 lb. bacon (cut in pieces)
Salt and pepper to taste
1 cup brown sugar
1 qt. tomato juice

If more liquid is needed, add some water. Bake in oven at 325° for 3 or 4 hours.

INDIANA BAKED BEANS

2 1/2 qt. dried navy beans (4 lb.) 3 1/2 tsp. prepared mustard
4 qt. water   2 cups ketchup
3/4 cup brown sugar   1 cup molasses
2 tbsp. salt   1 large onion (2 1/2 to 3" dia.)

Soak beans in large kettle overnight. Simmer about one hour in water in which they soaked. Mix together: sugar, salt, ketchup, molasses, and mustard. Add to beans. Lay onion on top. Bake covered in a slow oven, 300° for 5 hours. Add boiling water during cooking if necessary to keep beans from becoming dry. Remove the onion before serving or canning them.

BOSTON BAKED BEANS

2 cups small dried beans   3 tbsp. good brown bacon
2 tsp. salt   drippings
1/8 tsp. pepper   1 tsp. prepared mustard
1/2 cup brown sugar   2 cups tomato juice
1/2 cup minced onion   2 cups water or juice
                               from cooking beans

Soak beans overnight and cook until tender. Cubed ham may be added if desired. Combine all ingredients. Bake in a slow oven 325° for 6 to 8 hours or longer until beans are colored and tender. Add more water as necessary.
Variation: 1/4 cup brown sugar and 1/2 cup molasses instead of 1/2 cup brown sugar.

CANNED STRING BEAN DISHES

* Make layers of string beans and onion rings. Add mushroom soup. (Soup may be diluted with a little milk.) Top with bread crumbs. Bake. (Toasted bread crumbs may substitute for

onion rings.)

* Put in layers in baking dish with 5 or 6 cut up wieners. Add 1 can mushroom soup. Bake at 350° until soup bubbles.
* Fry or cook a few cut up raw onions into the beans with bacon chips sprinkled over the top.
* Dried bread crumbs browned in butter may be added to cooked green beans just before serving. This adds a delicious touch to an ordinary dish.
* Fry with flour, minus liquid. Before serving add a bit of celery seasoning and fried chicken seasoning, or any other seasoning with herbs. Adding leftover meat, cut fine, is also good.
* 1 can soup = 1 1/4 cups

FRIED OYSTER PLANT

Clean oyster plant. Cook in salt water until soft.
Dip in beaten eggs; roll in fine cracker crumbs and fry in butter until nicely browned on both sides.

FRIED CUCUMBERS

Beat 1 egg and add 1 cup milk. Peel and slice 2 or 3 cucumbers. Dip in about 2 cups cracker crumbs. Lay out to dry a little, then dip in egg-and-milk mixture and then again in cracker crumbs and fry. Sprinkle with salt to taste. Fry in butter or vegetable oil.

FRIED EGG PLANT

Pare 1/2 of an egg plant and slice 1/2 of an inch thick. Beat an egg with 1/4 cup milk. Dip the egg plant in egg, then in fine cracker crumbs. Fry in Crisco and butter, (half and half) until nicely browned. Do not fry too fast.

BAKED SWEET POTATOES

Put 4 cups cooked, salted and diced sweet potatoes in a greased casserole.
Add:
  1 cup brown sugar   1/2 cup cream
  1 tsp. flour

Bake at 350° 20 to 30 minutes or until sticky. Cover the top with small marshmallow bits and brown lightly until they begin to melt.

Most youngsters who turn up their noses at carrots, will love this.

BAKED CARROTS

2 1/2 cups cooked, mashed carrots
1 tbsp. onion, minced
1 tsp. salt
dash of pepper
3 eggs, separated

1/2 cup minced celery
1 cup bread crumbs
2 cups milk
2 tbsp. butter

Cook onions in butter till soft; add to carrots. Add beaten egg yolks, milk, celery, seasoning and bread crumbs. Beat egg whites and fold in. Place in greased baking dish and bake at 350° for 40 minutes.

SCALLOPED CARROTS

12 carrots
4 tbsp. butter
4 tbsp. flour
2 cups milk
1 diced onion
1/4 tsp. salt

1/4 tsp. celery salt
1/2 cup diced velveeta cheese
1 tsp. mustard
1/8 tsp. pepper
crushed potato chips

Slice carrots. Cook until tender but not too soft. Make white sauce with the butter, flour and milk. Add onion, salt, pepper, mustard and cheese. Pour carrots into casserole. Top with crushed potato chips. Bake at 350° for 45 minutes.

SCALLOPED CORN

1 qt. canned corn
2 eggs, beaten
salt and pepper to taste

1 cup cracker crumbs
1/2 cup milk

Put corn and cracker crumbs in layers in a casserole. Keep a few cracker crumbs for top. Mix eggs, milk and seasoning and pour over the corn. Add more milk, until corn is covered. Top with crumbs. Bake at 350° for 20 minutes or until brown. (For variation chopped onions may be added.)

* This scalloped corn may be made on the burner on top of the stove. Simply put all ingredients in a heavy saucepan and stir briskly with a fork. Set on low heat and heat until corn mixture has thickened. Do not stir while it is heating. If corn is on the burner it tends to become watery.

CORN FRITTERS

Cut 1/2 doz. big ears of corn over salad cutter.
Add:

2 eggs	1 cup flour
1/2 tsp. salt	1 cup milk
Pepper to taste	

Mix well and drop by tablespoons into frying pan with melted butter or lard.

CRUSHED CORN FRITTERS

1 pt. crushed corn	2 tsp. baking powder
2 eggs	Milk to moisten
1 cup flour or cracker crumbs	Salt and pepper to taste
2 tbsp. sugar	

Combine and mix well.   Fry in deep fat.

BAKED CORN

2 tbsp. lard	Paprika
2 tbsp. flour	2 cups corn pulp
1 1/2 cups milk	1 egg
1 tsp. salt	1 tbsp. Worchestershire sauce
1/4 tsp. mustard	Buttered crumbs

Make a sauce of lard, flour, milk and seasonings. Add corn, egg slightly beaten, and Worchestershire sauce. Pour into baking dish. Cover with buttered crumbs and bake in a moderate oven (350 - 400 degrees) 15 to 20 minutes.

TOMATO CASSEROLE

Slice raw, peeled tomatoes in a cake pan. On this arrange pepper and onion rings. Season with sugar, salt and pepper. Cover with bread crumbs, seasoned with salt, pepper and butter as for filling. Bake in moderate oven 1 hour to 1 1/2 hours.

TOMATO GRAVY

1 cup tomato juice	1/2 tsp. salt
1/2 cup water	1/2 cup cream
3 tbsp. flour	2 cups milk

Place juice and water in a saucepan and bring to a boil. Meanwhile blend the flour and salt with the cream. Add the milk and mix well. Pour into the hot juice, stirring constantly until it boils and is thickened. May be served with bread, toast, crackers or fried potatoes.

* 2 tbsp. sugar may be added if desired.

LEAH'S TOMATO SAUCE

Melt butter, the size of a walnut, in a pan. Add a rounded table-spoon of flour. Stir this into the melted butter, then add pure tomato juice, enough to make a slightly thickened sauce. Add sugar to taste. Serve hot with crackers or on top of toasted bread.

TOMATO BREAD

Heat one quart of tomato juice or whole tomatoes. Add sugar and pepper to taste and a lump of butter. Pour over broken toast just before serving. This is also delicious poured over broken up soda crackers.

ESCALLOPED POTATOES

6 cups medium potatoes	3 cups top milk
3 tbsp. butter	2 tbsp. flour
1 tsp. salt	pepper to taste
2 tbsp. chopped onions	1 tsp. parsley (optional)
(optional)	

Slice potatoes. Make a white sauce of butter, flour and milk. Place half of the potatoes in a greased casserole and cover with half of the sauce and seasonings. Add remaining potatoes and sea-soning, then remaining sauce. Cover and bake in a moderately hot oven (400°) about 1 hour. Uncover and continue baking until top forms a brown crust and potatoes are done.

* Potatoes may be boiled for 10 minutes to shorten baking time.

* 5 wieners or 1 cup diced ham, or 2 or 3 slices of bacon pieces may be added for extra flavor.

* Bake with 1 1/2 cups of diced Velvetta cheese.

* Raw sliced potatoes do not require a sauce, when top milk is used.

CRUSTY BAKED POTATOES

6 medium potatoes	1/2 cup cracker crumbs
4 tbsp. melted butter	1 tsp. salt

Pare potatoes, wash and wipe dry. Cut in halves and roll in melted butter, then in crumbs in which salt was added. Place in greased pan and bake at 350° for 1 hour.

PATCHES

Grind or grate 6 medium-sized raw, peeled potatoes and drain in a colander. Stir in 2 tbsp. flour and milk to make a thin batter. Add salt and pepper to taste. Parsley and onion may be added. Fry in a well oiled hot skillet.

FRIED NEW POTATOES

Put 1 quart unpeeled new potatoes through grater. Slice 1 onion. Fry together in 2 tablespoons oil.

BASQUE POTATOES

1/2 cup finely chopped onion
1/2 cup chopped celery
1/2 cup shredded carrot
1 clove garlic, minced
parsley, chopped

2 cups chicken broth
4 cups potatoes, pared
  and cubed
salt and pepper

Saute onion, celery, carrot and garlic in melted butter in a 10-inch skillet until tender. Add chicken broth, potatoes, salt and pepper to sautied vegetables. Cover; simmer for 10 minutes. Remove cover. Simmer, stirring occasionally, 20 minutes or until broth has thickened. Sprinkle with parsley. Makes 4 to 6 servings.

POTATOES WITH CHEESE SAUCE

Dice a dish of potatoes and cook until soft, in salt water. While it is cooking, make a sauce by melting butter in the skillet. Add flour, as for any white sauce. Next add milk. When it is thickened slightly, add cheese. (Onion may also be added.) Pour over the hot potatoes and serve.

POT LUCK POTATO CASSEROLE

2 lb. jacket boiled potatoes,
  peeled and chopped
4 tbsp. melted butter
1 tsp. salt
1/4 tsp. pepper

1 pt. sour cream
10 oz. (2 cups) grated, sharp
  cheddar cheese
2 cups crushed cornflakes mixed
  with 1/4 cup melted butter

1/2 cup chopped onion
1 can cream of chicken soup, undiluted

Combine potatoes and butter in large mixing bowl. Add salt, pepper, onion, soup, sour cream, cheese. Blend thoroughly. Pour into greased casserole 9 x 13. Cover with crushed cornflakes mixed with melted butter. Bake 350° for 45 minutes.

EGG & POTATO CASSEROLE

Make basic white sauce from **page 49** and mix in a dash of paprika, 6 cups grated potatoes and 6 sliced, hardboiled eggs. Pour into greased baking dish. Sprinkle top with grated cheese, buttered bread crumbs or cracker crumbs. Bake at 375° for 30 minutes.

ONION PATTIES

3/4 cup flour	2 tsp. baking powder
1 tbsp. sugar	1 tsp. salt
1 tbsp. cornmeal	3/4 cup milk
2 1/2 cups finely chopped onions	

Mix dry ingredients together then add milk. Batter should be fairly thick. Add onions and mix thoroughly. Drop by spoonsful into deep fat. Flatten slightly when you turn them.

ONION RINGS

Cut onions in rings. Dip in the following mixture and fry in deep fat, or oil.

1/2 cup flour	1 lightly beaten egg
1/4 tsp. salt	1/8 cup Mazola oil
1/2 tsp. baking powder	1/4 cup milk

CREAMED CAULIFLOWER

Cook cauliflower in salted water until soft. Make a white sauce. Add cheese (Velveeta is best.) Pour over top. Serve hot.

* Cheese sauce is good with different vegetables, such as asparagus and toast, etc.

SPINACH OMELET

Put butter in hot skillet. Add spinach, and heat until wilted (about 2-3 minutes). Pour 3 or 4 beaten eggs over the spinach. Cut. Add salt.

CREAMED ASPARAGUS

Cook asparagus stems until soft. Remove from water. Then make a thickening from the asparagus water. (This is also good made with whole wheat flour). Butter, salt, and pepper to taste. Put asparagus and large broken pieces of toast in dish. Pour the hot sauce over this and serve. Diced hard boiled eggs may be added.

ASPARAGUS AND KNEPP

Mix together: 6 eggs, 2 cups flour, 1 tsp. baking powder and
                3/4 tsp. salt.

Bring some water to a boil. Dip a spoon in your boiling water, then put the above mixture into the boiling water by the spoonsful. Cook for 15-20 minutes. Drain off some of the water and put the knepp in a dish. Top this with cooked, well-buttered asparagus. The knepp are also good topped with peas or brown-buttered hot dogs.

SQUASH COOKING HINTS

* When cooking corn on the cob, lay slices of peeled squash on top of the corn. First brush butter over the squash and sprinkle with salt and pepper. By the time the corn is ready, the squash is soft.

* When baking squash, scoop out the center but don't peel. Prepare hamburger with your favorite seasoning then fill the center of the squash with the meat. Cover with foil and bake at 350° until squash is soft.

* If you don't have hamburger, peel and grate raw potatoes fine. Put into the center of the squash. Add butter, salt, milk and pepper.

* Add leftover squash to caramel pudding.

* Use squash for pie, instead of pumpkin.

* Baked sliced squash: Brush with soft butter. Season with salt and pepper and with brown sugar if desired. Bake at 375° until brown. Turn once to brown on both sides.

COCONUT SQUASH

2 cups mashed squash (or pumpkin)	1/2 cup grated coconut
	2 well-beaten egg yolks

1 cup fine biscuit crumbs, or bread crumbs	3 tbsp. melted butter
	1 1/2 grated orange peel
1 1/2 cups milk	(optional)
1 cup sugar	1/2 tsp. nutmeg
	3/4 tsp. salt

Mix all ingredients thoroughly. Bake slowly in casserole until mixture thickens and is slightly browned. Make a meringue of the egg whites and 2 tablespoons sugar. Spread over pumpkin and brown.

BROCCOLI & BRUSSEL SPROUTS

Cover with water and bring to a good boil. Drain and add butter and small amount of water. Simmer until tender. Place several slices of processed cheese on top of the vegetables for variation. Or sprinkle with flour and stir, then add a bit of cream.

BROCCOLI WITH SAUCE

Cook broccoli in small amount of water. Drain. Put half of the broccoli in a buttered casserole. Add 2 cups chopped onions. Make cheese sauce of 4 tablespoons flour, 1 teaspoon salt, 2 cups milk and 1/4 lb. mild cheddar or American cheese. Cook sauce until thickened before adding the cheese. Stir until cheese melts. Pour 1/2 of the sauce on top of the broccoli in the casserole. Add the remainder of the broccoli, then the rest of the cheese sauce. Bake at 375° for about 45 minutes.

HARVARD BEETS

4 cups cooked diced beets	1/4 cup vinegar
1/2 cup sugar	1/4 cup water
1 tbsp. cornstarch	2 tbsp. butter
1 tsp. salt	

Mix the sugar, salt and cornstarch. Add vinegar and water and stir until smooth. Cook for 5 minutes. Add beets to hot sauce and let stand for 30 minutes. Just before serving, bring to a boil and add butter. (Omit salt when using canned beets which had been salted.)

* Harvard beets can also be made with canned pickled red beets by omitting the vinegar, sugar and salt. Use the beet water to make the sauce.

*   *These greens taste like bacon and eggs but it takes
a little practice to get them just right.*

DANDELION AND EGGS

Fry dandelion greens in butter till crisp. They will turn black
but they are not burnt — if you keep adding butter while frying.
Also add salt. As long as you can see some green they are not done
frying. When they are done, put eggs on top, cover and turn burner
to Off. Let set till eggs are done.

*Suggestion: When the dandelion stalk is too mature
and bitter, try fixing the flowers in this manner.*

DRESSING FOR GREENS

Cut up a few strips of bacon into a pan and fry. Use part of the
drippings to make pan gravy with 1 tablespoon flour. When brown,
stir in 1 cup water. Let boil, then add 1 tablespoon sugar, salt and
vinegar to taste. A bit of sour cream, or buttermilk may be added.
Fold in two hard-boiled eggs, diced. Add the greens just before
serving. Good with dandelion, lettuce, endive, etc.

SOUR CREAM CABBAGE

Grate 4 cups cabbage very fine. Simmer in tightly covered
saucepan with very little water until soft. With flour shaker,
sprinkle approximately 1 tablespoon flour over the cabbage. Add
2 tablespoons sour cream, salt and pepper to taste.

MEXICAN MIX-UP

1 1/2 lb. ground beef	2 cups kidney beans, drained
1 cup chopped onion	2 cups cooked macaroni
1/2 cup chopped green pepper	1/4 tsp. salt
1/2 tbsp. chili powder	1/8 tsp. pepper
1/2 clove garlic	1/2 cup shredded cheddar cheese
2 cups beef gravy	

In skillet brown beef and cook onion and green pepper with chili
powder and garlic until vegetables are tender. Add gravy, beans,
macaroni, salt, and pepper. Pour into 2 quart baking dish (12 x
8 x 2). Bake at 450° for 15 minutes. Stir. Top with cheese; bake
until cheese melts.

BAKED TURNIP

1 medium turnip (1 1/2 lb.)
3/4 tsp. salt
1 tbsp. sugar
1/8 tsp. ginger

2 tbsp. chopped parsley
1/4 cup water
3 tbsp. butter

Peel turnip and cut in 1/2 inch thick slices. Put in a buttered 1 quart baking dish. Combine seasonings and sprinkle over turnip. Pour water over all and dot with butter. Cover tightly and bake at 425° for 50 minutes or until done. Stir with a fork at least once.

CREAMED CELERY

1 qt. finely cut celery
1/2 tsp. salt

1/2 cup sugar
2 tbsp. vinegar

Cook together until tender, not using more water than necessary. Add a sauce made with 1 tablespoon flour and a little milk. Bring to a boil, then stir in 2 tablespoons salad dressing or mayonnaise.

BAKED MACARONI AND CHEESE

2 cups macaroni
2 tsp. salt
8 oz. cheese (Velveeta)

2 1/2 cups milk
Pepper to taste

Cook the macaroni with salt until tender. Put in casserole; add milk, cheese and dot with butter. Top with bread crumbs. Bake about 30 minutes at 325-350° or until brown.

* Chopped pepper, onions, celery or parsley may be added.

TUNA MACARONI

1 lb. elbow macaroni - cook according to directions. Pour part of the macaroni into a greased casserole dish. On top of this place cut up tuna chunks. Over this pour 1/3 of a can mushroom soup. Repeat procedure until dish is full. Pour milk over all until it covers the macaroni. Top with bread crumbs. Bake 1 hour in moderate oven. Cheese slices may be put on top for last 10 minutes of baking instead of bread crumbs.

MACARONI AND CHEESE

3 tbsp. butter
1/2 lb. velveeta cheese

1/4 tsp. pepper
2 1/2 cups uncooked macaroni

1 tsp. salt   1 qt. milk

Melt butter in baking dish; pour macaroni into the melted butter.
Stir until butter coats macaroni. Slice cheese and cut in four
pieces. Add salt, pepper, cheese and milk to macaroni. Bake at
325° for 1 1/2 hours. Do not stir while baking.

EGG DUTCH (omelet)

5 eggs   1 heaping tbsp. flour
1 tsp. salt   1 cup milk
Pepper to taste

Put in a bowl in order given and beat with a rotary beater. Pour
into a heated greased pan, cover with a tight lid. Place over
medium low heat. Cut and turn when about half done and finish
baking.

STARK CHEESE SOUFFLE

1 pt. milk   1 tsp. salt
1/4 cup tapioca (minute)   5 eggs, separated
1/2 lb. cheese

Scald milk in double boiler. Add tapioca and cook until transparent. Stir frequently. Add grated cheese and stir until melted.
Remove from boiler and add salt. Slowly add to thickly beaten egg
yolks. Mix thoroughly. Fold in stiffly beaten egg whites. Pour into a
well-greased pan. Set the pan into hot water to bake. Bake at
350° for 45 minutes, or until knife comes out clean when inserted.
Variation: Instead of grated cheese 1 finely cut green or red
             pepper may be added.

SCRAMBLED EGGS WITH CHEESE

Break 4 eggs into bowl. Add 1/4 to 1/2 cup diced cheese. Add
salt and pepper. Pour into a hot, greased frying pan. Stir roughly
with a fork, breaking the yolks. Fry, and serve immediately.

AMISH DRESSING

1 loaf bread, diced and toasted   1/2 tsp. salt
4 eggs   1/8 tsp. pepper
1 medium sized onion   1/2 tsp. sage
  chopped fine   1/2 tsp. thyme
3 1/2 or 4 cups milk as needed

3/4 cup diced potatoes (cooked) 1/2 cup shredded or diced and
2 cups, more or less,   cooked carrots for color
  diced chicken   3 stems celery, chopped fine

Put eggs in bowl and beat. Add salt, pepper, sage, and thyme.
Mix. Add 2 cups milk, onion, celery, potatoes, and diced chicken
and carrots. Add bread crumbs and enough milk to moisten well.
Substitute 1 cup chicken broth instead of milk to give it a good
flavor. Bake in a well greased casserole at 350⁰.

Variation: 2 cups cooked ham, cut fine instead of chicken. One
              large pepper, cut in short narrow strips. Parsley may
              be added.

WHOLE WHEAT SAUCE

Melt 3 or 4 tablespoons butter, or oil may be used. Add 2
rounded tablespoons whole wheat flour. Brown lightly, then add
milk to the right consistency (about 2 cups). Add herb seasonings,
a dash of red pepper, 1/8 to 1/4 teaspoon basil.

* This sauce is good over steamed asparagus tips and broken
  toast. Also good over string beans, peas, and other vegetables.

BASIC WHITE SAUCE

2 tbsp. melted butter   1/2 tsp. salt
2 tbsp. flour   1/8 tsp. pepper (optional)
2 cups milk

Melt butter in sauce pan. Stir in the flour, then add half of the
milk. Stir rapidly to remove all lumps, then add the remainder
of the milk. Cook for about 1 minute, stirring constantly.

* Add chopped dried celery leaves to the sauce. Cook a few minutes. Serve on boiled potatoes, or toast.

* Fry small pieces of bacon, then make white sauce from the
  bacon grease, or brown a diced onion before adding sauce.

* Add parsley or celery leaves and 4 or 5 chopped hard-boiled
  eggs.

CHEESE SAUCE

Make Basic sauce (slightly thinner) and add 1 cup diced cheese.
Stir until cheese is melted.

*Cheese sauce is good with many different vege-
tables..Pour it over the vegetables just before
serving.*

Here is a substitute for the bought cream soups.

INSTANT CREAM SAUCE

1 1/4 cups liquid (milk, beef or chicken broth) or liquid from canned vegetables, 1 1/2 tablespoons cornstarch (or 3 tbsp. flour), salt and pepper.

Bring to simmer 1 cup liquid. Shake thickening with 1/4 cup of remaining liquid in small jar, then stir into the hot liquid. Cornstarch will thicken immediately. Cook one minute while seasoning to taste, stirring occasionally (cook flour mixture 3 minutes).

This amount will substitute exactly for a can of cream soup. Season as you please, adding: meats or vegetables.

POTATO GRAVY

Pour the water from boiled potatoes into a sauce pan. While it is heating, make a thickening of 1 rounded tablespoon flour; dampen with milk, then stir in 1 egg yolk. Mix well, then add about 1/2 cup milk. Add to the potato water, stirring constantly. Add enough milk for right consistency. Add salt and pepper to taste and 1 tablespoon butter. Serve as any other gravy.

* When using the white of egg instead of the yolk in recipes, add about 1 tablespoon cold water to the yolk to keep it from drying out.

VEGETABLE HINTS

* *For more economical, nutritious and tasteful mashed potatoes, cook them with the skins. When soft, push them through a ricer, or foley mill. Stir hot milk in immediately. Add salt. They are also good minus the milk.*

* *In grandmother's day lard was often used on vegetables instead of butter. It is surprisingly good on cooked cabbage and on cooked navy, or snap beans.*

* *To get youngsters to eat more of the healthful salads, give them a serving when they are hungry and impatiently wait until dinner is ready.*

* Vegetables retain their flavor and value more when cooked with very little water, in a pan with a tight-fitting lid. When they begin to boil, lower the heat to the simmering stage.

* Add butter to your **RED BEETS** and they are not so apt to boil over.

* For something different, put the POTATOES through the cole slaw cutter. Add a finely cut red pepper, and then fry.

* New potatoes are delicious when washed with peelings, grated, then fried in oil- with or without onions. Salt and pepper.

* When cooking CORN ON THE COB, lay slices of squash on top of the corn. By the time the corn is ready, the squash is soft.

* Add herbs, Italian seasoning, fried chicken seasoning or other seasonings to string beans for a delightful new flavor.

* Cut all ASPARAGUS tops off beneath the ground, not on top. When the stalk is cut, the stump bleeds. Bleeding takes the strength out of the roots. When loose dirt covers the stump it can't bleed.

* Put extra value into your cooking by adding herbs. Parsley to creamed potatoes, chives to cottage cheese, mint to meat, sage and thyme to dressing, dill to pickles, and caraway seeds to rye bread. Herbs are easily grown and make nice shrubs or can be raised in flower boxes.

HOUSEHOLD HINTS

*Use adhesive tape to mend torn window shades, then color the tape with a crayon to match the color of the shade.

*Carry a pad and pencil along while at work to jot down your worth-saving thoughts. You will be surprised to see how many treasures you will gather.

*To remove paint or varnish use two parts ammonia and one part turpentine.

*To keep good old hickory knives from being lost, paint the handles a bright red or white.

*If your flat sheets are worn thin in the center, cut them apart lengthwise and sew the two outside edges together for the center. They'll last a long time yet.

*To save the chimneys on your oil stove, cut the top and bottom from empty tin, Karo cans, roll them up tight enough to slip inside the oil stove chimney.

*To clean a narrow-neck milk bottle, fill it up with water and a few drops of ammonia. Within a few minutes the bottle will be sparkling clean. This also works for cleaning meat jars.

*To brighten dull silver, rub it with a piece of potato dipped in baking powder.

*Save your potato water to soak your silverware in to brighten it.

*Line the martin's box on the inside with tinfoil to keep the sparrows and starlings away.

*To get mice out of a building and keep them out, place a few moth balls around — out of reach of little children who would be tempted to eat them. Mice can't tolerate the strong odor of moth balls.

*Give the Christmas cacti a teaspoon of castor oil each week in October to urge it to bloom in December.

*When picking nutmeats, save the shells and set them out for the birds. Their small beaks can pick out the hard-to-get pieces.

*Store your comforters and winter clothes in garbage bags if you have no cedar chest. Close with wire twists from bread packs. Garbage bags are roomy, cheap, and mothproof.

ONE DISH MEALS

IT SEEMS THERE'S NO END OF ONE-DISH MEAL recipes. Every mother who has a bit of an imagination can concoct such dishes on her own. The different meats and a great variety of vegetables make up many of the one-dish meals. And then there are many different herbs, spices, and sauces for flavoring. Lucky the mother who has a family that enjoys the various herbs and spices which give variety to each meal. Herbs are easily grown, healthy, and enrich the flavor of one-dish meals.

I well remember the time I visited an old grandmother's home. Her eyes sparkled as she pointed out the many different herbs that bordered her garden. There were hops which were used to begin her sourdough and which also make a soothing tea. There was common sage, good in dressings, and red flowering sage, used to heal a sore mouth. She also had bitter wormwood which "settled the stomach." (The wormwood's name fits well to its taste!) Plus there was peppermint, balsam, thyme, tansy and many others.

In grandmother's time such herbs were used more as medicinal teas than in cooking. Now it is not unusual to find thyme, marjoram, sage, dill, oregano and other herbs on the pantry shelf to add zest to a simple everyday meal.

DELICIOUS ONE-DISH DINNER

Peel potatoes, wash and slice. Grease casserole with butter. Put potatoes in layer. Next carrots if you wish, then a layer of sliced onions. Season with salt and pepper. Put dices of butter over top.

Next prepare **hamburger;** make patties and put over top. Add a little water. Cover with aluminum foil and bake one hour at 350°.

Variations:

* Ham may be used instead of hamburger.

* Turnips may be added.

* Canned tomato soup may be poured over all. Dilute with about half water.

MEATBALL STEW

1 1/2 lb. hamburger, 1 cup soft bread crumbs
1/4 cup finely chopped onions
1 beaten egg, 1 tsp. salt
1/2 tsp. marjoram, 1/4 tsp. thyme
2 tbsp. cooking oil
1 (10 1/2 oz.) can condensed tomato soup
1 (10 1/2 oz.) can condensed beef broth
4 medium potatoes, pared and quartered
4 carrots, scraped and cut in 1 inch chunks
8 small white onions, peeled
2 tbsp. chopped parsley

Combine the first 7 ingredients. Shape into 24 meatballs. Brown meatballs in oil in a 4-quart pan. Add condensed soups and vegetables. Bring to a boil; cover and simmer for 30 minutes or until vegetables are tender. Add parsley. Makes 6-8 servings.

SAUCY WINTER CASSEROLE

1/4 lb. bacon, diced
1/2 cup chopped onion
4 tsp. Worcestershire sauce
   or substitute vinegar
1 cup Karo
3/4 tsp. salt
Cooked spaghetti or macaroni

1/4 tsp. paprika
3/4 cup water
1 1/2 cups tomato sauce
1 lb. wieners
1 tbsp. cornstarch
2 tbsp. water

Combine bacon and onion in skillet; fry until bacon is crisp and onion is soft. Drain off extra fat. Stir in Worcestershire sauce, syrup, salt, paprika, water and tomato sauce. Bring to a boil.

Reduce heat, cover and simmer 10 minutes. Add wieners and simmer until they are hot. Blend cornstarch with 2 tbsp. water, stir into the sauce and boil one minute. Serve on hot spaghetti or any macaroni product.

SPAGHETTI DINNER

Take about one-half quart canned hamburger or that amount in fresh hamburger. Cook until liquid is almost taken up. Add one can of pizza sauce (page 269), simmer a little longer.

Meanwhile cook about one-half pound or more spaghetti in boiling salted water until tender. Put the meat sauce, and spaghetti together before serving.

BAKED SPAGHETTI

Cook 2 cups spaghetti in salted water. Drain and pour in a buttered baking dish.

Fry two slices bacon and one slice onion, and add to the spaghetti. Season one pint tomatoes with butter, salt and pepper. Pour over above ingredients. Sprinkle thickly with bread or cracker crumbs, put in oven till brown. Grated cheese may be added if desired.

CHOW MEIN (Chinese dish)

1 heavy chicken	1 tbsp. soya sauce
1 stalk celery	1 tbsp. Worcestershire sauce
2 onions	Salt and pepper to taste
1 tbsp. butter	

Cook chicken till tender. Remove bones. Fry chopped celery and onions in butter till brown. Add to chicken and broth; cook till celery is tender. Add soya, and Worcestershire sauce, salt and pepper, sugar if desired. Make thickening with 3 tablespoons cornstarch. Add to Chow Mein. Serve with Chow Mein Noodles.

TEXAS HASH

2 large onions (sliced)	3 tbsp. shortening
2 green peppers (cut fine)	1 lb. hamburger
1 cup spaghetti or macaroni	2 cups tomatoes
2 tsp. salt	1/4 tsp. pepper

Fry onions and green peppers slowly in shortening until onions are yellow. Add hamburger, until mixture falls apart. Add tomatoes, spaghetti and seasoning and mix. Put in a casserole. Cover and bake in oven 375 degrees for 45 minutes.

SPANISH RICE

Brown 1 pound hamburger, with 1 small chopped onion, if desired. Add 1/2 cup diced green pepper. Cook 1 cup rice until soft. Add to the hamburger and peppers. Add 1/2 cup diced cheese and salt and pepper to taste. 1/2 teaspoon chili powder and a dash of Italian seasoning may be added. Add tomato juice (diluted with 1/3 water) to cover. Bake for 1 hour at 350°.

* Peppers may be stuffed with the hamburger, rice, cheese, salt and pepper. Set in diluted tomato juice to bake.

STRAGANOFF CASSEROLE

2 cans (6 to 7 oz. each) tuna	1/2 cup sour cream
1 can cream of chicken soup	3/4 cup milk
2 cups cooked medium noodles	1/4 tsp. salt
2 tbsp. chopped parsley	dash of pepper
2 tsp. melted butter	3 tbsp. dry bread crumbs

Drain tuna and break into bite size chunks. Blend soup and sour cream. Stir in milk. Add tuna, parsley, noodles and seasonings. Pour into greased baking dish. Top with buttered crumbs. Bake at 350° for 20 to 25 minutes, or until bubbly.

* The cheaper canned fish such as mackeral can be used in fish dishes, but use a smaller amount for they're a little stronger in taste.

SUBSTITUTE FOR SOUR CREAM

Blend cottage cheese with blender or by hand until smooth. Use cottage cheese in many of the recipes instead of sour cream at about half the cost.

BUDGET BEEF-NOODLE CASSEROLE

1 lb. ground beef	3 cups cooked noodles
3 tbsp. onions	1 cup tomato juice
1/2 tsp. salt	2 tsp. Worcestershire sauce
1/2 cup diced cheese	1/4 cup ketchup
1 egg, beaten	

Mix all ingredients and pour into greased casserole. Top with 1/4 cup cracker crumbs. Bake at 350° for 1 hour or more.

YUMMASETTI

1 large pack noodles, cooked in salt water
3 pounds of hamburger, fried in butter with 1 onion
1 pint peas
2 cans mushroom soup
1 can cream of chicken or celery soup
1 cup sour cream
1/2 loaf toasted bread in butter

Mix together and pour into greased baking dish. Top with part of crumbs. Bake at 350 degrees for 1 hour.

SKILLET SUPPER

1 lb. bulk sausage
  (or 1 qt. canned)
1 onion, chopped
1 green pepper, chopped
1 qt. tomatoes

2 cups uncooked macaroni
2 tbsp. sugar
2 tsp. chili powder
1/2 cup water or tomato juice
1 tsp. salt

Brown sausage, onion and pepper, pouring off fat as it collects. Stir in remaining ingredients. Bring to a boil; cover. Simmer, stirring often until macaroni is tender. Two cups sour cream may be added before serving. Hamburger may be used instead of sausage.

HAMBURGER CASSEROLE

chopped onion
1 lb. ground beef,
  fresh or canned
salt and pepper
2 1/2 cups green beans

1 can tomato soup
5 potatoes, cooked
1/2 cup warm milk
1 egg, beaten

Fry onions and meat with salt and pepper until brown. Mix meat, beans and soup. Pour into 1 1/2 quart casserole. Mash potatoes. Add milk and egg and season to taste. Mix well. Spoon mounds of potatoes on meat mixture. Cover with cheese if desired. Bake at 350° for 30 minutes. If leftover mashed potatoes are used, then omit the milk.

GREEN BEAN DISH

4 large potatoes
1 lb. wieners cut up or
1 lb. browned hamburger

1 qt. canned green beans
1/2 onion

Sauce:

2 cups milk	1/2 lb. soft cheese
1/2 cup flour	2 tsp. salt

Heat milk enough to melt cheese and add flour and salt. Pour over potatoes and beans and bake at 300⁰ for 2 hours.

KINGBURGER KLOPS

Mix:

1 1/2 lb. hamburger	1 chopped onion
2 slices of bread soaked in	salt and pepper to taste
water, then squeezed dry	1 bay leaf (optional)
3 eggs	

Form into balls about 2 inch and place in pan of 1 1/2 quart boiling water. Cook 10 minutes. Place the balls in a roaster or casserole with 2 quarts of boiled potatoes cut in chunks. **Cover** with the following sauce:

1 cup strained water in which	4 tbsp. flour
the meatballs were boiled in	1 cup cold milk
1 cup sour cream	salt and pepper to taste
Season with salt and pepper	

Cook sauce and pour over the meatballs. Serve.

* Cream may be omitted and 2 cups milk used.

HANDY CASSEROLE

Put a layer of browned hamburger in a dish. Over this place a layer of sliced potatoes (cooked till about done), then a layer of canned vegetables. Add 1 can mushroom, celery or chicken soup. Top with a layer of cheese. Cover with foil. Bake at 350⁰ for 30 minutes.

VEGETABLE-RICE DISH

Cook together rice, onion to taste, small amount of carrots, red and green peppers, (optional). When rice is tender and almost dry, add enough milk till juicy, add drained peas, margarine and seasonings to taste and cubed Velveeta cheese. Heat until cheese melts and serve with fresh bread and butter and a salad or applesauce.

For variety substitute diced potatoes, noodles, or macaroni for the rice. Add ham, beef chunks, or almost any kind of meat, and green beans or peas. When potatoes are used, instead of adding plain milk, make a white sauce. The combination of any of the above ingredients and your imagination will make many nourishing meals.

CHICKEN & RICE CASSEROLE

Into a flat baking dish, place chicken or hamburger. Add chopped celery or other vegetables and uncooked rice. Add a can of cream of celery and cream of chicken soup. A white sauce could be used instead of soup. Bake until rice is tender.

VEGETABLE CHICKEN CASSEROLE

Take of each vegetable according to family size -- potatoes, carrots (cut small), and peas. Cook each separately till almost soft. Take a can of chicken, drain off liquid and make a thin gravy. Cut chicken off the bone and pour potatoes, carrots, peas and cut-up chicken into roaster or casserole and pour the seasoned gravy over the top of it. Mix slightly. Make a biscuit dough, and then drop the dough on top of the mixture. Put into oven till biscuits are done. This makes a delicious meal. Bake at 350° for 15 to 20 minutes. As a short cut, cook all vegetables together.

CHICKEN AND DRESSING

1 loaf of bread, toasted
1 large or 2 small onions, chopped
1 cup celery, diced
2 hardboiled sliced eggs
1 chicken, boned and diced

Make a thin gravy with the chicken broth. Mix all ingredients, adding salt and pepper. Put into a loaf pan or baking dish. Dot with butter. Bake at 350 degrees from 3/4 to 1 hour.

CHICKEN LOAF

3 cups diced cooked chicken	1/2 tsp. pepper
1 cup soft bread crumbs	3 eggs, separated
1/2 cup sweet milk	2 tbsp. melted butter
1 tsp. salt	1/4 cup chopped pimento

Let crumbs stand in the milk for ten minutes. Add the chicken, pepper, salt, egg yolks, butter and pimento. Beat egg whites till stiff and add to the chicken. Place in buttered pan and bake for 45 minutes at 350 degrees.

CHICKEN AND DUMPLINGS

Use a large kettle with a tight-fitting cover. Remove a quart of chicken meat from the bones; add broth and make gravy as usual.

Dumplings:

Beat one egg, 2 tbsp. milk, 1/2 tsp. salt, 3 tsp. baking powder, and enough flour to make a good stiff dough. Drop by spoonsful into the boiling gravy. Place lid on and let covered from 5 to 8 minutes. It is important that the lid be not removed once. Remove from stove. Take lid off and serve at once. Dumplings should be light and fluffy.

PORKY PIE

4 med. sweet potatoes	1 lb. ground pork
1 1/2 tsp. salt	1 1/2 cups water
2 tbsp. butter	2 tbsp. flour
1 1/2 tsp. cinnamon sugar	dash of pepper

Cook potatoes in salt water and peel. Mash slightly and add butter, 1/2 teaspoon salt and cinnamon sugar. Add a little milk if necessary. Brown pork patties and drain. (Canned sausage works fine, too.) Make a gravy with the water, flour, and pork broth. Pour over patties in a shallow baking pan. Spread sweet potatoes over top. Bake at 400° for 20 minutes.

FRYING PAN SUPPER

1 lb. hamburger, 1 small onion. Fry until it changes color, then add 2 cups potatoes - cut in strips, 2 cups shredded cabbage, 2 cups celery cut fine. Sprinkle with salt. Add 1/2 cup water. Cover and simmer for 20 minutes or until vegetables are done. Canned hamburger or chunk meat, cut up may also be used.

MEATBALL CHOWDER

2 lb. ground beef	2 bay leaves (optional)
2 tsp. salt	4-6 small onions, cut up
1/8 tsp. pepper	2 or 3 cups diced celery
2 beaten eggs	3-4 cups diced potatoes
1/4 cup chopped parsley	1/4 cup long grain rice
garlic salt (optional)	6 cups tomato juice
1/2 cup fine cracker or	6 cups water
bread crumbs	1 tbsp. sugar
2 tbsp. milk	1 tsp. salt
3-5 tbsp. flour	1 1/2 cup canned corn
1 tbsp. salad oil	

Mix thoroughly meat, salt, pepper, eggs, crumbs and milk. Form balls size of walnut. Dip in flour. Heat oil in large kettle.

Lightly brown meatballs on all sides. Add remaining ingredients (except corn). Bring to a boil. Cover and cook slowly until vegetables are tender. Add corn last. Cook 10 minutes. Serves 12 people. Carrots, peas and celery leaves can be used; also V-8 juice and less water.

LIMA BEAN BARBECUE

2 cups dried lima beans (or 4 cups cooked or canned)

2 tsp. salt	1/2 cup onion (chopped)
1 lb. pork sausage links	1 cup catsup
1 tbsp. prepared horseradish	1 tsp. Worcestershire sauce
1/4 cup liquid from cooked beans	

Add salt to beans and cook until tender. Drain. Fry sausage until brown. Mix all ingredients except sausage. Place half of bean mixture in 1 1/2 quart casserole dish. Cover with half of sausages. Add remaining bean mixture and sausages. Bake in hot oven 400° for 15 minutes.

BEEF AND CHEESE

1 lb. ground beef	2 tbsp. butter
1 small onion	3 tbsp. flour
1 1/2 cups uncooked spaghetti	2 cups milk
1 cup tomatoes	3/4 cup cheese

Cook spaghetti until tender, drain. In a skillet brown beef and onion in the butter. Add flour, seasoning, and milk. Cook until thick. Mix one-half cup cheese with spaghetti. Place half of spaghetti in baking dish. Put in meat mixture. Top with tomatoes. Put on the rest of spaghetti. Sprinkle with remaining cheese. Bake at 350 degrees 25 to 30 minutes.

WASHDAY DINNER

Use a large flat pan. Melt 1 tablespoon butter in it. Line the bottom of the pan with a thick layer of onion; then add a generous layer of potatoes. Sift 2 tablespoons flour over this. Pour a can of tomato juice over the whole. Slice sausages thinly to cover the top. Add boiling water to cover. Salt to taste. Bake slowly for 3 hours. If sausages get too brown, turn them over.

CHILI CON CARNE

1 lb. ground beef	1 small can kidney beans
2 tbsp. shortening	and liquid

2 onions (minced)   2 tsp. salt
1/2 green pepper   1 tsp. chili powder
1 small can tomatoes or tomato soup

Brown beef in shortening, add onions and diced pepper. Brown lightly. Stir in tomatoes, kidney beans, salt and chili powder. Simmer 1 hour.

PORCUPINE MEAT BALLS

1 lb. ground beef   1 onion (minced)
1/2 cup rice   1 small can tomato soup
1 tsp. salt   1/2 cup water
1/2 tsp. pepper

Wash rice. Combine meat, rice, salt, pepper and onion. Shape into small balls. Mix soup and water and pour over meat balls. Use pressure cooker, if possible, and cook 12 minutes, if not, cook 30 minutes, closely covered.

DRIED BEEF CASSEROLE

1 8 oz. pkg. noodles   1 cup milk
1 can cream of mushroom soup   1/4 lb. dried beef
Buttered bread crumbs

Fry beef in butter until slightly browned. Add mushroom soup and milk. Cook noodles in salt water until tender. Drain. Combine this and beef in buttered casserole. Cover with buttered bread crumbs. Bake in moderate oven until brown.

BAKED BEEF STEW

2 lb. beef cut in cubes   6 med. potatoes thinly sliced
1/4 cup flour   2 med. carrots thinly sliced
1/4 tsp. celery seed   1 1/2 cups hot water
1 1/4 tsp. salt   4 tsp. beef bouillon
1/8 tsp. pepper   1 tsp. Worcestershire sauce
4 medium onions, sliced   Butter or margarine

Mix flour and seasonings and dredge meat in them. In a large casserole with tight fitting cover, arrange in layers, meat and vegetables. Add bouillon to hot water and add Worcestershire sauce. Pour evenly over casserole. Dot with butter, cover and bake at 325° for 3 hours. Leftover beef broth may be used instead of the water and bouillon.

SUEY STEW

Take a roast or stew meat cut in chunks. Trim off fat. Cut potatoes in cubes. Carrots and onions and any vegetable you like — take according to size of family. Pour over vegetables and meat: 1 can cream of celery, 1/2 can water, 1 can cream of chicken, 1/2 can water. Do not mix. Bake 5 hours at 275°.

BUSY DAY CASSEROLE

1 1/2 cups cubed ham 　　or hamburger	1 cup diced **carrots** 1/2 cup peas (**canned**)
1 cup diced potatoes	1/2 cup green beans (**canned**)

Brown the ham. Add potatoes, carrots and water. Cook until tender. Add peas, beans and boiling water to cover. Into this stir 1 tbsp. flour mixed with a little water. Put this mixture into a large casserole or small cake pan. Top with favorite biscuit dough, dropped by tablespoon in ham mixture. Cheese may be added to the biscuits. Bake from 20 to 30 minutes at 350° until done.

CALIFORNIA RICE

1 cup raw rice	1 cup chopped celery
1 cup chopped onion	1 cup cooked, diced chicken
1 lb. bulk sausage	salt and pepper
1 can mushroom soup	1 can water

Brown sausage, celery, onion and rice. Add chicken, soup, water and seasonings. Put in greased casserole. Bake 2 hours at 325°. The ingredients need not be browned if preferred otherwise.

TAMALE PIE

1 can whole grain corn	1 1/2 tbsp. butter
1 pt. tomatoes	1 1/2 tsp. salt
1/2 lb. ground beef	1/2 to 1 tbsp. chili powder
1/4 lb. ground pork	1/2 garlic bud (may be omitted)
1 small onion	

Boil all together for 15 minutes. Remove from heat and add:
3/4 cup sweet milk   1 egg, beaten
1 cup granulated cornmeal

Mix well and pour in buttered casserole. Bake 1 hour in moderate oven, 325 degrees.

BAKED PORK CHOPS

Put a layer of thinly sliced potatoes in a baking dish, cover with shredded onions, salt and pepper. Lay over this as many pork chops as needed. Season well on both sides. Add enough milk to moisten and bake until all food is done. 400 degree oven.

SCHNITZ UN KNEPP

3 lb. ham
1 qt. dried apples
2 tbsp. brown sugar
2 cups flour
4 tsp. baking powder

1/4 tsp. pepper
1 egg, well beaten
3 tbsp. melted butter
1 tsp. salt

Milk (enough to make a fairly moist stiff batter).

Wash dried apples. Cover with water and soak overnight. Cover ham with boiling water and boil 3 hours. Add apples and water in which they were soaked and boil 1 hour longer. Add sugar.

Make dumplings by sifting flour, salt, pepper and baking powder. Stir in beaten egg, milk and shortening. Drop by tablespoon into hot ham and apples. Cover and cook 15 minutes. Serve hot.

WIGGLERS

5 slices bacon
1 1/2 lb. hamburger
2 onions
1 1/2 cups diced potatoes
1 1/2 cups celery

2 cups peas
1 can mushroom soup
3/4 qt. tomato juice
1 1/2 cups carrots, diced
1 1/2 cups spaghetti, cooked

Cut bacon up small and fry with hamburger and sliced onions until brown. Drain off fat. Put in roaster with all other vegetables that have been cooked. Stir in juice and soup. Lay slices of Velveeta cheese on top and bake 1 hour at 350°.

MOCK TURKEY

2 lb. hamburger, browned in butter
2 cans cream of chicken soup
1 can cream of celery soup
4 cups milk
1 loaf of bread, broken

Add salt and pepper to taste. Mix together and place in pan. Bake at 350° for 45 minutes.

MEAT PIES

Grind 3 or 4 cups of cooked meat. Add hardboiled eggs and chopped onions, and salt and pepper to taste. A desired sauce may be added to moisten the meat, such as salad dressing, ketchup or mayonnaise.

Dough:

1 cup milk	2 eggs
2 tsp. baking powder	2 tbsp. lard
1 tsp. salt	2 cups flour

Mix dough lightly. Roll out and cut in squares. Put meat on and fold over, and press down. Deep fat fry.

LITTLE BEEF PIES

1 beef bouillon cube	1 1/2 tsp. salt
2 cups boiling water	1 tsp. sugar
3 1/2 cups chopped	1/2 tsp. paprika
cooked beef	1/4 tsp. pepper
2 tsp. Worcestershire sauce	1/4 cup flour

1 pkg. (10 oz.) frozen mixed vegetables (canned may also be used)

Heat oven to very hot (450°). Dissolve bouillon cube in boiling water; add beef, Worcestershire sauce, salt, sugar, paprika and pepper. Add vegetables; cook 5 minutes. Combine cold water and flour; slowly stir into mixture and cook until thickened. Then spoon into 6 or 8 oz. oven proof casseroles.

Pastry:

1 cup flour	1/3 cup shortening
1/2 cup cornmeal	4 tbsp. cold water
3/4 tsp. salt	

Sift together flour, cornmeal, and salt. Cut in shortening, until mixture resembles coarse crumbs. Sprinkle water by tablespoons over mixture. Stir lightly with a fork until just dampened. (If necessary, add another tablespoon of cold water to make dough hold together.)

Form into a ball. Divide pastry into 6 parts. Roll each part to form a circle large enough to fit the top of the casserole. Place pastry circle over filling. Turn edges under; flute. Make several cuts in pastry to allow steam to escape. Bake in a preheated oven (450°) 12-15 minutes.

MEATS

MEAT SAUCES

MEAT CANNING

MEAT CURES

SEA FOODS

PIZZAS

BUTCHERING DAY IS STILL THE JOYFUL DAY it was years ago, and is not yet out of style. Neighboring men brave the cold, early on a winter's morning to scald, scrape, and hang up the hogs while inside the house the women are making hurried preparations for dinner, and are cleaning casings. Children delightedly blow through spools and watch the cleaned casings spring to life. Mothers thoroughly check for holes, for you can't make sausage with weak casings.

There are many enjoyments on butchering day. One is the cooking of the liver to make liverworst. The warm cooked liver is delicious with salt sprinkled on it. And after the lard has been make, the cracklings become a good afternoon snack for the children.

Meat has become an expensive item on the table. To some it has become somewhat a necessity to have their daily portion. But there are still families who take a more economical way and substitute cheese, eggs, soybeans or cooked beans for meat on some days.

Soybeans especially are a cheap, but very good protein food. Soybeans can be added to extend the meat supply, as can be soybean flour; or they may be used as any other beans: in salads, baked beans, or with ham bone for soup.

CHICKEN BARBECUE SAUCE

1/4 cup butter or margarine, melted	1 cup water
	2 1/4 tbsp. salt
1 cup vinegar	1 tbsp. Worcestershire sauce

Bring to a boil. Brush the sauce on the meat with a brush to keep meat damp while barbecuing.

SPAGHETTI SAUCE

1 small chopped onion	1/2 tsp. garlic salt
1 - 8 oz. can tomato sauce	1/4 tsp. pepper
1 can tomato soup	1 tbsp. parsley

Mix onions, tomato soup and 1 1/4 cup water. Simmer for 10 minutes. Mix seasoning and parsley into the sauce. Place meatballs in the sauce and simmer uncovered for 25 minutes turning occasionally. Mix with hot, cooked spaghetti. Top with grated cheese.

* This sauce is very good with a cut-up stewing hen instead of hamburger. Cook the hen until almost done. Finish cooking in the spaghetti sauce.

HOT DOG SAUCE

1/2 green pepper	2 tbsp. brown sugar
medium sized onion, chopped	3/4 cup ketchup
2 tbsp. prepared mustard	1 tbsp. Worcestershire sauce
3/4 tsp. salt	

Mix all ingredients, then add 1/2 to 1 pint of water. Cook 15 minutes, then add your wieners and cook till wieners are good and hot. This sauce is very good on top of mashed potatoes.

CHICKEN BARBECUE SAUCE

1/4 cup butter, margarine or oil	1 cup water
	2 tbsp. vinegar
1 tsp. salt	2 tsp. brown sugar
dash of pepper	2 tbsp. Worcestershire sauce

Mix, then bring to a boil. Baste meat with sauce.

BARBECUE SAUCE

1/2 cup catsup
1 tbsp. vinegar
1 tbsp. sugar

1 tbsp. mustard
1 tbsp. Worcestershire sauce

Mix well. If too strong, use less catsup, and some tomato juice.

BARBECUED CHICKEN

Cut fryers into serving pieces. Place in shallow baking dish, brush with oil and bake in moderate oven 375°, 45 minutes or until browned. Pour barbecue sauce over chicken, continue baking 45 minutes longer. Baste frequently.

BARBECUED HAMBURGER

Brown 1 pound hamburger with 1 sliced onion. Add 1 teaspoon salt and a dash of pepper. When brown add barbecue sauce and steam for 10 minutes. Serve with buns.

BEEF BAR-B-Q

5 lb. ground beef (browned)
1 large bunch celery
1 lb. onions
3 14 oz. bottles catsup
5 tsp. Worcesterchire sauce

1 cup brown sugar
2 tbsp. chili powder
2 tbsp. salt
1 tbsp. pepper
1/2 cup flour

Finely mince celery and onions; simmer until tender. Add catsup and seasonings. Make thickening of flour, adding it to celery -- onion mixture. Cook at low temperature for 10 minutes. Add browned beef to finish barbecue.

Caution - This mixture should not be placed on high heat, as it will burn easily. It may be stored in a closed container and warmed up as needed.

LIVER PATTIES

If your beef liver is tough, try grinding it. Season with salt; pepper, if desired. Fry like hamburger patties. A little flour may be added, or sprinkle the liver with flour before turning. Delicious! Chopped onion and beaten egg may be added to the liver.

(Add a small amount of vinegar to the water when cold packing meat to keep cans free from grease.)

BEEF BARBECUE (for canning)

10 lb. ground beef	3/4 cup prepared mustard
5 cups chopped onions	1 1/2 cups brown sugar
1/2 cup salt (scant)	2/3 cup Worcestershire sauce
1 1/4 tbsp. pepper	5 cups catsup
1 cup vinegar	

Brown hamburg and onions. Add the other ingredients and 4 cups beef broth or water, (or more if necessary). Steam 10 minutes. Pack in jars and seal. Makes about 9 quart. Boil 1 to 2 hours.

BARBECUED BONE MEAT

1 1/2 lb. bone meat	1/2 cup onions, chopped
1 cup celery, chopped	1 cup catsup
2 tbsp. Worcestershire sauce	1 tbsp. mustard
1 tbsp. brown sugar	3/4 tsp. salt
(Tomato juice may be added).	

Mix, then cold pack one hour.

Large Batch:

12 cups celery, chopped	18 lb. meat, ground if wished
6 cups onion, chopped	1 1/2 cups Worcestershire sauce
3/4 cup mustard	3/4 cup brown sugar
3 qt. catsup	3 tbsp. salt

Makes about 40 pints.

CANNED MEAT LOAF

15 lb. ground beef	1 cup oatmeal
1/2 cup salt	3 cups water or milk, or
4 slices bread	tomato juice
36 Premium Crackers	4 eggs

Mix well and pack in jars. Chopped onion may be added if desired. Boil 3 hours. May be formed into balls and fried before canning.

* To stretch hamburger, crumble about 5 or more slices of bread into a pound of the meat. Add a little milk or tomato juice, or an egg, and seasoning. Mix and form into patties. Fry.

SAVORY MEAT LOAF

1 1/4 lb. ground beef and 1/4 lb. ground pork, or 2 lb. ground beef (omitting the ground pork).

1/4 cup onions, minced	1/4 tsp. pepper
1 cup oatmeal or crackers	1 tsp. mustard
2 1/2 tsp. salt	1/4 cup catsup
1 beaten egg	1 cup tomato juice

Mix, and then form into a loaf. Put a few bacon slices on top. Pour tomato juice over all. Bake at 350° to 375° for 1 hour.

* May be pressed into a cake pan and topped with catsup. Bake for about 1 hour.

* Spread glaze over loaf.

GLAZE FOR MEAT LOAF

1/2 cup brown sugar	1 tbsp. Worcestershire sauce
1 1/2 tsp. prepared mustard	

Add enough vinegar to make a slight thickening. Spread over meat loaf.

HAM LOAF

Mix the following:

2 lb. smoked ham (ground)	1 1/2 cups bread crumbs
2 lb. fresh pork (ground)	1 tsp. salt
2 eggs	1 tsp. pepper
1 1/2 cups milk	

Make into loaf. Pour syrup over top. Bake at 375° for 2 hours.

Glaze:

1 1/2 cups brown sugar	1/2 cup water
1 tsp. dry mustard	1/2 cup vinegar

SAUSAGE LOAF

1 1/2 lb. pork sausage meat	2 tbsp. horseradish
1 1/2 cups bread or	2 tsp. prepared mustard
cracker crumbs	1 egg, slightly beaten
2 tbsp. grated onion	1/2 cup milk
2 tbsp. catsup	

Mix sausage and cracker crumbs, add onion, catsup, horseradish, mustard and egg. Moisten with milk. Shape into loaf and bake at 350° for 1 hour.

VEAL LOAF

1 lb. beef, ground fine
1 cup bread or cracker crumbs
1/2 cup cream
1 tsp. sugar

2 eggs, beaten
1 tsp. butter
Salt and pepper to taste

Mix well. Make a long loaf. Bake 1 1/2 hours to 2 hours at 350-375°.

MEAT PATTIES

2 lbs. ground pork, or
    hamburger
2 eggs
1 onion
1 cup cracker crumbs

1 cup milk
1 tsp. salt
1/2 tsp. pepper

Make into patties. Fry.

BEEF ROAST

If 3 lb. roast, mix 2 teaspoons salt, a small amount of pepper, 2 teaspoons brown sugar and rub well into all sides of the meat. Place into casserole. Add a small amount of water (approx. 3 tbsp.). Roast at 325° for 1 hour, or until done. Cover until done. (Roasting time is approximately 30 to 35 minutes per pound of beef. If it's a boneless, rolled roast, increase time about 10 minutes per pound.)

YORKSHIRE PUDDING

2 eggs
2 cups sour milk
1 cup sweet milk
2 tsp. baking powder

1 tsp. salt
1 tbsp. sugar
2 cups sifted flour or
    enough to make stiff batter

Pour out the broth from the meat, leaving about 1 inch in pan. Pour batter in broth around roast and bake 25 minutes. Thicken rest of broth, cut pudding in blocks and pour gravy over it and serve with beef.

CHUNK BEEF PATTIES

Grind up 1 quart chunks. Add about 5 double white crackers (crushed), 2 eggs, a little parsley, hamburger seasoning, or whatever seasoning your family likes. Add enough milk to make a soft pattie. Mix. Fry in patties.

HAMBURGER PUFFS

1 good sized onion (chopped)	1/2 green pepper (chopped fine)
1 tbsp. butter or oil	1 tsp. salt
4 large slices of bread	1/4 tsp. pepper
1 cup milk	1 lb. ground beef
2 eggs, beaten	

Saute onions in butter until lightly browned. Crumble bread into milk and let stand until milk is absorbed. Add onions and remaining ingredients to bread and milk. Mix well and press patties into greased muffin tins. Allow to set for 15 minutes. Bake in oven for 25 or 30 minutes at 400°. Place muffin tins on cookie sheet if necessary. Serve with gravy or catsup. (A can of cream soup heated with 1/2 can of milk makes a nice sauce to use with the puffs.) Makes 8 or 9 puffs.

HAMBURGER-EGG CASSEROLE

6 eggs, beaten	3 cups milk
1 lb. ground beef	1 tsp. salt
1/4 tsp. pepper	1 tsp. Worcestershire sauce
1/2 tsp. dry mustard	6 slices cheese, cut up (optional)
12 slices bread, cut up	

Mix everything together. Put in casserole. Place dish in pan of water. Bake at 350° for 1 1/4 hours.

WAGON WHEEL HAMBURGER

2 lbs. hamburger	1/4 cup chopped onion
1/2 cup barbecue sauce	1/4 cup chopped green pepper
1/2 cup dry bread crumbs	1 tsp. salt
2 beaten eggs	

Combine and mix lightly, put into an 8-inch skillet. On top make a spoke design with barbecue sauce, and sprinkle a little brown sugar over the whole top. Bake at 325° for 50 minutes or until done.

SOUR CREAM BEEFBURGERS

1 1/2 lb. ground beef	1 cup sour cream
1/4 cup Worcestershire sauce	1 tbsp. chopped onion
1 1/2 tsp. salt	

Mix together, then add the following:
1 1/2 cups crushed cornflakes or bread crumbs. Form into pat-

ties. Broil for 5 minutes; turn; broil 3 more minutes. 10-12 burgers.

STEAK SUPREME

2 lbs. hamburger	2 tsp. salt
2 eggs	6 tbsp. onions chopped fine
1/2 cup dry bread crumbs	Some pepper if desired

Heat lard in skillet; press meat into skillet to about 1 inch thickness. Brown on both sides. Add a can of mushroom soup and the same of water. Cover tightly and simmer 20 minutes.

HAPPY CHANGE MEATBALLS

Mix lightly until blended:

1 tsp. salt	1/2 cup cracker crumbs
1 1/2 lbs. ground beef	1/2 cup milk
1/4 tsp. pepper and nutmeg	2 eggs, slightly beaten

Shape into small balls, place into a large shallow baking pan. Bake at 350° for 30 minutes. Drain off excess fat. Combine in a bowl:

2 cups tomato juice	2 tbsp. flour

Mix well then add:

3/4 cup catsup	1/4 cup water
1/2 tsp. Worcestershire sauce	

Mix until blended then pour over meat balls and bake 30 minutes longer.

OLD-FASHIONED POULTRY STUFFING

1 cup chopped celery	1 can (10 1/2 oz.) condensed
1/2 cup chopped onion	cream of chicken soup or
1/2 tsp. poultry seasoning	1 1/4 cups chicken gravy
1/4 cup butter or oleo	8 cups dry bread cubes

Cook celery, onions, and poultry seasoning in butter until vegetables are tender. Add soup. Mix lightly with bread cubes. Makes about 4 cups stuffing or enough for a 5 to 6 lb. bird.

CHICKEN ROLL (or Ham Roll)

Use biscuit dough. Roll out, then spread with cut-up cooked chicken. Roll up, as you do to make rolls, and then cut in slices. Place in a greased pan and bake at 350°. Make gravy with the chicken broth.   Top the hot rolls with the gravy.

This can be made with ham also, using the same method.   For the gravy, a simple white sauce should be made.   Stir Chef's Delight or cheese spread into this while hot.   Serve hot over rolls.

CRUNCHY CHICKEN

3 to 4 lb. broilers.   Dip pieces of raw chicken into melted margarine then roll into finely crushed equal parts of cracker and cornflakes crumbs.   Place in flat, well oiled baking pans, laying pieces side by side -- not crowding.   Sprinkle with salt and favorite chicken seasoning.   Bake in 375⁰ oven for an hour or until the meat is brown and tender.

BAKED CHICKEN

1/2 cup flour	3 tsp. salt
2 tsp. paprika	1 cut-up broiler or
1 tsp. pepper	young chicken
1/4 tsp. dry mustard	

Mix dry ingredients well in plastic bag and then dust cut-up chicken parts.   In cake pan, melt 1/4 lb. butter.   Place chicken parts in pan, not crowding.   Bake at 350⁰ for 1 1/2 hours or 2 hours or until done.

Make your own-

SHAKE AND BAKE

1 cup flour	2 tsp. paprika
a bit of pepper	1 tsp. baking powder
1/2 tsp. salt	

Mix, then shake and bake.

CHICKEN BOLOGNA

Cut the meat from the bones (use 25 lbs. meat).   Add 1 lb. tenderquick.   Grind twice; let set 24 hours, then add 1 oz. black pepper, 1/2 cup sugar, 2 tsp. salt petre, 2 tsp. garlic powder and 3 tbsp. liquid smoke.   Mix well and grind again, then process as any fresh meat (such as stuffed sausage), or stuff into cloth bags and boil in water 30 minutes.   Let cool then slice and can, adding the water used to cook.   Liquid smoke may be omitted and the meat smoked after stuffing.   Then boil and slice and put in jars to can.   Cold pack 2 1/2 hours.

CANNED CHICKEN

Cut into bite size pieces. Add salt. **Fry, then can.** When unexpected company comes, this can be opened, a thickening added
to provide a meat and gravy dish.

* When dressing a quantity of chickens, place 6 fowls (after scalding, picking and singeing), 3 towels, and soap in the wash machine and cover with warm water. Run the machine for 10 minutes. The chickens come out nice and clean.

* When cleaning chickens use a ball made of nylon netting instead
  of a knife. Nothing better.

SLOPPY JOES

2 lbs. hamburger	1 small bottle catsup
1/2 cup onion, chopped	2 tbsp. brown sugar
1/2 cup celery, chopped	1 cup tomato paste
1/2 cup vinegar	salt and pepper to taste
2 tbsp. dry mustard	

Add 1 cup water to hamburger. Cook. Add the rest of the ingredients and continue cooking. Serve with hamburger buns.

BEANBURGERS

Brown 2 pounds ground beef in 2 tablespoons oil; add 1 small
onion, chopped, 1/2 cup catsup and 1 teaspoon Worcestershire
sauce. Add sufficient water to prevent burning and simmer 20
minutes. Add 1 pint cooked kidney beans, drained; salt and pepper
to taste, 1/2 teaspoon garlic powder and 1/2 teaspoon chili powder, or 1 teaspoon oregano may be added. Continue simmering
about 30 more minutes. Serve on buns, using only one half of bun.
Top with a slice of cheese and melt in hot oven. Serve hot.

CHEESEBURGERS

Make hamburger patties. Fry. After they have been turned,
place a slice of cheese on top of each one and continue frying until
done. Serve on bread immediately.

HOT HAM AND CHEESE BUNS

Cut a 1/2 pound slice ham and 1/2 pound sharp cheese into 1/4
inch cubes. Combine with 1/3 cup sliced onions, 2 hard boiled

eggs sliced, and 1/2 cup sliced pepper or stuffed olives. Top with
3 tablespoons salad dressing blended with 1/2 cup chili sauce. Mix
well and spread mixture in 10 split wiener buns. Wrap each in foil.
Twist ends securely. Bake for 10 minutes in 400° oven or until
buns are hot.

HAM SALAD SANDWICHES

2 cups ground, cooked ham	1/4 tsp. onion powder
3 stalks celery	1/2 cup mayonnaise
1 large dill pickle	1/2 tsp. salt
1/4 tsp. dry mustard	1 tbsp. lemon juice

Put ham, celery, and pickle through coarse blade of food chopper, add remaining ingredients and mix.

CHICKEN SALAD SANDWICHES

1 qt. **cold, boiled chicken**	Salt and pepper to taste
1 pt. celery	**4 or 5 hard-boiled eggs**
Mayonnaise or other dressing	3/4 cup chopped olives (optional)

Put chicken, celery, and eggs through coarse blade of food chopper. Add remaining ingredients.

SOUPERBURGERS

1 lb. ground beef	1/2 cup chopped onion
1 tbsp. shortening	1 can (10 oz.) vegetable soup
2 tbsp. ketchup	1 tsp. prepared mustard
Dash pepper	6 buns split and toasted

In skillet brown beef and onion in shortening. Stir to separate
meat. Add remaining ingredients. Cook 5 minutes stirring now
and then. Serve on buns. This is also delicious served with
mashed potatoes.

SWISS STEAK

Salt and pepper a 2 or 3 inch steak, beat on both sides all the
flour it will take. Sear on both sides, cover with sliced onions,
pour over a small bottle of tomato catsup. Add enough water to
cover steak and bake in oven 2 hours.

If catsup is not desired, sear and add 1 tablespoon vinegar, 1
tablespoon salt and a small amount of pepper. When steak is
browned, cover with boiling water or cream and simmer slowly
until very tender.

CORNED BEEF

50 lbs. beef (Roasts, Steaks, or any choice cut)
3 qts. salt

Place meat in a large crock or similar suitable container in layers. Salt each layer. Let stand overnight. Then rinse off roughly and pack in crock again.
Make a brine of:

1/4 lb. baking soda	2 lbs. brown sugar
1/4 lb. salt petre	2 tbsp. liquid smoke

Water enough to cover meat well.

Place meat in brine. It will be cured and ready for use in 2 weeks. It can then be cut in suitable pieces and canned (cold pack 3 hours) or put in freezer. If crock is kept in a cool place, meat may be kept in brine and used anytime within 3 months. Flavor is improved when kept over 6 weeks.

SCALLOPED WIENERS

1 lb. wieners	4 1/2 cups milk
5 cups (coarsely crushed)	Pepper to taste
crackers	4 large tbsp. butter
2 eggs	2 tsp. salt

Add a small amount of water to the wieners and cook for 10 minutes. Slice the wieners. Make alternate layers of crackers and wieners in a casserole. Beat egg and add seasoning and milk. Pour over the crackers and wieners. Dot the top with butter. Bake at about 450° for 30 minutes or until done. This will fill a very large casserole or 2 smaller ones.

SCALLOPED HAM

1 1/2 cups ground ham	3 cups milk
1/2 cup ham broth	1 tbsp. butter
2 cups cracker crumbs	1 tsp. salt
2 eggs, beaten	Dash of pepper

Brown ham and cook until tender, then grind. Line bottom of casserole with layer of cracker crumbs, then a layer of half of the ground ham, then crackers, making two layers of each. Mix milk, seasonings and eggs and pour over meat. Dot the top with butter. Bake at 375° for 30 minutes or until done.

POOR MAN'S STEAK

1 lb. hamburger	1 cup cracker crumbs
1 cup milk	1 tsp. salt
1/4 tsp. pepper	1 small onion, chopped fine

Mix well and shape in a narrow loaf. Let it set for at least 8 hours, or overnight. Slice in pieces and fry till brown. Put slices in layers in a roaster and spread mushroom soup on each piece. Use one can of soup. Bake one hour at 325°. (Pan gravy may be used with the mushroom soup.)

BEGGAR'S DISH

Take 1 pound or more of hamburger with a bit of onions. Fry until good and done, then take a can of red kidney beans. Drain off liquid. Put beans in with meat. Mix in well, then fry until good and done. This is an economical dish when meat is so expensive.

* For variation a can of condensed tomato soup may be added with the beans. Delicious!

PIZZA PIE (with biscuit mix)

3/4 cup warm water	1 pkg. yeast
2 1/2 cup biscuit mix	

Dissolve yeast in water, add mix, mix well; then knead, roll out, put in pan and let rise for 1/2 hour.
Filling:

3/4 cup chopped onions	2 cups tomato sauce
1 lb. ground beef, cooked	1/2 cup chopped green
1 tsp. oregano	pepper
salt and pepper to taste	

Cook ground beef, onions and green pepper together. Add rest of ingredients. Cook together. Pour into crust and bake. Cheese and/or mushrooms may be put on top.

YEAST PIZZA

1 pkg. dry yeast	1 tsp. sugar
1 cup warm water	1 1/2 tsp. salt
3 cups flour	1/4 cup salad oil

Dissolve yeast in warm water, add sugar, salt, and oil, mix

thoroughly. Add 1/2 of the flour and beat until no lumps. Gradually add remaining flour. Knead dough for 5 minutes. Take half of the dough, roll out to a circle 12 inches in diameter. Place on a greased cookie sheet, leave edges a little thicker than middle, repeat with other half of dough. Put on second cookie sheet, let rise 20 to 30 minutes. Brush the tops with salad oil. Cut one lb. cheese in fine pieces and sprinkle over top. Put two cups tomato sauce lightly over the cheese. Bake at 450° for 15 minutes or until edges are brown and cheese is melted.

JIFFY PIZZA

Dough:

2 cups flour	2/3 cup milk
1 tbsp. baking powder	1/3 cup salad oil
1 tsp. salt	

Sauce:

6 oz. tomato paste	1/4 tsp. pepper
1/4 cup water	1/2 tsp. salt
1 tsp. oregano	2 tbsp. sugar
Cheese, finely chopped	1 lb. browned hamburger
	1 tsp. garlic powder (optional)

Sift flour, baking powder, and 1 tsp. salt. Add milk and oil. Pat dough on bottom of pizza pan. Mix **sauce ingredients** and spread on dough. Crumb the meat on top and sprinkle with finely cut cheese. Bake 25 to 30 minutes at 425°. Serves 6 or more.

CRAZY CRUST PIZZA

Mix 1 cup flour, 1 teaspoon salt, 1 teaspoon oregano, 1/8 teaspoon pepper, 2 eggs, 2/3 cup milk. Grease and flour pizza pan or cookie sheet with sides. Pour in batter and tilt pan to cover bottom. Arrange drained, cooked hamburg (1 quart) over batter; onions and mushrooms. Bake at 400° 20-25 minutes. Remove from oven. Drizzle on 1 cup pizza sauce and slices **Velveeta** cheese. Bake till cheese melts. Instead of pizza sauce, you can use tomato sauce, 1 1/2 teaspoon oregano and pepper.

SPARERIBS AND SAUERKRAUT

4 lbs. or 2 sides spareribs	2 tbsp. brown sugar
salt and pepper	1 tbsp. caraway seeds
1 qt. sauerkraut	1 onion, sliced

1 apple, chopped   2 cups water

Cut ribs and brown in skillet and season. Pour off fat. Place kraut mixed with apples, sugar, caraway, and onion in a kettle. Place ribs on top. Pour water around the meat and kraut. Cover tightly and simmer 1 1/4 to 1 1/2 hours or until ribs are very tender.

BARBECUED SPARERIBS

Add canned ribs to the Tennessee Barbecue Sauce and simmer 15-20 minutes. Sausage may be substituted for ribs.

TENNESSEE BARBECUE SAUCE

1 bottle chili sauce   1 bottle ketchup
2/3 cup brown sugar   3 tbsp. dry mustard
2 tbsp. Worcestershire sauce   1 1/2 cups water
3 medium-sized onions

Mix all ingredients and simmer 15 minutes.

BRINE FOR CANNING STUFFED SAUSAGE

Combine:
 2 qt. water   1/2 tsp. pepper
 1/4 cup salt   1/2 tsp. salt petre
 1/4 cup sugar

Bring mixture to a boil, then add meat. Boil 20 minutes. Pack in jars and cover with liquid. Cold pack for 3 hours.

KRAMER SAUSAGE

50 lbs. meat   12 oz. salt
2 tbsp. black pepper   2 tbsp. sage
1 level tbsp. red pepper

Smoke 3 hours, if preferred, then cold pack for 3 hours.

SUMMER SAUSAGE

25 lbs. beef   1 cup white sugar
10 lbs. pork   2 tsp. salt petre
2 tbsp. garlic powder   1 1/2 cup warm water

Grind the meat and mix all the above ingredients together, then make the following brine:

6 cups salt

5 cups brown sugar

6 heaping tsp. salt petre

3 gal. water

Mix, and bring to a boil. Let cool. Stuff the meat in long narrow bags (bologna size) then place in brine for 3 weeks. Remove from brine and place in cold water overnight. Hang up and smoke in the bags. When smoked, paraffin the bags well, then hang in a cool place. The bags may be hung in the cellar stairs but not in the cellar. Slice and eat cold.

MINCE MEAT (for canning)

1 qt. ground meat

2 qt. sliced apples

2 qt. cider (grape juice
   may be used)

1 qt. sour cherries (optional)

5 cups sugar

1/2 tsp. cinnamon

1/4 tsp. ground cloves

1/4 tsp. allspice

Juice and rind of 2 oranges
   (optional)

Salt to taste

2 cups raisins

Mix all ingredients and cook 15 minutes. Stir frequently to prevent scorching. Add more cider if necessary. Pour into hot sterilized jars and seal at once. Process 30 minutes in hot bath.

CANNED MEAT BALLS

5 lbs. hamburger

3 tsp. salt

1/8 tsp. pepper

Mix well and form in balls the size of walnuts; fry in skillet. When brown pack in jars. When done frying make a brown gravy and divide in jars. If they are not full add water to fill up. Boil in pressure cooker at 10# for 1 hour.

To can meat balls to cook with Spaghetti: Put the meat balls in cans raw, but seasoned, and add water. Cook 1 hour and 25 minutes at 10# in pressure cooker.

CANNING BEEFBURGER

Brown hamburger as for casseroles; add salt, pepper, and whatever seasonings you prefer. (1 lb. salt and 3 tbsp. pepper to 25 lbs. meat) Add chopped parsley, diced celery, chopped onions or the vegetables of your choice (or make some plain). Put in jars and cold pack 1 hour. This is very handy to use in many different dishes.

LEBANON BOLOGNA

50 lbs. beef   1 lb. salt

Let stand 4 days. Then grind meat twice and add:

3 tbsp. pepper   2 1/2 lbs. sugar
2 tbsp. nutmeg   1 1/2 lb. salt
1 1/2 tbsp. salt petre   9 oz. peanut oil or
                                      1/2 lb. lard

The secret is, let your meat season before grinding and stuffing.
Mix when butchering. Cut meat to grind, then put it in large container, making alternate layers of meat and of the mixed seasoning. Let stand a week or 10 days, turning the meat on top every
day or so to prevent drying out. Grind to your desire, add 1/2
pound melted lard to 25 pounds meat. Mix in wooden or enamel
containers. Stuff and let hang 2 or 3 days to settle, then smoke.
Do not overheat with smoke fire.

SUMMER BOLOGNA

60 lbs. beef   1 lb. lard
1 tsp. salt petre   1 qt. salt
1/3 cup pepper (scant)   3 lbs. brown sugar
1 qt. molasses

Let beef stand till just a little old. Soak in strong salt water
about 30 minutes. Smoke 1/2 day. Grind and add the above mixture and mix. Grind again. Stuff in bologna sized bags. Smoke
7 to 10 days.

This is very good if venison is used instead of beef.

BEEF AND PORK BOLOGNA

60 lbs. beef trimmings   1 1/2 oz. coriander or
40 lbs. pork trimmings   1 oz. curry powder
3 lbs. Tender Quick   1 oz. mace
3 to 4 oz. black pepper   Onions if desired

Mix 2 pounds Tender Quick with the 60 pounds chilled beef trimmings and grind, using the coarse grinding plate. After grinding,
spread the meat in a cool place and let it cure for 48 hours. Grind
the 40 pounds chilled pork trimmings with 1 pound Tender Quick
and let cure. After 48 hours, regrind the cured beef, using 1/8"
hole plate. Then add the pork and grind the mixture again. Add
the seasoning and mix thoroughly. A small amount of water will
help to mix. 30 to 40 minutes is not too long for thorough mixing.
Stuff the meat tightly into beef or muslin casings and allow to hang

in a cool place overnight. Then hang the bologna in a smoke house, heated 110 to 120 degrees, and smoke to a rich brown color, about 2 or 3 hours. Put the hot smoked bologna immediately into water heated 160 to 175 degrees and cook until they float or squeak when the pressure of the thumb and fingers on the casings is suddenly released. The cooking time ranges from 20 to 90 minutes, depending on the size of the casings. Plunge the cooked sausage into cold water to chill. Hang in a cool dry place for future use.

DRIED BEEF

(For 20 lbs. beef)

4 1/2 gal. water	20 lbs. beef
Salt enough to carry an egg	2 lbs. brown sugar
1 oz. salt petre	

Put weight on top to keep meat in brine. For large pieces soak 60 hours, small pieces 48 hours. Smoke.

MEAT CURE

2 lbs. brown sugar	2 oz. pepper
4 gal. water	1 oz. salt petre
6 lbs. salt	

Bring to a boil, then cool. Pack meat in tub or crock as tightly as possible. Put weight on top to keep meat in brine. Leave hams in 4 weeks, bacon only 5 or 6 days. Then smoke, and wrap in paper or cloth.

A RECIPE FOR MAKING LARD

To a kettle of fat add:

3 tbsp. soda

5 medium size potatoes, peeled and sliced

Fry out as usual. This is to make a nicer, whiter lard and keeps it from getting a strong taste so soon.

MEAT — for immediate use, or later

Spine, ribs and bacon can be put in salt water (strong enough to float an egg). To use, soak in clear water overnight so it will not be too salty.

Hams can also be put in salt water and may be kept for 6 weeks before smoking.

MEAT CURING HINTS

Trim your meat then chill thoroughly through and through at 40°. Never put salt on the meat before it is thoroughly chilled for salt blocks the body heat. If the body heat does not escape the inside bones may sour before the salt or cure penetrates. Be careful the meat does not freeze.

For 100 pounds of meat, use 7 pounds salt, 2 pounds brown sugar, 2 ounces salt petre. For hams use 1/2 the required amount and about a week later the remainder 1/2. For bacon use 1/2 of the cure recipe. Apply the meat cure only once for bacon and also for the 100 pounds of meat. Using a cup measure, fill it slightly rounding with the cure for every 10 pounds of meat (bacon and hams), putting a second cup on the hams a week later.

HOW TO CURE HAM

When curing hams, poke cure around the bones, especially the shank end, with your fingers and finish by patting the remainder on the meat side. Put the meat in a wooden box which has a few drain holes. Place in a cool cellar or room, keeping the temperature between 45 and 36°, if at all possible, and not below freezing. Two days are required for curing, for every pound of hams. A 25 pound ham requires 50 days. The curing time may be shortened somewhat for a very large ham. Bacon: curing time is 1 1/2 days for each pound of meat.

After the meat is cured, soak it in cold water for 1/2 to 1 hour; then scrub to remove excess salt and mold which forms if your curing room is too warm. This mold won't hurt the meat. TO SMOKE: Pass a twine through shank of hams or shoulders. For bacon: Push a stiff wire through one end to hold it stiff. Put a twine through the meat under the wire to hang it up. Meat will color better when dipped in hot water a few seconds, scrubbing it briskly.

When the meat is cured and smoked, wrap it in a large paper bag. Double the top over and tie it tightly so no flies can enter. The skipper fly which lays eggs to hatch worms, can't be kept out of a room with regular window screens. Hang the meat in a reasonably dry room as this will prevent it from becoming moldy. If it molds, just brush it off. Never wrap your cured meat in plastic.

After you begin cutting a ham, swab some vegetable oil on the cut. This will prevent mold to some extent. This way hams can be kept a long period of time. Some people say they are better the second year than the first. Preferably, they should be aged several months as they will lose their saltiness. If still too salty, soak or cook lightly and pour off the first water.

EASY HAM CURING

Add enough salt to water so that an egg floats. In this brine soak the untreated hams for 6 weeks, then smoke them.

To preserve them, slice or cut the ham into pieces. Dip each piece in soft, partly melted lard. Place in jar. Pour melted lard on top, completely covering the meat. Put lid on jars and set them on the cellar floor.

HOW TO CLEAN COW STOMACH (Tripe)

First rinse stomach in clear cold water. Cut up stomach in parts, then soak it in 1/2 to 1 gallon of fresh lime in cold water from 1/2 to 1 hour or until the inner lining peels off easily.

Clean all the lining off then rinse several times in clear water. Let it set in salt water a day or two before cooking to eat. If cleaned proper it is nice and white and leaves no odor.

SCALLOPED OYSTERS

4 cups crackers (coarsely crushed)
2 cups milk   1 egg
1 (10 oz.) can of oysters   Pepper to taste
1 tbsp. salt (scant)   1/3 cup butter

For a 1 1/2 quart casserole, line bottom with crackers, then oysters and crackers making 2 layers of each. Add milk to the eggs. Pour over it. Do not add milk until just before baking. Arrange butter in thin slices on top. Bake in moderate oven until well heated (aprox. 45-60 minutes).

FRIED OYSTERS

3 doz. oysters   1/2 tsp. salt
2 eggs, beaten   1 tbsp. water
1/2 cup fine cracker crumbs

Drain oysters. Dip in seasoned crumbs, then in a beaten egg diluted with water and then in crumbs again. Fry with butter until golden brown.

FRIED SALMON PATTIES

2 cups cracker crumbs   2 eggs, beaten
1 cup salmon   1 1/2 cups milk
1 tsp. salt (scant)   Pepper to taste

Roll crackers until fine. Mix with other ingredients. Drop by tablespoons and fry with butter.

SALMON LOAF

Fix Amish Dressing (page 48), omitting the chicken and chicken broth. Add 1 can salmon, cut fine. Mix and form into a loaf, or press into a casserole. Bake at 350° from 1 to 1 1/2 hours.

SALMON SOUFFLE

Mince 1 can of salmon   1 cup bread crumbs
2 egg yolks   1/2 tsp. vinegar
1 1/4 cup milk

Mix all together; add beaten egg whites. Put in casserole. Bake 30 minutes in 400° oven.

CANNED FISH

Cut up and pack fish into jar. Add salt and about 1/3 cup vinegar to each quart. Seal and cold pack 3 1/2 to 4 hours. (The bones will soften within 4 weeks and can be eaten.) Serve with a little vinegar and pepper.

MEAT HINTS

* *Add vinegar to the water when coldpacking meat to keep cans free from grease.*

* *To stretch hamburger, crumble about 5 or more slices of bread into a pound of the meat. Add a little milk or tomato juice (or an egg). Mix and form into patties. Fry.*

* *Put a handful of soda in scalding water to scald chickens. This will help remove pin feathers.*

* *To make chickens easier to defeather, the water should be heated to 150 degrees.*

SALADS

MY KITCHEN

God bless my little kitchen,
  I love its every nook
And bless me as I do my work,
  Wash pots and pans and cook.

And the meals that I prepare
  Be seasoned from above,
With Thy blessing and Thy grace,
  But most of all Thy love.

As we partake of earthly food
  The table for us spread.
We'll not forget to thank Thee, Lord,
  Who gives us daily bread.

So bless my little kitchen, God,
  And those who enter in,
May they find nought but joy and peace
  And happiness therein.

                   -Unknown

TOSSED SALADS
* *Add several handfuls of the LEFTOVER BREAD CUBES*
  (toasted) to tossed salads, adding it last.

* *When jello is too solid to whip, put the egg beater*
  in hot water before whipping.

COLESLAW

2 cups cabbage, finely shredded	3 tbsp. vinegar (approx.)
3/4 cup sugar	1/2 tsp. salt
2 tbsp. water	

Mix all ingredients thoroughly until sugar is dissolved. 1/2 cup finely chopped celery or peppers may be added if desired.

The following two salads will keep a long time in the ice box.

DUTCH SLAW

1 large head cabbage, chopped	1/2 cup chopped onions
1/2 cup vinegar	2 cup sugar
1 cup diced celery	1 green pepper, diced
2 tsp. salt	1 tsp. celery seeds
1/2 cup mustard seeds	

Mix and put in glass jar and screw on lid. Ready to serve.

CABBAGE SALAD

4 qts. shredded cabbage	1 pepper (optional)
2 medium onions	

Bring this to a boil then pour over cabbage. Mix.

1 1/2 cup sugar	3/4 cup vinegar
3/4 cup salad oil	1 tbsp. salt
1 tsp. celery seeds	

COLE SLAW DRESSING

1 cup salad dressing	1 tbsp. celery seeds
1/2 cup sugar	2 tbsp. vinegar
1 tsp. garlic powder	1 tsp. salt

Blend well and serve on cole slaw.

KRAUT SALAD

1 qt. sauerkraut, drained
1 cup celery, cut fine
1 small mango, cut fine
1 small onion, cut fine

1/2 cup cooking oil
1 cup sugar
1/2 cup vinegar

Mix.

POTATO SALAD

1 qt. cooked, diced and salted potatoes
10 (or less) hard boiled, sliced eggs
1/2 cup finely chopped celery, if desired
2 cups Velvet salad dressing (page 100)
1 small minced onion

Mix and serve.

MACARONI SALAD

Use well-cooked macaroni instead of potatoes and prepare same as potato salad. Macaroni and potatoes may also be combined and used for Macaroni-Potato Salad. Cooked navy beans may also be added.

HAM-RONI SALAD

1 cup diced ham
2 cups (quick cooked) macaroni
3/4 cup chopped celery
1 cup grated carrots
1/4 cup chopped green pepper

1/4 cup chopped onion
3 tbsp. mayonnaise
1 1/2 tbsp. barbecue sauce
1 tsp. prepared mustard
Salt and pepper

Combine ham, macaroni, celery, carrots, pepper and onion. Combine mayonnaise, barbecue sauce (optional), catsup and mustard. Mix thoroughly and add to other mixture.

CARROT SALAD

1 box orange jello. Mix as directions on box, using slightly more water. When jello starts to thicken, add 1/2 cup finely grated carrots and 1 cup crushed pineapple. If more sweetness is desired, add 2 tbsp. sugar. Stir and let set.

* Raisins may also be added.

QUICK LETTUCE SALAD

Spread lettuce leaves on individual plates; place a pineapple slice or a spoonful of pineapple chunks on each plate. Top with cottage cheese. On this put a spoonful of mayonnaise. Sprinkle nutmeats on top or garnish with a maraschino cherry.

GOLDEN SALAD

1 envelope Knox unflavored gelatine
3/4 cup pineapple juice   1/4 tsp. salt
1/4 cup orange juice   1/4 cup sugar
1 cup drained, diced pineapple   1/4 cup vinegar
1/2 cup orange sections, cut in small pieces
1/2 cup coarsely grated, raw carrots

Mix gelatine, sugar and salt thoroughly in a saucepan. Add pineapple juice. Place over low heat, stirring constantly until gelatine is dissolved. Stir in orange juice and vinegar after removing from heat. Fold in pineapple, oranges and carrots. Put in mold.

PERFECTION SALAD

1 tbsp. gelatine   1 cup cabbage, finely shredded
1/2 cup cold water   2 cups celery, finely cut
2 cups boiling water   2 pimentoes, finely cut
1/2 cup sugar   1/4 cup red or green peppers,
1/2 cup mild vinegar   finely cut
2 tbsp. lemon juice   1 tsp. salt

Soak gelatin in 1/2 cup cold water about 5 minutes. Add boiling water, sugar, vinegar, lemon juice, and salt. When mixture begins to stiffen, add remaining ingredients. Turn into a wet mold and chill. Remove to bed of lettuce. Garnish with mayonnaise.

CARROT CRACKER SALAD

3 cups grated carrots   1 tbsp. sugar
1 1/2 cups soda cracker crumbs   Salt and pepper to taste
3 eggs, chopped   1 cup mayonnaise (approx.)
1 small onion

Mix and serve.

Most any vegetables of the salad variety may be used in the following recipe.

SUMMER SALAD

Take several tablespoons olive oil, cooking oil, or sour cream. Add vinegar or lemon juice, and then salt to taste. If a sweet salad is desired, honey or sugar may be mixed in with the oil.

Add 1/2 banana, finely diced. Mix and then add any of the following vegetables or add of your own choice:

lettuce	1/2 cup carrot, finely diced
radishes	tomatoes
cucumber	onions
celery	spinach

Mix thoroughly and then add 1 handful of raisins and a handful of crushed peanuts (optional).

Variation: Lettuce and onions only
             Lettuce and apples, diced

GREEN BEAN SALAD

Wash, cut off and discard ends from 1 lb. green beans; then cut into 1-inch pieces. Cook for 15 to 20 minutes or until beans are tender. Drain thoroughly, and put beans into a bowl. Keep beans warm. Meanwhile, clean 2 small onions and cut into 1/8 inch thick slices. Separate the onion rings and put them into the bowl with the beans.

Dice and fry 6 slices of bacon until crisp, without pouring off drippings. Then add the following to the bacon: 1/3 cup vinegar, 2 1/2 tbsp. sugar, and 1/2 tsp. salt.

Heat the mixture to boiling, stirring well. Pour the bacon-vinegar mixture over the beans and onions and toss lightly to coat thoroughly.

3-BEAN SALAD

1 cup vinegar	2 tbsp. oil
1 cup sugar	Salt and pepper to taste

Let stand while you slice:
1 sweet onion   1 green or red sweet pepper
1 to 1 1/4 cup celery, diced
1 can yellow beans, cooked and drained
1 can green beans, cooked and drained
1 small can dark red kidney beans, washed and drained

Mix all vegetables together. Add vinegar mixture and let stand 24 hours before serving.

* Salad dressing may be used instead of the vinegar mixture.

PEA SALAD

1 cup cooked peas, drained   1/2 cup sweet pickles, chopped
1 cup celery, cut fine   1/2 cup diced cheese

Season with salt, pepper, and sugar. Mix with a good mayonnaise.

TURNIP SALAD

Take 3 cups finely grated turnips. Add mayonnaise, sugar, salt, and pepper to taste. Add enough milk for the right consistency.

FRUIT SALAD

1 medium jar maraschino cherries
2 qt. peaches   3 lb. sugar
10 oranges   3 cups water
1 qt. crushed pineapples   2 pkg. gelatine
2 lbs. red grapes   soaked in 1 cup water
2 lbs. green grapes   3 lbs. bananas, sliced

Boil sugar and water 2 or 3 minutes. Add a few drops yellow food coloring and gelatine which had been soaked in 1 cup cold water. Pour crushed pineapples over sliced bananas. Stir gently so pineapple juice touches all sides. This will keep bananas from turning brown. (Lemon juice will do the same.) Add the bananas and pineapple to the gelatine. Add other fruit, mix and chill.

PINEAPPLE FRUIT SALAD

1 can pineapples   Heat:
1/2 doz. bananas   Juice of the pineapples
1 doz. marshmallows   1/2 cup sugar
1 cup mixed nuts   1 tbsp. butter

Mix 1 tbsp. flour with cold water, enough to make a smooth paste. Add 1 egg, stir into the paste. Add heated juice, sugar and butter; mix and then boil until it thickens slightly. Cool. Pour over fruit mixture. Serve with whipped cream.

LETTUCE-PINEAPPLE SALAD

Follow the above recipe but omit the bananas, nuts and whipped cream. Instead, add cut up lettuce, marshmallows and pineapple.

CHRISTMAS SALAD

First part:
2 pkg. lime jello   3 1/2 cups water   1 medium can crushed
                                          pineapple, drained
    Mix jello, using the 3 1/2 cups of water instead of following package directions. Add crushed pineapple. Pour into 9" x 13" cake pan and chill until firm.

Second part:
    Bring pineapple juice to a boil. Soften 2 pkg. Knox gelatin in 2/3 cup cold water. Add to boiling pineapple juice. Cool until partially set. Soften 1 small package Philadelphia cream cheese and add to gelatin mixture. Whip 1 cup cream and sweeten to taste. Add to pineapple-cheese mixture and pour over firm lime jello. Refrigerate until firm.

Third part:
2 pkg. strawberry jello   3 1/2 cups water
 Mix jello, using the 3 1/2 cups of water instead of following package directions. Chill until partially set. Pour over second part and chill until firm.

  * If desired, half of the crushed pineapples may be added to strawberry jello instead of putting them all into the lime jello.

TRIPLE TREAT SALAD

First layer:
    Prepare 1 small pkg. strawberry jello according to directions. Pour into 9 x 9 inch pan. Slice 2 bananas into the jello. Let set until firm.

Second layer:
    Take 1 small pkg. lemon jello and dissolve in 1 cup hot water. Add 1 small pkg. Cream Cheese and 1/3 cup mayonnaise. Beat well. When partially set, pour over the first layer.

 Third layer:
    Dissolve 1 small pkg. lime jello in 2 cups water. When cool, add 1/2 cup crushed pineapple. Chill. When partially set, pour on top of the other two layers.
    Slice in cubes when ready to serve.

CROWN JEWEL JELLO

Prepare separately a pkg. of raspberry, lime and black cherry jello, using 1 cup hot water and 1/2 cup cold water for each. Dissolve in hot water, then add the cold water. Let set until firm. Heat 1/4 cup sugar and 1 cup pineapple juice to boiling. Dissolve 1 pkg. strawberry jello in the hot liquid. Add 1/2 cup cold water. Chill until syrupy. Whip 2 cups cream. Fold cream and 1/2-inch cut jello cubes into syrupy jello. Pour into dish and chill.

MARY'S LIME SALAD

Melt 16 marshmallows and 1 cup milk in a double boiler. Pour hot mixture over 1 pkg. lime jello. Stir until dissolved. Stir in 2 (3 oz.) pkg. cream cheese. Stir till cheese dissolves. Add 1 (No.2) can crushed pineapples and cool until mixture becomes syrupy. Blend in 1 cup whipped cream and 2/3 cup salad dressing. Chill until firm.

RIBBON SALAD

Layer I-
Prepare 1 small pkg. red jello. Pour into oblong cake pan.

Layer II

1 small can crushed pineapple	1 box lemon jello
2/3 cup milk	1 cup whipping cream
16 marshmallows	2/3 cup nuts
1 8 oz. cream cheese	

Heat milk, marshmallows and cheese in double boiler until melted. Add lemon jello. Let cool and add pineapple, nuts and cream, whipped. Pour over layer of red jello after it has set. Chill.

Layer III
Prepare orange jello as to directions and pour on top. Let set until firm.

COTTAGE CHEESE SALAD

1 3 oz. pkg. orange jello	1 small can mandarin oranges
1 pt. creamed cottage cheese	1 small can crushed pineapple
1 pkg. Dream Whip or 1 cup cream whipped	

Drain fruits. Make Dream Whip according to directions. Mix cottage cheese and dry jello thoroughly. Add fruit and Dream Whip. Beat and serve the same day.

WHITE FRUIT SALAD

2 tbsp. gelatine
1 cup hot fruit juice
1/2 can white cherries
1/2 cup chopped nuts
1/4 cup powdered sugar

1/2 cup cold fruit juice
1/2 cup pineapple slices
1 cup mayonnaise
1 cup cream, whipped

Soak gelatine in cold fruit juice, drained from canned fruit, for about 5 minutes. Dissolve in hot fruit juice. When mixture begins to stiffen, add mayonnaise and beat in cream and powdered sugar. Add pineapples and cherries, cut in small pieces, and nuts. Put in wet molds. Serve with lettuce and mayonnaise mixed with a little whipped cream. Serves 12.

PINEAPPLE AND CHEESE SALAD

1 pkg. lime jello
1/2 cup nuts

1 small can crushed pineapple
2 cups cottage cheese

When jello begins to set, whip as you would whipping cream. Fold in pineapple, cheese and nuts, cut fine. Chill.

* 1/4 cup sugar and 1 can whipped evaporated milk may be added.

APRICOT SALAD

Prepare as 3-Layer Salad, but use 2 boxes apricot jello, 2 diced bananas, and 2 cups mashed apricots (apricots instead of pineapple on bottom layer)

APPLE SALAD

6 apples, diced
1/2 cup diced celery
4 bananas

1/2 cup nuts, cut fine (peanuts
may be used)

Filling: Mix 1 cup white sugar, 2 tbsp. flour and 1 egg with enough cold water to make a thickening. Add 1 cup hot water and boil. Add a little salt and vinegar and 1 tbsp. butter. Cool and mix with apples, etc. Whipped cream may also be added.

* Marshmallows and pineapple may also be added.

3-LAYER SALAD

Fix 2 small boxes jello according to directions. Add 1 cup drained crushed pineapple. Put into the bottom of oblong cake pan.

Let set until firm.

Cook: 1/2 cup sugar, 2 tbsp. cornstarch, and 2 egg yolks. Blend with 1/2 cup cold water. Pour into 1 1/2 cups hot pineapple juice. Cook until thick. Cool, then pour onto the jello. Chill.

When ready to serve, top with 1 large pkg. Philadelphia cream cheese blended with 1 cup Marvel cheese (page 298) and 1 cup cream, whipped. Add sugar to whipped cream if desired.

PERFECT SALAD DRESSING

1/2 cup sugar	2 tbsp. vinegar (scant)
1 tsp. salt	2 tbsp. salad dressing

Mix, then add 1/3 cup milk or cream. Mix until sugar is dissolved. Serve with cut up lettuce.

FRENCH DRESSING

1 can condensed tomato soup	1 cup cooking oil
1/2 cup sugar	3/4 cup vinegar

1 tsp. of each of the following: paprika, salt, onion salt, pepper, garlic salt, dry mustard, horseradish (optional).

Put ingredients in jar and shake. Keep cool.

* 2 tbsp. Worcestershire sauce and 1 small chopped onion may be added.

SUSAN'S SIMPLE SALAD DRESSING

1 cup white sugar	1 cup salad oil
1/2 cup vinegar	1/4 cup lemon juice
3/4 cup catsup	3 tbsp. grated onion
1 tbsp. salt	1 tsp. celery seed
1/2 tsp. paprika	

Mix all together well. Keep in ice box.

TOSSED SALAD DRESSING

1 1/3 cup white sugar	2 tsp. salt
2 tsp. paprika	1 cup vinegar
2 tbsp. dry mustard	1 cup salad oil
1 tsp. celery seed	1 small onion, grated

VELVET SALAD DRESSING

1 tbsp. flour or Clear Jel	1 egg
1/2 cup sugar	1 tsp. prepared mustard
1 tsp. salt	4 tbsp. vinegar
1 cup cold water	3 tbsp. butter

Beat egg well and add dry ingredients, vinegar and water. Cook in double boiler until thick. Remove from heat and beat in 3 tbsp. butter. This dressing is good for lettuce and potato salad. Cream or 2 tbsp. mayonnaise can be added.

HOMEMADE MIRACLE WHIP

3/4 cup cooking oil	1/2 tsp. dry mustard
1 tbsp. lemon juice	2 tsp. salt
2/3 cup sugar	1 egg plus water to make
	3/4 cup

Beat water and egg thoroughly with egg beater.
Cook the following in a qt. saucepan:

2/3 cup flour	1/2 cup vinegar
1 cup water	

Bring to a boil, then blend in the other ingredients. Beat hard until smooth.

SALAD DRESSING

Heat:
  1 pt. milk, 1/2 cup sugar and 1/2 tsp. salt.
Moisten 5 tbsp. flour with milk and stir into hot milk mixture. Stir until boiling. Add 3 tbsp. vinegar, 2 tsp. mustard and 1/2 tsp. turmeric dissolved in hot water. Let stand until cold, then beat and add cream to consistency desired.

ELLA'S SALAD DRESSING

1/4 cup vinegar	1/3 cup catsup
1/2 cup oil	1/2 cup sugar
1 tsp. salt	1 tbsp. miracle whip

Shake well. Will keep quite awhile in the ice box.

HOMEMADE MUSTARD

1/2 cup vinegar	1/2 cup sweet cream
1/2 cup sugar	2 tbsp. dry mustard
2 tbsp. flour	1 egg

Mix all ingredients, then boil in the double boiler until thick. To color, add a shake of turmeric.

MONOTONY BREAKER

Mix together 1 1/4 cup boiling water and 1 box cherry jello. Grind cranberries— enough to make 1 cup; add 1 cup sugar and about 1/4 cup water. Cook cranberries, sugar and water until cranberries are soft. When cool, blend the 2 mixtures and add 1 cup apples (ground) and 1 cup pineapples (crushed) and broken nuts.

CRANBERRY SAUCE

1 lb. cranberries	4 cups sugar
8 apples	1 can crushed pineapple, if
2 oranges or 2 tsp. Tang	desired
dissolved in a little water	

Grind all together; do not heat. Let stand a few days to sweeten.

COOKED CRANBERRY SAUCE

1 lb. cranberries. Add 1 1/2 cups water and boil together cranberries and 18 apples. Put through ricer or food mill. Add 4 or 5 cups sugar or according to taste. Stir while cooling. Grate the rind of 2 oranges. Extract the juice. Add both when cool.

FRUIT GLAZE

Soak 1 tbsp. gelatine in 2 tbsp. water. Thaw 1 1/2 cups frozen sweetened fruit or use fresh fruit. Press through sieve. Bring to a boil in saucepan. Remove from heat and add gelatine. Stir until gelatine is dissolved. Chill until set but not firm. Pour over a dessert such as puddings, pies or whatever desired.

BEATITUDES FOR HOMEMAKERS

Blessed is she whose daily tasks are a work of love; for her willing hands and happy heart transform duty into joyous service to all her family and God.

Blessed is she who opens the door to welcome both stranger and well-loved friends; for gracious hospitality is a test of brotherly love.

Blessed is she who mends both stockings and broken toys and broken hearts; for her understanding is a balm to her husband and children.

Blessed is she who scours and scrubs; for well she knows that cleanliness is one expression of godliness.

Blessed is she whom children love; for the love of a child is of greater value than fortune or fame.

Blessed is she who sings in her work; for music lightens the heaviest load and brightens the dullest chore.

Blessed is she who dusts away doubt and fear and sweeps all the cobwebs of confusion; for her faith will triumph over all adversity.

Blessed is she who serves laughter and smiles with every meal; for her cheerfulness is an aid to mental and physical digestion.

Blessed is she who introduces Jesus Christ to her children; for Godly sons and daughters shall be her reward.

Blessed is she who preserves the sacredness of the Christian home; for hers is a divine trust that crowns her with dignity.

—Ella May Miller

CAKES

CUPCAKES

GINGERBREAD

JELLY ROLLS

CAKE HINTS

* Much less sugar can be used in some of the cake, cookies, or dessert recipes, and the food is no less tasty. In many instances, molasses or honey can be substituted for sugar. Someone said we pay twice for sugar or sweets- when we buy the sugar and candy and again when we pay the dentist bill.

* To substitute honey for sugar in a cookie or cake recipe, reduce the amount of liquid 1/4   cup for each cup of honey used. When honey is substituted in baked goods, add 1/2 teaspoon baking soda to the recipe for every cup of honey used and bake at a lower temperature.

* When making a bought READY-MIX CAKE add 1 tablespoon cooking oil. This brings out more of the flavor and will make the cake more moist.

* Measure shortening before molasses in baking and it will not stick to the cup.

TIPS ON MAKING ANGEL FOOD CAKES
* Have all ingredients at room temperature.
* Use cake flour only.
* Egg whites must be clean and should not contain a part of the yolks.
* Have the sugar clean if bea en with the egg whites. Only a bit of flour might damage the cake.
* Fold in flour and sugar mixture gently. <u>Do not beat</u>. Fold in with a cake scraper.
* Bake in an ungreased tube pan. When baked, turn upside down to cool.
* Be careful not to over-bake.

LYDIA'S ANGEL FOOD CAKE

1 1/2 cup egg whites (11-12)	1 cup cake flour
1 1/2 cup white sugar	1/2 tsp. salt
1 1/2 tsp. cream of tartar	1 tsp. almond flavor

Sift together 3/4 cup of the sugar and the flour three times. Set aside. Beat egg whites until frothy, then add salt and cream of tartar. Beat until it stands in peaks. Add 3/4 cup of the sugar about 3 tablespoons at a time, beating well with egg beater each time after adding the sugar. Lightly fold in the sugar-flour mixture, adding about 1/2 cup at a time. Add flavoring. Bake at 375° for about 35-40 minutes or until done.

CHOCOLATE ANGEL FOOD CAKE

2 cups egg whites (14-16)	1 tsp. cream of tartar
1 1/2 cups sugar	3/4 cup cake flour
1/4 tsp. salt	1 tsp. vanilla
1/4 cup cocoa	

Sift flour, cocoa and salt together. Add cream of tartar to egg whites and beat until they will hold peaks. Add vanilla, then sugar gradually and fold in flour mixture. Put in ungreased tube pan and bake 40-45 minutes at 350 to 375 degrees.

NUT ANGEL FOOD CAKE

Use Lydia's Angel Food Cake recipe. Omit almond extract and add 1/2 cup ground walnuts to the flour and sugar mixture.

MARASCHINO CHERRY ANGEL FOOD CAKE

Grind 1 small jar maraschino cherries (about 2/3 cup). Fold into Lydia's Angel Food Cake batter and bake.

BUTTERSCOTCH OR CHOCOLATE CHIP ANGEL FOOD CAKE

Use a white angel food cake recipe. Add 3/4 cup Butterscotch Bits or Chocolate Chips to the batter.

FOR JELLO ANGEL FOOD CAKE

Mix in 2 or 3 tablespoons any flavor jello into the Angel Food Cake batter.

BROWN SUGAR ANGEL FOOD CAKE

2 cups egg whites (14-16)   1 tsp. salt
2 tsp. vanilla   2 cups brown sugar
1 1/2 tsp. cream of tartar   1 1/2 cups sifted flour

Beat egg whites with cream of tartar and vanilla and salt till stiff peaks form. Gradually sift 1 cup sugar over egg whites and beat. Sift remaining cup of brown sugar with flour. Fold into egg whites. Turn into ungreased 10 inch tube cake pan. Bake in 350° oven 45 to 50 minutes.

YELLOW SPONGE CAKE

Sift together:
1 1/2 cup sifted flour   1/2 tsp. baking powder
1 cup sugar   1/4 tsp. salt
Blend:
6 egg yolks   1 tsp. vanilla
1/2 cup sugar

Beat yolks with sugar and vanilla until fluffy. Then add the flour mixture and 1/2 cup cold water— first flour, then alternately with the water. Fold in 6 stiffly beaten egg whites. Pour into a tube pan and bake approximately 1 hour in 350 degree oven.
Cooked Icing:
3/4 cup milk and 1/3 cup flour cooked until real thick.
Let get cold then beat in 1 stick butter or oleo, 3/4 cup sugar and 1 teaspoon vanilla. Beat until real fluffy like whipped cream. Ice the cake and cover with coconut or fine nutmeats.

SPONGE CAKE

1 1/2 cups sugar   1/2 cup cold water
1 1/2 cups flour   1 tsp. baking powder
5 eggs, well beaten   1/4 tsp. salt
        separately   3/4 tsp. cream of tartar

Sift all dry ingredients together except cream of tartar. Beat water with egg yolks until thick then fold in the dry ingredients. Beat egg whites with the cream of tartar until it stands in peaks. Fold into the other mixture. Bake in tube pan 1 hour at 350°.

LEMON SPONGE CAKE

1 cup sifted cake flour   3/4 cup sugar
1 tsp. baking powder   2 egg whites

1/2 cup cold water

2 tsp. grated, lemon rind

2 egg yolks, beaten

1 tsp. lemon juice

2 tbsp. sugar

1/2 tsp. salt

Sift dry ingredients, flour, baking powder and salt 4 times.

Add water and lemon rind to egg yolks and beat until lemon colored.

Add sugar (2 tsp. at a time) beating after each addition.

Add dry ingredients, slowly stirring to blend. Beat egg whites until they peak. Add lemon juice and 2 tablespoons sugar, beating until well blended. Fold egg whites into the rest of the batter. Pour into a tube pan and bake 1 hour at 350°.

LEMON CHIFFON CAKE

2 eggs, separated

1 1/2 cups sugar

2 1/4 cups sifted flour

3 tsp. baking powder

1 tsp. salt

1/3 cup cooking oil

1 cup milk

2 tsp. lemon juice

Grated rind of 1 lemon

Sift 1 cup sugar with flour, baking powder and salt. Add the oil, half of milk and lemon juice and rind. Beat until fluffy, then add egg yolks and remaining milk, beating until smooth.

Beat egg whites until frothy; gradually beat in 1/2 cup of the sugar, beating until stiff and glossy. Fold this into the batter.

Bake at 350 degrees for 30 minutes.

SPICE CHIFFON CAKE

1 3/4 cups and 2 tbsp. All-Purpose flour

1 1/2 cups sugar

3 tsp. baking powder

1 tsp. salt

1 tsp. cinnamon

1/2 tsp. nutmeg

1/2 tsp. allspice

1/2 tsp. cloves

1/2 cup salad oil

5 egg yolks

3/4 cup water

2 tsp. vanilla

1 cup (7-8) egg whites

1/2 tsp. cream of tartar

Sift together the flour, sugar, baking powder, salt and spices. Beat well the egg yolks, water and vanilla, then add to dry ingredients and oil. Beat egg whites stiff with cream of tartar. Fold in last. Pour into ungreased 10-inch tube pan. Bake at 325° for 55 minutes, then at 350° for 10 minutes more.

WHOLE WHEAT COCOA CHIFFON CAKE

1/2 cup cocoa   3/4 cup boiling water
Stir until smooth, then set aside to cool.
7 or 8 eggs — separate eggs until there is 1 cup whites. Set yolks
aside. Add 1/2 teaspoon cream of tartar to the whites and whip
until very stiff peak forms.
Measure and sift together into mixing bowl:
1 3/4 cups whole wheat flour   1 tsp. salt
1 1/2 cups raw sugar   3 tsp. baking powder
Make a well and add in order:
1/2 cup salad oil
the egg yolks   the cooled cocoa mixture
                                 1 tsp. vanilla

   Beat until smooth and creamy. Pour egg yolk mixture gradually
over whipped egg whites while gently folding with rubber scraper
just until blended. Bake in a tube pan for 55 minutes at 325°. Increase to 350° for 10 to 15 minutes.

CHOCOLATE 2-EGG CHIFFON CAKE

2 eggs   3/4 tsp. salt
1 1/2 cups sugar   1/3 cup cooking oil
1 3/4 cups sifted cake flour   1 cup buttermilk
3/4 tsp. soda   2 sq. unsweetened chocolate
                                    (2 oz.) melted

   Heat oven to 350°. Grease well and dust with flour two round
layer pans— 8 inch by at least 1 1/2 inches deep or 9"x 1 1/2" or
one oblong pan 13"x 9 1/2"x 2".
   Beat egg whites until frothy. Gradually beat in 1/2 cup of the
sugar. Continue beating until very stiff and glossy. Sift remaining sugar, flour, soda, and salt into another bowl. Add oil and
half of buttermilk. Beat 1 minute medium speed on mixer or 150
vigorous strokes by hand. Scrape sides and bottom of bowl constantly. Add remaining buttermilk, egg yolks, chocolate. Beat
1 more minute scraping bowl constantly. Fold in meringue. Pour
in prepared pans. Bake layers 30 to 35 minutes.
   Sweet milk may be used instead of buttermilk.

GERMAN SWEET CHOCOLATE CAKE

1 bar (4oz.) Baker's German Sweet Chocolate
1/2 cup boiling water   1 tsp. vanilla
1 cup butter or margarine   1/2 tsp. salt
2 cups sugar   2 1/2 cups sifted cake flour

4 egg yolks, unbeaten

1 cup buttermilk

1 tsp. baking soda

4 egg whites, stiffly beaten

Melt chocolate in boiling water. Cool. Cream butter and sugar until fluffy. Add egg yolks, one at a time, and beat well after each addition. Add melted chocolate and vanilla.

Sift together flour, salt and soda. Add alternately with buttermilk to chocolate mixture, beat well. Beat until smooth. Fold in whites. Pour into 3 layer pans (8 or 9 inch) which have been lined on bottoms with paper. Bake in moderate oven 30 to 40 minutes. Cool. Spread with coconut pecan frosting.

Instead of Baker's German Chocolate you can use: 6 tbsp. cocoa, 2 tbsp. margarine and 3 cups flour instead of 2 1/2 cups.

CHOCOLATE FUDGE CAKE

1 1/2 cups sugar

1/2 cup butter

2 eggs

1 tsp. soda with a little
vinegar to moisten

2 squares of chocolate

2 1/2 cups flour

1/2 cup buttermilk

1 tsp. vanilla

Cream butter and sugar, then 1 egg at a time. Alternate buttermilk and flour.

LAZY WIFE CAKE

1 1/2 cups pastry flour

1/4 tsp. salt

2 tsp. soda

1 tsp. vanilla

3 tbsp. cocoa

1 cup white sugar

7 tbsp. cooking oil

1 tbsp. vinegar

Sift the above ingredients into a 9 x 9 ungreased cake pan. Mix with fork. Make three holes in the dry ingredients. Into one put the vanilla, the next the oil, and into the third the vinegar. Pour over all this 1 cup cold water. Mix with a fork. Do not beat. Bake at 350° for 25 to 30 minutes or until done.

COCOA CAKE

6 tbsp. butter or oleo

2 cups sugar

2 cups sour milk or buttermilk

2 tsp. soda

2 tsp. vanilla

3 cups flour (scant)

1/2 cup, or less, cocoa

Melt the butter and mix with sugar. Add the sour milk in which the soda has been dissolved. Add vanilla. Then add the flour and cocoa which have been sifted together. Bake 40-45 minutes at 350°.

SUGARLESS CHOCOLATE CAKE

2 beaten eggs
1 cup hot water
1 cup table syrup or honey
1 cup melted lard

1/2 cup cocoa
2 tsp. soda
2 1/4 cups flour
1/4 tsp. salt

Sift dry ingredients together. Add hot water, a little at a time, and stir well after each addition. Add the lard, syrup and beaten eggs. Mix well. Bake at 350° for 30 to 40 minutes.

DELUXE COCOA CAKE

1 cup granulated sugar
2 cups sifted flour
1 tsp. soda
1/2 cup brown sugar
   firmly packed
1/2 cup shortening

2/3 cup buttermilk or sour milk
1 tsp. vanilla extract
2 eggs
3 squares unsweetened chocolate,
   cut up and melted in 1/2 cup
   boiling water.

Have shortening at room temperature. Stir just enough to soften. Add sugar, forcing through a sieve to remove lumps (if necessary). Mix sugar and shortening. Add flour, soda, and granulated sugar. Add 1/2 cup of sour milk, the vanilla, and eggs. Mix until all flour is dampened, then mix one minute or 100 strokes. Add remaining liquids. Blend and beat the same amount as before. Add chocolate mixture and beat 1 minute longer. Scrape bowl and spoon often to make sure all batter is well mixed. Turn batter into 2 greased and floured 9 inch layer pans. Bake in moderate oven (350°) for 30 minutes.
   May be baked in loaf pan.

MARBLE CAKE

Sift together:
2 1/2 cups flour
1 1/2 tsp. baking powder
1 2/3 cup sugar
Mix in small bowl:
1 sq. chocolate, melted
2 tbsp. hot water
Stir to soften:
3/4 cup shortening

1 1/2 tsp. soda
1 tsp. salt

1/4 tsp. soda
1 tbsp. sugar

Stir flour mixture into shortening, mixing alternately with 3/4 cup sour milk.

Add: 2 unbeaten eggs. Beat well. Add chocolate mixture to 1/4 of batter. Put large spoonful of batter into cake pans alternating plain and chocolate mixtures. Then with knife cut through batter in a wide zig-zag course. Bake at 350° till done.

AUNT FRONIE CAKE

2 cups sugar
Cream together, then add:
2 beaten eggs
2 cups flour
1 tsp. baking powder
1/2 cup sour milk

1/4 cup shortening

4 tbsp. cocoa
1/2 tsp. salt
2 tsp. soda

Mix all ingredients, then add 1 cup boiling water. Mix thoroughly. Bake at 350° for about 30 minutes or until done.

CHOCOLATE MINT DREAM CAKE

2 cups flour
3/4 tsp. salt
1 1/2 cup white sugar
3 tsp. baking powder
1/2 cup cocoa

2/3 cup shortening
1 cup milk
1 tsp. vanilla
2 eggs

Sift all dry ingredients together. Add shortening, milk, vanilla. Mix, then add 2 eggs. Beat well. Bake at 350° for 30 to 35 minutes. Cut the top of the cake off through the center with a thread and add the following filling, or place the filling on top as icing.

Peppermint whipped cream filling:

Beat 1 pint whipped cream until stiff. Add 1/3 cup icing sugar and 1/2 teaspoon peppermint flavor. Tint with green food coloring.

VELVET CHOCOLATE CAKE

2 cups cake flour
1/2 tsp. salt
2 cups brown sugar
1/2 cup shortening
2 well-beaten eggs

1/2 cup cocoa
1 cup cold water
1 tsp. vanilla
1 tsp. soda dissolved in
2 tbsp. boiling water
1 cup chopped nuts may be added.

Sift flour once, measure and mix with salt and cocoa and sift again. Cream shortening, add sugar gradually, beating thoroughly after each addition. Add vanilla, then well-beaten eggs and beat until fluffy. Beat in flour mixture alternately with the water. Add the dissolved soda and beat well. Bake in layer cake pans 350 degrees for 30-35 minutes.

FIVE STAR FUDGE CAKE

1 1/2 cups butter or margarine
4 1/2 cups sugar
3 tsp. vanilla
6 eggs
6 (1 oz.) sq. unsweetened
 chocolate

6 cups sifted cake flour
3 tsp. soda
1 heaping tsp. baking powder
1 1/2 tsp. salt
3 cups ice water

Cream butter, sugar, eggs and vanilla until fluffy. Blend in melted chocolate. Sift together dry ingredients, add alternately with water to chocolate mixture. Pour batter into three 8-inch layer pans which have been greased and lined with wax paper. Bake in a moderate oven 30 to 35 minutes.

EASY CHOCOLATE CAKE

Pan size			
small	med.	large	
8 x 8	13 x 9 1/2	14 x 9 1/2	Measure and sift:
1	2	3	heaping cups sifted flour
1	2	3	rounded tbsp. cocoa
1	2	3	tsp. soda
1/8	1/4	1/2	tsp. baking powder
1/8	1/4	1/2	tsp. salt
			Beat:
1	2	3	eggs
			Add:
1/4	1/2	3/4	cups shortening
1	2	3	cups sugar. Cream well.
			Add alternately with dry ingredients; mix well:
1/4	1/2	3/4	cup buttermilk or sour milk
1/2	1	1 1/2	cup boiling water
1	2	3	tsp. vanilla

Dough will be thin. Bake in hot oven 375 or 400 degrees.

CHOCOLATE MAYONNAISE CAKE

2 cups flour
1 cup sugar
1/2 cup cocoa
2 tsp. soda

1 cup boiling water
1 tsp. vanilla
1 cup salad dressing
(homemade miracle whip on
page 100, may be used.)

Sift together: flour, sugar, cocoa, and soda. Mix all together.
Bake at 325° to 350° for 45 minutes.

CARAMEL CAKE

Cream together:
  2 cups brown sugar
Next add:
  2 eggs unbeaten
  1 tsp. vanilla

1/2 cup lard

2 cups flour (all-purpose)

Put 1 tsp. cocoa in a cup. Add 2 tsp. hot water. Fill the cup
with sour milk, then add 1 tsp. soda. Stir this mixture until
cocoa is well dissolved. The cup will run over so be sure to hold
it over the mixing bowl while stirring. When cocoa is dissolved
pour in with the other ingredients and mix. Bake in 350° oven.

CREME VELVET CAKE

1/2 cup margarine or crisco
1 1/2 cup sugar
1/2 tsp. salt
1 cup water

2 1/2 cups cake flour
2 1/2 tsp. baking powder
3 egg whites
1 tsp. vanilla

Cream margarine and gradually add sugar, creaming well. Add
salt and water, alternately with sifted flour with baking powder.
Last fold in stiffly beaten egg whites and vanilla. Bake at 350° for
35 to 40 minutes.

WHITE AS SNOW CAKE

2 1/2 cups sifted cake flour
4 1/2 tsp. baking powder
1 1/2 cup sugar
1 tsp. salt

1 cup milk
1/2 cup shortening
4 egg whites - at least 1/2 cup-
                 unbeaten
1 tsp. vanilla extract

Sift all the dry ingredients into mixing bowl. Add shortening
(soft but not melted) and 2/3 of the milk. Beat until batter is well

blended and glossy, 150 strokes by hand. Add remaining milk, egg whites, flavoring. Beat until smooth — about 150 strokes. Pour into 2 well greased and floured 8-inch layer cake pans. Bake in moderate oven 30 minutes at (350°). May also be baked in loaf pan. Nuts may be added.

AMISH CAKE

Cream: 1/2 cup butter and 2 cups brown sugar (packed). Add 2 cups buttermilk or sour milk with 2 teaspoons soda. Add 3 cups flour and 1 teaspoon vanilla. Bake at 375°. Spread the following topping on top after cake is done. Return to oven and bake until bubbly, or 1 minute.
Topping:

6 tablespoons soft butter, 4 tablespoons milk, 1 cup brown sugar, 1/2 cup nuts.

PRALINE CAKE

1 cup butter or veg. shortening	3 cups sifted flour
2 cups sugar	1 tsp. cream of tartar
4 eggs, separated	1 tsp. soda
	1 cup buttermilk

Cream shortening and sugar until light. Add egg yolks, one at a time, and beat till fluffy. Sift dry ingredients and add alternately with buttermilk. Fold in stiffly beaten egg whites. Bake in 9"x13"x2" greased and floured cake pan at 350° for 50 minutes. Remove from oven and spread with Praline topping on page 130. Place under broiler or in a hot oven for 1 or 2 minutes.

FEATHER CAKE

1/2 cup shortening	1 cup milk
2 cups sugar	3 cups self-rising flour
3 whole eggs or 5 egg whites	1 tsp. vanilla

Cream shortening, add sugar, and beat again. Add milk and flour alternately and vanilla. Last add the eggs. Mix and bake in pans of your choice. If using plain flour add 3 teaspoons baking powder and 1/2 teaspoon salt.

SUNSHINE CAKE

8 eggs	1/2 tsp. salt
1 1/2 cup raw sugar	1 cup whole wheat flour

1 1/2 tsp. lemon extract
1/2 tsp. cream of tartar

2 tbsp. water
1/2 cup chopped nuts

Separate eggs. Beat whites until frothy. Add cream of tartar. Gradually add 1 cup sugar. Continue beating until very stiff peaks form. Beat yolks until very thick, add salt, flavoring and 1/2 cup sugar. Continue beating — add water and whole wheat flour alternately. Beat well. Fold yolks into whites, very gently. Fold in nuts. Pour into Angel Food Cake pan. Bake at 325 to 350 degrees for 1 1/2 hours. Invert on funnel. Cool one hour. Remove from pan. May be eaten unfrosted, or frosted with Sea Foam frosting.

HANDY MADE CAKE

2 cups sugar
1/2 cup butter or margarine
3 eggs, beaten
1 cup milk

2 1/2 cups bread flour
3 tsp. baking powder
1 tsp. salt
1 tsp. vanilla

Cream shortening and sugar. Add eggs. Sift flour, baking powder, and salt together, then add alternately with milk. Add vanilla. Bake at 350 for 35-40 minutes.

VELVET CRUMB CAKE

1 1/3 cup biscuit mix
3/4 cup sugar
3 tbsp. soft shortening

1 egg
3/4 cup milk
1 tsp. vanilla

Heat oven to 350°. Grease and flour a square pan (9"x9"x 1 1/2"). Mix biscuit mix and sugar. Add shortening, egg and 1/4 cup milk. Beat 1 minute. Stir in the rest of milk gradually. Add vanilla; beat 1/2 minute. Pour into pan. Bake 35 to 40 minutes. Cover with broiled topping while warm.

BROILED TOPPING:

Mix 3 tbsp. soft butter, 1/3 cup brown sugar, packed, 2 tbsp. cream, 1/2 cup wheaties or coconut, 1/4 cup chopped nuts. Spread on baked cake, then place under low heat until bubbly and brown, 3 to 5 minutes.

CRUMB CAKE

2 cups brown sugar
1/2 cup shortening
2 1/2 cups flour
1 cup thick sour milk

2 eggs
2 tsp. baking powder
1 tsp. soda
1 tsp. vanilla

Mix sugar, flour, shortening, baking powder and soda together. Then take out 1 cup of crumbs for top. Mix and add remaining ingredients. Pour batter into greased pan. Sprinkle crumbs over top and bake.

BLACK WALNUT CAKE

2 cups sugar
2 eggs, separated and beaten
1 cup sweet milk
2 1/2 cups flour
Add egg whites last

2 1/2 tsp. baking powder
1/2 cup ground walnuts
1/2 cup butter or lard
1 tsp. vanilla

NUT CAKE

2 cups sugar
1/2 cup butter
1 cup milk
2 1/2 cups flour

2 tsp. baking powder
1 cup nuts
3/4 tsp. salt
3 eggs
1 tsp. vanilla

Cream sugar and butter. Add eggs and vanilla; beat well. Sift together flour, salt, and baking powder, and add alternately with milk. Fold in nuts. Bake at 350° for 30 minutes.

LEMON LAYER CAKE

2/3 cup butter
1 3/4 cups sugar
3 cups sifted cake flour
1 1/4 cups milk

2 eggs
1 1/2 tsp. vanilla
2 1/2 tsp. baking powder
1/2 tsp. salt

Cream butter and sugar. Add eggs and vanilla and beat until fluffy. Sift flour, baking powder and salt. Add alternately with milk, beating after each addition. Beat thoroughly. Pour into 2 greased and floured 9-inch round pans. Bake at 350° for 30 to 35 minutes. Cool, then remove from pans. Fill with lemon filling and top with Fluffy White Frosting.

LEMON FILLING

Combine: 3/4 cups sugar, 2 tablespoons cornstarch and 1/2 tsp. salt in a saucepan. Add 3/4 cup water, 2 slightly beaten egg yolks, and 3 tablespoons lemon juice. Cook and stir over medium heat till thick. Remove from heat then add 1 teaspoon grated lemon peel and 1 tablespoon butter.

COCONUT CAKE

1 1/2 cups sugar
1/2 cup butter
1 cup milk
4 egg whites (well beaten)
1/2 cup coconut

1 tsp. coconut flavor
1 tsp. vanilla
1/2 tsp. salt
4 tsp. baking powder
2 cups flour

Cream butter and sugar; add eggs and beat until batter is creamy. Add milk, salt, coconut, flour and baking powder.

ORANGE COCONUT CAKE

3/4 cup shortening
2 cups sugar
2 egg yolks
3 1/4 cups flour
1/2 tsp. salt
4 tsp. baking powder

1 1/2 tsp. grated orange rind
1/2 cup orange juice
3/4 cup water
1/2 cup coconut
4 egg whites

Cream shortening, add sugar gradually. Beat until fluffy. Add orange rind and beaten egg yolks. Beat again, then mix in the orange juice and water. Sift flour, salt and baking powder twice. Add dry ingredients. Fold in coconut and stiffly beaten egg whites. Pour in layer pans and bake.

GOLDEN FLUFF CAKE

2 cups sifted flour
3 1/2 tsp. baking powder
1 tsp. salt
1 1/3 cup sugar
1/3 cup shortening

1/2 tsp. lemon, optional
1/2 tsp. vanilla flavor
1 cup milk
1/3 cup egg yolks or
(4 medium yolks)

Sift together dry ingredients. Add shortening (which should be at room temperature), lemon and vanilla extracts and 2/3 of the milk. Beat 200 strokes. Add remaining 1/3 cup milk and egg yolks. Beat same amount as before. Pour batter in 2 greased and floured 8-inch layer pans. Bake 30 to 35 minutes in moderate oven (350°). May also be baked in a loaf pan.

TOASTED SPICE CAKE

1/2 cup shortening
2 cups brown sugar
2 egg yolks
2 1/2 cups cake flour

1 tsp. baking powder
1 1/2 tsp. cinnamon
1 tsp. cloves
1 1/4 cups sour milk

1/2 tsp. salt   1 tsp. vanilla
1 tsp. soda

Cream together shortening and sugar. Add egg yolks and beat well. Sift flour once. Measure and add salt, soda, baking powder and spices. Sift again. Add dry ingredients to first mixture alternately with milk and flavoring. Beat well after each addition. Pour in greased flat pan (8"x 12"x 1 1/4").

Spread the following meringue mixture over the batter before baking. Beat 2 egg whites till stiff enough to hold peaks. Slowly add 1 cup light brown sugar to whites, beating until smooth. Spread over cake batter and sprinkle with 1/2 cup finely chopped nuts or 1/2 cup shredded coconut. Bake at 350° for 40 minutes.

SOUR CREAM SPICE CAKE

1/2 cup shortening	2 tsp. cinnamon
2 cups brown sugar	1 tsp. cloves
3 eggs, separated	1 tsp. allspice
1 cup sour cream	1 3/4 cups flour sifted with
1 tsp. vanilla	1/2 tsp. salt
1 tsp. soda	

Cream shortening and sugar; add egg yolks. Add flour, soda and spices. Add sour cream and beat well. Add vanilla and fold in stiffly beaten egg whites. Bake in greased 8-inch layer pans 25 minutes at 350 degrees.

SUGARLESS SPICE CAKE

2 1/4 cup sifted cake flour	1 tsp. lemon rind
2 1/4 tsp. baking powder	1 tsp. vanilla
1/4 tsp. salt	1/2 cup shortening
1 1/4 tsp. cinnamon	1 cup corn syrup
1/4 tsp. nutmeg	1/2 cup milk
1/4 tsp. cloves	2 eggs unbeaten

Sift together flour, baking powder, spices and salt. Cream the shortening. Add a little flour at a time until all the flour has been stirred in. Add syrup and eggs and beat well. Add the milk, lemon rind and vanilla. Bake 30 minutes at 350°.

NUT SPICE CAKE

3 cups cake flour	2/3 cup shortening
1 1/2 tsp soda	1 cup granulated sugar

3/4 tsp. salt	1 cup brown sugar
3/4 tsp. allspice	3 eggs
3/4 tsp. cloves	1 1/2 cups buttermilk
1 1/2 tsp. cinnamon	1/2 cup chopped nuts

Sift flour, soda, salt, spices together. Cream shortening; add sugars gradually. Cream well. **Add eggs,** 1 at a time, and beat well after each addition. Add sifted dry ingredients alternately with buttermilk. Add nuts with last addition of dry ingredients. Pour into two greased paper-lined 9 inch layer pans. Bake in oven at 350⁰ for 35 to 40 minutes.

OLD SPICE CAKE

1 tbsp. or 1 cake yeast	1 cup warm water
1 tsp. sugar	2 beaten eggs
1/2 cup lard	1 cup raisins
2 1/2 cups flour	1 cup sugar
1 tsp. soda	1 tsp. salt
1/2 tsp. each of cinnamon, nutmeg, cloves, allspice	

Dissolve the yeast in the warm water and 1 teaspoon sugar. Mix together the eggs, lard, and raisins. Stir in the yeast. Sift together all the dry Ingredients and add to the other mixture. Let set in a warm place for about 25 to 30 minutes and then bake at 350° for 30 minutes.

PUMPKIN SPICE CAKE

1/2 cup shortening	2 tsp. cinnamon
1 1/4 cup sugar	1/2 tsp. ginger
2 eggs, beaten	1/2 tsp. nutmeg
2 1/4 cups sifted flour	1 cup pumpkin
2 1/2 tsp. baking powder	3/4 cup milk
1/2 tsp. soda	1/2 cup chopped nuts
1 tsp. salt	

Cream shortening; add sugar gradually, creaming till light and fluffy. Blend in beaten eggs. Sift together the dry ingredients. Combine pumpkin and milk. Add dry ingredients alternately with pumpkin mixture, beginning and ending with dry ingredients. Stir in chopped nuts. Bake in 2 greased 9-inch layer pans, 350° for about 30 minutes. Frost with your favorite butter cream icing using orange juice for the liquid and grated orange rind for added zest.

ZUCCHINI SQUASH CAKE

1 cup oil	3 eggs
3 cups flour	1 tsp. soda
2 cups sugar	1 tsp. salt
2 cups peeled drained	1 tsp. baking powder
zucchini squash, mashed	2 tsp. vanilla
1/2 cup raisins	nuts (optional)

Mix same as the pumpkin cake preceding this one. Put in 2 small loaf pans or one large one. Bake 1 hour at 350°.

CARROT CAKE

2 cups sugar	2 tsp. baking powder
1 1/2 cup cooking oil	1 tsp. salt
4 eggs	2 tsp. cinnamon
2 cups flour	3 cups raw carrots, shredded
2 tsp. soda	1/2 cup chopped nuts

Cream together sugar and cooking oil. Add eggs and beat well. Sift flour, soda, baking powder, salt and cinnamon together. Then add to the creamed mixture. Fold in carrots and nuts. Bake in a moderate oven.

CREAM CHEESE ICING: 4 tbsp. butter, 8 oz. cream cheese, 2 tsp. vanilla, 1 lb. powdered sugar. Mix together until smooth.

ORANGE CARROT CAKE

2 cups whole wheat flour	1 tsp. salt
1 cup brown sugar	1 1/4 cup vegetable oil
1 cup white sugar	1- 12 oz. can of frozen
2 tsp. baking powder	unsweetened orange juice
2 tsp. soda	(save 1/4 of can)
2 tsp. cinnamon	4 eggs
1 tsp. nutmeg	2 1/2 cups grated raw carrots
	1/2 cup chopped nuts

Sift dry ingredients. Add oil and orange juice (Save 1/4 can orange juice for the glaze). Mix well. Add eggs and beat well. Stir in carrots and nuts. Bake at 350° for 1 hour or until well done.

Glaze: Brown 6 tbsp. butter. Add rest of juice and 2 cups powdered sugar. Spread over cake while warm.

OATMEAL CAKE

1 1/4 cup boiling water
1 cup quick oatmeal
1/2 cup shortening
1 cup brown sugar
1 cup white sugar
2 eggs

1 1/2 cup flour
1 tsp. nutmeg, if desired
1 tsp. cinnamon
1 tsp. soda
1/2 tsp. salt
1 tsp. vanilla

Pour boiling water over oatmeal and let set 20 minutes. Cream shortening and sugar well. Add unbeaten eggs, one at a time, beating well after each one. Blend in oatmeal mixture. Sift flour, spices, soda and salt together and fold in. Add vanilla. Bake in greased and floured pan 350° for 30 to 35 minutes.

While cake is still hot from oven, pour on the following topping and put under broiler for about 2 minutes or until brown:

2/3 cup brown sugar
1 cup chopped nuts
1 cup coconut
Mix well.

6 tbsp. melted butter
1/4 cup cream
1 tsp. vanilla

CAROB OATMEAL CAKE

1 cup quick rolled oats   1/4 cup carob powder, or cocoa
Pour 1 1/2 cups boiling water over the above. Stir until smooth.
Let cool.

1 1/2 cups raw sugar
2 eggs, beaten
1/4 tsp. salt

1/3 cup cooking oil
1 tsp. vanilla
1 tsp. soda

1 cup flour (You can take 1/2 cup unbleached and 1/2 cup whole wheat flour if you wish.)

Sift soda and salt with flour. Cream oil and sugar. Add beaten eggs and vanilla. Then add carob mixture and flour. Bake in an 8 x 12 greased pan at 350° about 45 minutes. Top with coconut and sunflower seeds before baking, using this instead of frosting. This cake will stay nice and damp for a week. (Carob powder may be bought at a health food store.)

BANANA NUT CAKE

1 cup white sugar
1/2 cup butter
4 tbsp. sour milk
2 well beaten eggs
2 cups flour
1 cup mashed bananas

1 tsp. soda
2 tsp. baking powder
1 tsp. cream of tartar
pinch of salt
1 tsp. vanilla
1/2 cup chopped nuts

Cream sugar and butter, add the eggs, milk and vanilla. Add sifted dry ingredients. Add bananas and nuts. Bake at 375° about 40 minutes or until done.

RAISIN NUT CAKE

1 1/2 cups white sugar	1/2 tsp. nutmeg
1 1/2 cups brown sugar	1/2 tsp. cinnamon
1/2 cup shortening	1 tsp. baking soda
2 eggs	3 cups flour
1 1/2 cups warm raisin juice	1 cup chopped nuts
1/4 tsp. salt	1 cup cooked raisins

Cook raisins, using enough water to make 1 1/2 cups juice when finished cooking. Cream sugar and shortening. Add eggs and beat well. Add sifted dry ingredients and warm raisin juice. Stir in raisins and nuts. Bake in greased loaf pan at 350° for 45 minutes to one hour.

DATE CAKE

Put into mixing bowl over heat 1 1/2 cups whole dates (pitted) and 2 cups boiling water. Cook until dates are soft. Add 2 teaspoons soda. 1 cup brown sugar, 2 tablespoons butter, 1 teaspoon salt. After this mixture has cooled off a little, add 2 eggs (beaten), 1 1/4 cups flour and nut meats, if desired. (A cake that is good without frosting.) Bake at 350° until done.

FRUIT CAKE

Mix the following in a bowl and let stand one hour:

8 oz. mixed fruit peel	3 3/4 cups golden raisins
2 1/4 cups nuts	1/2 cup grape juice

Mix the following together in a large bowl:

2 cups brown sugar	1/2 cup soft butter
1 tsp. almond flavor	5 eggs

Sift the following together and add to the sugar mixture:

2 cups flour	1/2 tsp. cinnamon
1/2 tsp. mace	1/4 tsp. baking powder

Add fruit mixture and mix thoroughly. Pour into greased 10" tube pan lined with wax paper. Bake at 275° until firm and evenly browned — about 3 hours and 20 minutes. Remove from oven. Cool 1/2 hour. Turn out on cooling rack. Cool thoroughly. Wrap cake in vinegar-soaked cloth. Store in airtight container one week.

MIRACLE FRUIT CAKE

Combine the following in a saucepan:

1 1/2 cups chopped dates
1 1/2 cup raisins
1 1/2 cups brown sugar

2/3 cup butter or substitute
4 tbsp. molasses or corn syrup
1 1/2 cups hot water

Boil gently 3 minutes. Cool in a large mixing bowl. Beat 2 eggs and add to fruit mixture. Add candied fruit (using candied fruit recipe below) and 1 cup chopped nuts.

Sift together 4 times the following dry ingredients:

3 cups white flour
1 1/2 cups whole wheat flour
3 tsp. soda

1 1/2 tsp. nutmeg
2 tsp. cinnamon
2 tsp. baking powder

Add to fruit mixture, stirring well. Pour into wax paper-lined loaf pans, or bread pans. Bake in moderate oven until toothpick comes out clean when inserted.

(Make your own candied fruit. Melt 1/2 cup butter or margarine in saucepan; add 1 cup brown sugar. To this mixture add 2 cups drained cherries (sweet or sour) and 1 medium-sized can crushed pineapples (drained). Let this mixture stand for about 15-20 min.)

APPLESAUCE CAKE

1 cup sugar (white or brown)
1/2 cup shortening
1 egg
1 cup sifted cake flour
1/2 tsp. salt
1/2 tsp. baking powder
1 cup applesauce

1 tsp. soda
1/2 tsp. cloves
1 tsp. cinnamon
1 tsp. allspice
1 cup raisins
1/4 cup chopped nuts

Cream shortening. Add sugar, beat until light. Add egg and beat until fluffy; add applesauce and mix. Sift flour, salt, baking powder, soda, cloves, cinnamon and allspice together and add raisins and chopped nuts. Combine the two mixtures. Bake in an oven at 350° for 40-45 minutes.

GLAZE FOR APPLESAUCE CAKE

In a small saucepan stir together 1/2 cup white sugar, 2 tablespoons cornstarch, and 1/4 teaspoon cinnamon. Stir in 1/2 cup canned applesauce, 1/2 cup water, and 1 teaspoon lemon juice. Cook over moderate heat, stirring constantly until thickened. Cool slightly and put on cake when lukewarm or cold.

OLD TIME MOLASSES CAKE

2 cups flour   1/2 cup buttermilk or sour milk
3/4 cup molasses, fill cup with sugar
2 tsp. soda   1/2 cup hot water
1 egg

Mix thoroughly. Bake at 325° to 350° for 30-40 minutes.

BROWN STONE FRONT CAKE

2 cups brown sugar   1 cup stewed raisins
1/2 cup butter   2 1/2 cups flour
3 egg yolks   1 tsp. soda
1 cup sour milk or buttermilk   1 tsp. cinnamon
1 cup chopped walnuts   1/2 tsp. nutmeg
1/2 tsp. allspice   3 egg whites stiffly beaten

Sift flour and spices together. Add soda. Cream butter and
sugar. Add egg yolks. Add dry ingredients and milk alternately.
Add nuts and raisins and egg whites. Bake at 350° till done.

BURNT SUGAR CAKE

Sift together:
2 1/4 cups sifted cake flour   1 tsp. salt
3 tsp. baking powder   1 cup sugar
Blend:
1 cup milk, 1/3 cup burnt-sugar syrup (directions on page 309),
and 1 tsp. almond extract

Add 2/3 of this liquid to dry mixture. Then add 1/2 cup shortening. Beat until batter is well blended and glossy, then add the remaining liquid. Put in 2 eggs, unbeaten. Beat until batter is very
smooth. Bake in moderate oven 350°. Frost with Burnt-Sugar
Cream Frosting.

SHOO-FLY CAKE

Take 4 cups flour, 3/4 cup shortening, and 2 cups brown sugar.
Mix thoroughly. Take out 1 cup crumbs and keep for top; to the
rest of the crumbs add 2 cups boiling water, 1 cup molasses, and
1 tablespoon soda.
Mix well, then pour into greased cake pan. Sprinkle remaining
crumbs on top and bake at 350° until done.

SORGHUM MOLASSES CAKE

2 cups sorghum molasses
2 eggs
3 cups self-rising flour
1/2 tsp. salt
1/2 tsp. allspice
1 tsp. cinnamon

1 cup cooking oil
1 1/2 cups milk
1/2 tsp. cloves
1 tsp. nutmeg
Raisins or nuts may be added

Mix the above ingredients, then bake at 350° for 30-35 minutes or until done.

FRUIT COCKTAIL CAKE

2 cups flour
1 1/3 cups sugar
3 tsp. soda
(1 lb. 1 oz.) fruit cocktail

2 eggs
1 tsp. vanilla
1/2 tsp. salt

Mix all ingredients together and blend well. Pour in 9 x 13 pan. Bake at 350° for 45 minutes or until broke away from pan. Boil topping 5 minutes and put on cake.

Topping for cake:
8 tbsp. butter
1 cup brown sugar

1/2 cup milk
coconut or nuts (optional)

PINEAPPLE UPSIDE DOWN CAKE

Spread 3 tbsp. brown sugar and 3 tbsp. butter in skillet. Heat and melt. Arrange 5 slices of pineapple on top of this. Cover with sponge cake batter below:
Beat thoroughly 3 egg yolks. Add 1/2 cup sugar, 1/4 cup boiling water and 1/2 tsp. lemon flavoring. Mix one minute. Sift together and add 3/4 cup cake flour, 1 tsp. baking powder, 1/4 tsp. salt. Beat quickly about 1/2 minute. Bake 25-30 minutes at 350°. Turn upside down on a plate to serve. Other fruit may be used.

APPLE DAPPLE

Mix:
2 eggs
2 cups white sugar
1 cup cooking oil

Sift:
3 cups flour (scant)
1/2 tsp. salt
1 tsp. soda

Add sifted ingredients to egg mixture, then add 3 cups chopped apples, 2 teaspoons vanilla, and nuts (optional). Mix well. Pour into greased cake pan and bake 45 minutes or until done at 350°.

ICING:

1 cup brown sugar, 1/4 cup milk, 1/4 cup butter or margarine. Cook 2 1/2 minutes. Stir a little after removing from stove, but do not beat. Dripple over cake while cake and icing are still hot. A few chopped nutmeats may be sprinkled over the icing.

ROYAL APPLE CAKE

Sift together and set aside:

3 cups flour	1 tsp. baking powder
1 tsp. soda	1/2 tsp. salt
2 tsp. cinnamon	1 tsp. nutmeg

Combine and mix well:

1 cup oil	2 cups sugar
2 eggs	

Add alternately the flour mixture and 1 cup water. Then add: 1 cup nuts, 1 cup raisins, 2 cups diced apples. Spread into a greased pan. Bake at 350°.

PENNSYLVANIA DUTCH HUSTLE CAKE

1/3 cup milk	1 egg, beaten
1/4 cup sugar	1 1/3 cups sifted flour
1/2 tsp. salt	1 1/2 cups apple slices
1/4 cup butter or margarine	2 tbsp. brown sugar
1/4 cup lukewarm water	1/4 tsp. cinnamon
1 package dry yeast	1/4 tsp. nutmeg

Scald milk. Stir in sugar, salt and half of butter or margarine. Cool to lukewarm. In a mixing bowl dissolve yeast in warm water. Stir in lukewarm milk mixture. Add egg and flour. Beat until smooth. Spread dough evenly in greased 9 x 9 inch pan. Arrange apple slices on top. Sprinkle with mixture of sugar, cinnamon and nutmeg. Dot with remaining butter or margarine. Cover. Let rise in warm place, free from draft for 40 minutes or longer, until doubled in bulk. Bake at 400° for 25 minutes.

ROMAN APPLE CAKE

1 cup sugar (brown)	1 egg
1/2 cup shortening	1/2 cup milk
1 tsp. vanilla	1 1/2 cups flour
1/4 tsp. baking powder	1/4 tsp. soda
1/4 tsp. salt	

Mix well; fold in 4 medium apples (chopped).

Topping for Cake:

1 tbsp. melted butter	2 tsp. cinnamon
1/2 cup brown sugar	2 tsp. flour
1/2 cup chopped nuts	

Mix, then sprinkle crumbs over cake. Bake 45 minutes at 350°. Serve warm.

FRESH BLUEBERRY CAKE

1/2 cup butter or margarine	1 cup sugar
2 eggs	2 cups flour
3 tsp. baking powder	1/2 tsp. salt
1 cup milk	1 cup blueberries
Cinnamon and sugar to taste	

First cream the butter or margarine, then add the sugar, a little at a time and cream again. Add the eggs and some of the sifted flour, salt and baking powder. Blend this slowly, adding the milk and rest of flour. Wash the berries and dry them on a towel and dust with some flour. Add berries just before placing the cake into the oven. Pour into greased and floured sheet pan, 9"x13"x 2". Sprinkle with sugar and cinnamon, nutmeg, cloves, or whatever is desired. Bake at 325° for 45 minutes. Serve with whipped cream or ice cream. (If blueberries are scarce, raisins or currants can be substituted.)

COCOA CRUMB

2 cups flour	1/2 cup butter or margarine
1 1/2 cups brown sugar	

Mix like pie crust. Reserve 3/4 cup for topping.

To the rest of the crumbs add:

1 beaten egg	1 tsp. soda
1 cup buttermilk	1 tsp. vanilla
2 large tbsp. cocoa (optional)	

Bake in large cake or pie pans with crumbs on top. Bake at 350° from 30 to 40 minutes.

TROPICAL GINGERBREAD

1/2 cup shortening	1 tsp. ginger
1/2 cup sugar	1/2 tsp. cloves
1 egg	1/2 tsp. salt

2 1/2 cups flour
1 1/2 tsp. soda
1 tsp. cinnamon

1 cup baking molasses
1 cup hot water

Melt shortening and cool. Add sugar and egg. Beat well. Sift together flour, soda, salt and spices. Combine molasses and hot water. Add alternately with flour to first mixture. Bake in 350° oven for 50 to 60 minutes. (9"x 9"x 2" pan)

ANGEL GINGERBREAD

1 cup white sugar
1/2 cup shortening
1/2 cup baking molasses
2 eggs
2 cups sifted flour

1/2 tsp. salt
1/2 tsp. ginger
1/2 tsp. cinnamon
1/2 tsp. nutmeg

Mix and beat well and add last, 3/4 cup of boiling water, in which 1 tsp. soda has been dissolved. Bake in moderate oven (350°) 25 to 30 minutes or until done. Serve with whipped cream.

EASY CHOCOLATE ROLL UP

1/4 cup butter
1 cup chopped pecans

1 1/3 cups flaked coconut
1 can (15 1/2 oz.) Eagle
    Brand milk

CAKE:

3 eggs
1 cup sugar
1/3 cup cocoa
2/3 cup flour (all purpose)

1/4 tsp. salt
1/4 tsp. baking powder
1/3 cup water
1 tsp. vanilla

Line 15 x 10" jelly roll pan with foil. Melt butter in pan. Sprinkle nuts and coconut evenly in pan. Drizzle with condensed milk. Beat eggs at high speed for 2 minutes until fluffy. Gradually add sugar. Continue beating 2 minutes. No need to sift flour. Spoon into cup. Level. Add remaining ingredients. Blend 1 minute, beating lightly. Pour evenly into pan. Bake at 375° for 20-25 minutes until cake springs back when touched in center. Sprinkle cake in pan with powdered sugar. Cover with towel. Put cookie sheet lightly over towel. Invert. Remove pan and foil. Roll up jelly roll fashion, starting on 10" side. Use towel to roll cake.

ICINGS

ICINGS
* *A teaspoonful vinegar beaten into a boiled frosting when flavoring is added will keep it from being brittle or breaking when cut.*

* *To keep icing soft, add a pinch of baking soda to the whites of eggs before beating them then beat in the usual way and pour hot syrup over beaten eggs. Frosting will be soft and creamy.*

GRANDMA'S CARAMEL FROSTING

Cook 2 cups brown sugar and 1 cup top milk over medium heat to the soft ball stage (230°).   Remove from stove and add 1/4 teaspoon cream of tartar.   Stir very little to blend cream of tartar. Set aside to cool to lukewarm.   Do not let it get too cold.   Beat until it thickens enough to spread on cake.   Work fast when the right consistency.

BURNT-SUGAR FROSTING

Cream together:
3 tbsp. soft butter or margarine	1 egg yolk, beaten

Beat in alternately:
5 tbsp. burnt sugar syrup (Page 309)	2 tbsp. cream
4 cups sifted confectioners sugar	1 tsp. almond extract

Beat until smooth and creamy enough to spread.

NUT ICING

2 cups brown sugar	1/2 cup hickory nuts
1 cup sweet cream	

Boil sugar and cream together to soft ball stage.   Set aside until cold, then add ground nuts, lump of butter and 1 tsp. vanilla.

PRALINE TOPPING

Mix 1/2 cup brown sugar, 1 cup chopped nuts or 1/2 cup coconut, 1/4 cup melted butter and 3 tbsp. cream.   Mix, and place on top of cake.   Place under broiler or in a hot oven for 1 or 2 minutes.

COCONUT-PECAN FROSTING

Combine:

1 cup evaporated milk, or cream	1 cup sugar
	3 egg yolks
1/2 cup butter or margarine	1 tsp. vanilla

Cook and stir over medium heat until thickened (about 12 min.). Add:

1 1/3 cup shredded coconut	1 cup chopped pecans

Beat until thick enough to spread. Makes 2 1/2 cups.

CREAMY ICING

1/4 cup sugar	1 tsp. salt
2 tbsp. water	1 tbsp. cocoa
2 1/3 cups confectioner's sugar	1 egg
1/2 cup Crisco	1 tsp. vanilla

Boil the water and sugar together for 1 minute. Mix confectioner's sugar, salt and egg. Blend the 2 together. Add Crisco, cocoa and vanilla. Beat until creamy.

JELLO FROSTING

3 tbsp. Jello	1 cup sugar
2 small egg whites	1/8 tsp. cream of tartar
1/4 cup water	

Put jello and water in top of double boiler. Beat whites of eggs. Mix sugar and cream of tartar together then add to jello mixture. Beat until it peaks while still on boiling water. Take off heat and beat one minute and spread.

SUGARLESS FROSTING

1 1/4 cups corn syrup	1 tsp. baking powder
3 egg whites	2 tsp. flavoring
	(vanilla or other flavoring)

Boil corn syrup in a saucepan over direct heat until it spins a thread when dropped from a spoon. Beat egg whites foamy. Add baking powder and beat until stiff. Add corn syrup slowly, beating vigorously while adding. Add flavoring and continue beating until frosting is stiff and stands in peaks. This makes frosting for two 9-inch layers, one medium loaf cake, or 16 large cup cakes.

FLUFFY WHITE FROSTING

Put 2 egg whites in top of double boiler, add 1/2 cup sugar and 1/2 cup white syrup. Beat over boiling water until thick enough to support the egg beater upright. Then spread on cake and swirl. Will stay soft.

MAPLE CREAM ICING

Mix:

1 cup brown sugar   3 tbsp. milk
1/4 cup butter or oleo

Put on stove and bring to full boil, no more! Remove from heat and add 1 cup powdered sugar and 1 teaspoon vanilla. Stir until dissolved and spread on cake.

1/2 tsp. maple flavor may be added.

SOFT ICING

3 tbsp. flour   2/3 cup milk
    Cook in saucepan until thick. Then cool.
Cream together:
3/4 cup Crisco   3/4 cup granulated sugar
Flavoring

Mix all together. Beat vigorously until smooth.

CREAMY CARAMEL FROSTING

Melt 4 tbsp. margarine in saucepan. Blend in 1 cup firmly packed brown sugar and 1/4 teaspoon salt. Cook over low heat stirring constantly for 2 minutes. Stir in 1/4 cup whole milk; continue stirring until mixture comes to a boil. Remove from heat; blend in about 2 1/2 cups powdered sugar gradually. Add 1/2 teaspoon vanilla. Thin with a small amount of canned milk if necessary.

MINUTE FUDGE ICING

1/4 cup butter   1/4 cup cocoa (scant)
1 cup sugar   1/4 cup milk

Melt butter in saucepan and add other ingredients. Stir over low heat till dissolved. Bring to a rolling boil and boil one minute. Remove from heat and beat until creamy enough to spread.

COCOA ICING

1 cup sugar

4 tsp. cocoa

2 tbsp. corn starch

1 cup boiling water

Boil till thick, then add 2 tablespoons butter and vanilla.

CHOCOLATE FUDGE ICING

2 sq. Baker's unsweetened
   chocolate

1 1/4 cup milk

Dash of salt

1 tbsp. light corn syrup

3 tbsp. butter

1 1/2 tsp. vanilla

2 cups sugar

Add chocolate to milk and place over low heat. Cook until smooth and blended, stirring constantly. Add sugar, salt and syrup. Stir until sugar is dissolved and mixture boils. Continue boiling until mixture forms a very soft ball in water. Cool to lukewarm; add vanilla and beat until consistency to spread. If it hardens too soon, add small amount of hot water.

BUTTER-CREAM FROSTING

1 lb. box powdered sugar

1/4 tsp. salt

1/4 cup butter or oleo

1/4 cup cocoa

1 egg

3 tbsp. hot water

Blend all together and beat to spreading thickness. Makes enough to frost top and sides of 8-inch layer cake.

SEAFOAM FROSTING

1 egg white

3/4 cup raw sugar

pinch of salt

1/4 tsp. cream of tartar

2 tsp. honey

Beat in top of double boiler until peak forms.

MARSHMALLOW FROSTING

1 egg white

7/8 cup sugar

3 tbsp. water

1 to 2 cups moist coconut

1 tsp. vanilla

12 marshmallows cut in pieces

Put unbeaten egg white, sugar and water in double boiler. Beat constantly with egg beater six minutes. Remove from heat, add vanilla and marshmallows. Beat until consistency to spread. Add coconut, reserving enough to sprinkle on top.

LEMON FROSTING

1/2 cup butter or margarine   4 cups confectioner's sugar
Dash of salt   4 tsp. lemon juice
1 tsp. grated lemon rind   1/3 cup milk

Cream butter, salt and rind. Add part of sugar gradually. Add remaining sugar alternately with lemon juice, then with milk until right consistency to spread.

ORANGE ICING

1/4 cup oleo or butter   3/4 cup granulated sugar
1/4 cup orange juice   3/4 cup sifted powdered sugar
1/4 cup orange jello

Melt oleo; add sugar and orange juice then jello. Boil 1 minute. Beat in powdered sugar, when slightly cooled and beat until spreading consistency.

ORANGE ICING

3 cups powdered sugar   Grated rind of 1 orange
4 tbsp. orange juice   2 tbsp. melted butter

Combine sugar, juice and rind. Beat well and add melted butter. Stir until well blended.

CREAM CHEESE FROSTING

1 8 oz. pkg. of cream cheese   1 lb. powdered sugar
8 tbsp. margarine   2 tsp. vanilla

Cream cheese and margarine. Add sugar and vanilla and stir until creamy.

BEAT-N-EAT FROSTING

1 egg white, unbeaten   1 tsp. vanilla
3/4 cup sugar   1/4 cup boiling water
1/4 tsp. cream of tartar

Mix the first four ingredients well. Add the boiling water and beat rapidly with an egg beater 4 or 5 minutes till thick. Delicious for quick topping.

ORANGE CAKE FILLING

Juice and rind of 1 orange	2 egg yolks
1 cup cold water	1 tbsp. corn starch
1 cup sugar	

Cook until thick and clear.

CARAMEL FILLING FOR SPONGE CAKE

Two tablespoons white sugar melted in pan without water. Put in 1 cup water, and boil to syrup, add 1 tablespoon butter, 1 cup sugar, and pour over three beaten eggs to which has been added 2 tablespoons flour. Beat well then bring to a boil, stirring constantly. Spread on sponge cake. (This filling, or any other filling, may be used for jelly rolls.)

CHOCOLATE FILLING

Shave chocolate fine, about 2 squares. Put into a vessel into which has been added 1 cup rich milk, 1 1/2 cup sugar, butter size of an egg. Boil all together until thickness desired.

CREAM FILLING

1 pt. milk	2 tbsp. cornstarch
1 egg	1 lump butter
1/2 cup sugar	

Cook the above until thick. Cool and spread between layers of cake.

CLEAR LEMON FILLING

Mix together in saucepan:

3/4 cup sugar	1 1/2 tbsp. grated lemon rind
3 tbsp. cornstarch	6 tbsp. lemon juice
1/3 tsp. salt	1 1/2 tbsp. butter
	3/4 cup water

Bring to a boil and boil 1 minute, stirring constantly. Chill.

HOUSEHOLD HINTS

*A handy household tool is a crochet hook, a fine and a large one. Keep them handy for unplugging wash machine drains, sink traps, etc.

*If you're bothered with cold feet when going away in winter, place a piece of styrofoam insulation in the bottom of the buggy box.

*For a cheaper window cleaner put vinegar in a spray bottle. Wipe dry with a cloth.

*Put hot water in large plastic jugs and use them to keep hands and feet warm when going away in winter. Or use for a warm bed in a cold room or to keep chicks warm.

*Vinegar in water with a dash of ammonia makes a good window spray cleaner.

*Season your new skillet to prevent rusting, and food sticking to the bottom. To season, wash and dry the skillet, then rub the inside with vegetable oil or shortening; heat for several hours on top of the range at a low temperature, or in the oven at 250 or 300 degrees. Reseason skillet whenever necessary.

*Remove stains from pie plates by soaking them in a strong solution of borax and water.

*Paint your oil stove with 1/2 pint car enamel.

*Have the comfort cover open at the sides to get more wear from it, for either end can be used at the top.

*Cut holes in tin pie plates and strip them over your gas burner. They will be under the stove top and will help keep burners clean.

*When a new stove pipe is handled without gloves, it leaves messy finger prints. After all is set up, take a soft cloth wrung out of warm soap water and wipe off the whole stove pipe. Then wipe dry with a soft dry towel. This makes it sparkle for it washes off the oil that is put on the pipes to prevent rusting.

*Cut insoles from old felt hats and put in your shoes to keep your feet warm.

COOKIES

MOTHER'S RECIPES

Most women have a pantry filled
  With spices, herbs, and stuff;
Salt and sugar, yeast and flour—
  But that's not quite enough.

My mom's the finest cook around,
  And she told me long ago,
That bread's no good unless you add
  Some loving to the dough.

"And when you're baking pies," says she,
  "A pinch of faith and trust,
If added to the shortening — makes
  A tender, flaky crust.

"You must add a cup of patience
  When making cookie dough,
With temperance as your partner
  Place them in a neat row.

"Add some kindness to your yeast
  And when the doughnuts rise
They'll sweeter be — (though made in grease);
  You'll meet a glad surprise!

"And Compassion by the spoonful
  In the batter of a cake,
Makes it come out light and fluffy,
  Just the finest you can make."

Now these things can't be purchased
  In the store across the way;
But Mother keeps them in her heart
  And uses them each day!

                  -Adapted

WHOOPIE PIES

4 cups flour	1 cup cocoa
2 cups sugar	2 eggs
2 tsp. soda	2 tsp. vanilla
1/2 tsp. salt	1 cup thick sour milk
1 cup shortening	1 cup cold water

Cream together: sugar, salt, shortening, vanilla and eggs.

Sift together: flour, soda and cocoa. Add this to the first mixture alternately with water and sour milk. Add slightly more flour if milk is not thick. Drop by teaspoons. Bake at 400°.

Filling:

1 egg white, beaten	2 cups confectioner's sugar
1 tbsp. vanilla	or as needed
2 tbsp. flour	3/4 cup Crisco or margarine
2 tbsp. milk	Add marshmallow creme
	(optional)

Beat egg white, sugar, and vanilla, then add the remaining ingredients. Beat well. A few drops peppermint flavor may be used in place of vanilla.

SOUR CREAM CHOCOLATE COOKIES

2 cups brown sugar	1 cup sour cream
3/4 cup shortening	Pinch of salt
2 eggs	2 tsp. soda
1 tsp. vanilla	4 or 5 cups flour
	2 sq. chocolate

Cream together sugar, shortening, eggs and vanilla. Melt chocolate over hot water and add to sugar mixture. Put soda in 1/2 cup of cream and add alternately with flour and remaining cream. Make dough as soft as can be handled. Chill for a few hours. Roll 1/4 inch thick. Cut and bake in moderate oven.

SOFT CHOCOLATE COOKIES

1 tsp. salt	3 sq. (3 oz.) unsweetened
1 tsp. soda	chocolate
2 tsp. pure vanilla extract	2 eggs, unbeaten
1 cup shortening	2 1/2 cups sifted all-
2 cups light brown sugar	purpose flour
3/4 cup sour milk	1 cup chopped nuts

Blend first 3 ingredients with shortening. Gradually mix in sugar. Melt chocolate over hot water and add. Beat in eggs. Add flour alternately with milk. Stir in nuts. Drop heaping teaspoons of batter, 2 inches apart on lightly greased cookie sheets. Bake in moderate oven (375 degrees) 10 to 12 minutes, or until done. Cool and store in air-tight container. Yields 5 dozen.

SOFT CHOCOLATE CHIP COOKIES

1/2 cup shortening
1 cup sugar
2 eggs if large, or 3 small
1/2 cup milk
2 1/2 cups flour

1 tsp. baking powder
3/4 tsp. baking soda (in milk)
1 small bag chocolate chips (for
  variety try butterscotch
                    morsels).

Mix and drop by teaspoon on greased cookie sheet. Bake at 400° until slightly brown around edges.

CHOCOLATE MACAROONS

2 egg whites
1 cup sugar
1/8 tsp. salt
1/2 tsp. vanilla

1 1/2 cups shredded coconut
1 1/2 sq. unsweetened
  chocolate

Beat egg whites until stiff and gradually beat in sugar and salt. Beat well after sugar is added. Add vanilla, fold in coconut and chocolate which has been melted over hot water. Drop by teaspoons on a greased cooky sheet. Bake at 275 degrees, about 30 minutes. Makes 1 1/2 dozen cookies.

CHOCOLATE PINWHEEL

1/2 cup sugar
1/2 cup shortening
1 egg yolk
1 1/2 tsp. vanilla
1 1/2 cups flour

1/4 tsp. salt
1/2 tsp. baking powder
3 tsp. milk
1 sq. unsweetened chocolate
                    (melted)

Mix all but chocolate to a smooth dough. Divide dough into two equal portions. To one portion add melted chocolate. Roll white dough 1/3 inch thick on floured surface. Roll chocolate dough the same size and place on top of the first dough. Roll like a jelly roll. Chill, then cut in slices and bake at 350°.

BUTTERSCOTCH COOKIES

6 cups brown sugar
1 1/2 cups butter

1 1/2 tbsp. soda
2 tbsp. baking powder

4 eggs, beaten   1 tbsp. vanilla
6 to 7 cups all-purpose flour

Cream the brown sugar and butter together until smooth, then add the eggs.

Sift the soda and baking powder with the flour, and add to the first mixture. Shape into rolls and chill. Slice and bake at 350° for 15 to 20 minutes.

OLD-FASHIONED GINGER COOKIES

2 cups shortening   2 tbsp. soda
3 cups (Grandma) baking   1 tsp. ginger
    molasses   1 tsp. cinnamon
1 cup sugar   2 cups sour milk
10 cups flour, 1/2 pastry   or buttermilk
  and 1/2 bread flour
1 tsp. salt

Heat molasses and sugar together, add shortening and stir until smooth. Remove from heat. Sift dry ingredients together, and add alternately with sour milk. Stir until a smooth dough. Work with hand for 5 minutes. Chill. Roll 1/2 inch thick. Glaze cookies with a beaten egg. Bake at 350 degrees for 20 to 25 minutes. Makes 8 dozen cookies.

SOFT GINGER COOKIES

6 to 8 cups flour   1 cup sugar
3/4 tsp. salt   1 egg
1/2 tsp. cinnamon   2 cups dark baking molasses
2 tbsp. ginger   2 tbsp. vinegar
1 cup lard   4 tsp. soda
1 cup boiling water

Sift 6 cups flour with salt and spices. Cream lard and sugar; add the egg. Beat until light. Add molasses and vinegar, then dry ingredients and soda dissolved in boiling water. If necessary add more flour to make a soft dough. Drop by teaspoons on greased cooky sheet. Sprinkle with sugar. Bake 10 minutes in a moderate oven 350 degrees.

GINGER SNAPS

Heat:
  1 cup sugar   1 cup lard
  1 cup dark baking molasses   Cool and stir frequently.

Add 1 egg and stir
Add:

1 tsp. ginger	1 tsp. soda
1/2 tsp. cinnamon	4-5 cups flour

Use enough flour to make a stiff dough. Roll very thin and bake in a quick oven. They will taste like bakery cookies.

GINGER CREAMS

2/3 cup shortening	1 tsp. cinnamon
1 cup molasses	1/2 tsp. cloves
1 tsp. soda	2 tsp. bone meal powder
1 1/4 cup brown sugar	1 cup hot water
1/2 tsp. salt	1 cup raisins, nuts,
1 tsp. ginger	if desired

5 1/2 cups flour or 4 1/2 cups flour and 1 cup wheat germ

Cream shortening and sugar. Add molasses, then the soda in hot water. Add sifted dry ingredients, then the raisins and nuts. Bake at 350° for 15-20 minutes or until done.

MOLASSES DROP COOKIES

1 cup lard	1 1/2 cups sweet milk
1 1/2 cup brown sugar	3 tsp. soda
2 eggs	1 tsp. ginger
1 cup Brer Rabbit molasses	2 tsp. cinnamon
1 cup table syrup	6 cups flour

Drop from spoon. Bake in moderate oven.

MOLASSES SUGAR COOKIES

3/4 cup shortening	2 tsp. soda
1 cup sugar	1 tsp. cinnamon
1/4 cup molasses	1/2 tsp. cloves
1 egg	1/2 tsp. ginger
2 cups sifted flour	1/2 tsp. salt

Cream together sugar and shortening. Add molasses and egg; beat well. Sift together flour, soda, cinnamon, cloves, ginger and salt. Add to first mixture. Mix well. Chill. Form into one inch balls. Roll in granulated sugar and place on greased cookie sheets, two inches apart. Flatten with spoon or fork. Bake in moderately hot oven, 350° for 8 to 10 minutes. Makes four dozen.

LITTLE HONEY CAKES

Cream:
 1 1/2 cups lard   2 cups sugar
Add: 4 beaten eggs
Blend in:
 1 cup molasses   1 cup hot water
 1 cup honey
Add:
 2 tsp. cinnamon   2 tbsp. baking powder
 1 tsp. ginger   Flour to stiffen (5 cups approx.)
 2 tbsp. soda

 Chill dough overnight. Roll or drop. Bake at 350° until brown.

SOFT MOLASSES COOKIES

3/4 cup shortening   2 1/4 cups flour
3/4 cup brown sugar   2 tsp. soda
2 eggs   1/2 tsp. salt
3/4 cup molasses   1/2 tsp. cinnamon
3/4 cup sour cream   1 1/2 tsp. ginger (optional)

 Cream shortening and sugar. Add well-beaten eggs, molasses,
and sour cream and stir until smooth. Mix the dry ingredients together and add gradually. Chill the dough. Drop by spoonsful on a
greased baking pan. Bake at 350° for about 10 minutes.

CHURCH COOKIES

5 cups sugar   4 eggs
2 1/2 cups lard   2 tsp. vanilla
1 cup molasses   2 tsp. ginger & dash of
1 cup hot water   cinnamon (optional)
                                         1 tsp. baking powder

 Dissolve 3 tablespoons soda and 1 teaspoon salt in hot water.
12 to 15 cups flour. Mix in order given. Roll out and bake at
375°.

RAISIN DROP COOKIES

1 cup raisins and 1 cup water. Boil down to 1/2 cup liquid.
Cream:

3/4 cup margarine
1 egg
Add: 1 tsp. vanilla
      1 tsp. soda

1 cup sugar

3 cups sifted all-purpose flour
with 1 tsp. baking powder
Pinch of salt

Mix alternately with raisins and liquid. Drop by tablespoon.
Bake in 375° oven about 15 minutes.

RAISIN FILLED COOKIES

Filling:
2 cup chopped raisins
2 tbsp. flour
1 cup water
1 cup sugar
1 tbsp. lemon juice (optional)
  Boil till thick

Dough:
2 cups brown sugar
1 cup sweet milk
4 tsp. cream of tartar
1 cup shortening
7 cups flour
2 tsp. soda
2 tsp. baking powder
2 eggs
2 tsp. vanilla

Roll the dough, cut with round cutter. Put 1 teaspoon filling on
cookie. Place another cookie on top, which has a hole in the middle.
(Make hole with thimble.) Do not press together. Bake at 350° for
20 minutes or until done.

EASY FILLED DROPS

1 cup shortening
1 cup brown sugar
2 eggs
1/2 cup water, sour milk
  or buttermilk
3 1/2 cups sifted flour

1 tsp. salt
1 tsp. soda
1/8 tsp. cinnamon
1 tsp. vanilla

Heat oven to 400°. Mix well: shortening, sugar and eggs. Stir
in water and vanilla. Sift together and stir in flour, soda, salt and
cinnamon. Drop with teaspoon onto ungreased baking sheet. Place
1/2 teaspoon date filling (below) on dough. Cover with 1/2 teaspoon dough. Bake 10 to 12 minutes. Makes 5 to 6 dozen.
Date Filling:
  Cook until thick stirring constantly, 2 cups dates, cut small,
3/4 cup sugar and 3/4 cup water. Add 1/2 cup chopped nuts. Cool.

DATE PINWHEELS

Filling: Dough Part:
2 1/2 cups dates   1 cup shortening
1 cup sugar   2 cups brown sugar
1 cup water   4 eggs
Cook slowly for 15 min.   4 to 5 1/2 cups flour
Add 1 cup chopped nuts   1/2 tsp. salt
Cool.   1/2 tsp. soda

Cream the shortening, add the brown sugar gradually. Add well-beaten eggs and beat until smooth. Add dry ingredients sifted together and mix well. Chill thoroughly. Divide mixture into two parts and roll each out separately into rectangle shape, less than 1/4 inch thick. Spread each dough with date filling and roll up as for jelly roll into 2 long rolls. Chill overnight. Cut with a sharp knife into slices 1/4 inch thick. Bake in moderate oven (400°) for 10 to 20 minutes.

DATE-FILLED OAT COOKIES

2 cups shortening, half butter   1 tsp. salt
3 cups brown sugar   2 tsp. soda
6 cups flour   1 cup buttermilk
4 cups rolled oats   1 tsp. vanilla

Cream sugar and shortening together. Add vanilla. Sift flour. Measure and add salt, soda, and rolled oats. Add dry ingredients alternately with buttermilk. Mix thoroughly. Chill in ice box for several hours. Turn out on lightly floured board and roll to 1/8 inch thickness. Cut with round cookie cutter and place 1 inch apart on greased baking sheet. Bake at 375° until a golden brown. Makes 8 dozen cookies. When cookies are cold, spread with the following filling:

2 cups finely chopped dates   1 cup water
1 cup sugar   2 tbsp. water

Combine ingredients and cook until thick. Let cool before spreading on cookie. Top with another cookie.

DATE COOKIES

8 cups flour   1 tsp. salt
4 cups sugar   2 cups shortening
2 tsp. soda   6 large eggs
2 tsp. cream of tartar

Blend all together and drop on cookie sheet. Bake at 375°.

When cool, spread date filling between two cookies. Cookies seem a little hard at first but several hours after the filling has been spread they are soft and delicious.

Date Filling:

2 tbsp. cornstarch
2 cups water
1 cup cut-up dates

2 cups brown sugar
juice of 2 lemons or
2 tbsp. Realemon

Bring to a boil and cook until thick. Cool and spread between cookies.

CARROT COOKIES

1/2 cup shortening
1 cup brown sugar
1/2 cup granulated sugar
1 egg
1 cup cooked carrots,
  mashed and cooled

2 cups flour
1/2 tsp. baking powder
3/4 cup raisins
1 tsp. vanilla
Pinch of salt

Cream shortening and sugar together. Add vanilla, egg, carrots, and the remaining ingredients, adding the raisins last. Drop on cookie sheet and bake at 375°.

PUMPKIN NUT COOKIES

1/2 cup shortening
1 cup sugar
2 eggs, beaten
1 cup pumpkin
2 cups sifted flour
4 tsp. baking powder

1 tsp. salt
2 1/2 tsp. cinnamon
1/4 tsp. ginger
1/2 tsp. nutmeg
1 cup raisins
1 cup chopped nuts

Cream shortening; add sugar gradually. Cream till light and fluffy. Add eggs and pumpkin; mix well. Sift flour, baking powder, salt and spices together. Stir in dry ingredients and mix until blended. Add raisins and nuts. Drop by teaspoonsful on greased cookie sheet. Bake in a 350° oven about 15 minutes. Makes 4 dozen cookies.

PUMPKIN COOKIES

1 cup lard
1 cup pumpkin
1 tsp. cinnamon
1 tsp. baking powder
1 egg

1 cup brown sugar
2 cups flour
1 tsp. soda
1/2 tsp. salt

Mix together sugar, lard, and egg. Add pumpkin. Mix well.
Sift dry ingredients. Add to mixture and beat well. Drop on
cookie sheets. Bake at 350⁰ , 10 to 20 minutes. When slightly
cooled frost with this icing. Cream: 1 teaspoon butter, add 1
tablespoon milk, 1/4 cup pumpkin and add 10 x sugar. A very
delicious and moist cookie.

FAVORITE SOUR CREAMS

5 cups brown sugar	3 tbsp. baking powder
2 cups shortening (scant)	3 tbsp. soda
2 cups thick sour cream	1 tsp. vanilla
4 eggs, beaten	Flour to make a soft dough
1 cup sweet milk	

Mix all ingredients in order given. Bake at 350⁰ for 20 minutes
or until done. Makes from 90 to 100 cookies.

SOUR CREAM COOKIES

3 cups brown sugar	1 tsp. salt
1 cup lard or shortening	2 tsp. soda
4 eggs	2 1/2 tsp. nutmeg
2 cups sour cream (thick)	1 tsp. baking powder
2 tsp. vanilla	6 to 7 cups flour

Cream lard and sugar well, add eggs, beating well after each
addition. Add sour cream, vanilla. Sift dry ingredients together,
mix well. Bake at 375⁰ .

Icing: 3/4 cup butter, browned
         3 cups powdered sugar
         2 tsp. vanilla

Mix and add hot water until spreading consistency.

KEUFELS

To make dough mix following ingredients with fork.
1 cup plus 2 tbsp. flour
1/2 cup margarine or butter
1 - 3 oz. pkg. cream cheese

Form into 24 small sized balls and with finger press and shape
into small sized muffin tins. Then mix the following:

1 cup brown sugar	1 egg
2 tbsp. melted butter	1/4 tsp. salt
1 tsp. vanilla	3/4 cup chopped nuts

Fill muffin tins. Bake at 350⁰ for 20 minutes.

MINCEMEAT COOKIES

1 cup shortening
1 cup brown sugar
1 cup white sugar
1 tsp. soda
1 tsp. cinnamon
1/2 tsp. cloves

1/2 tsp. nutmeg
3 eggs
3 cups flour
1/2 tsp. salt
1 cup mincemeat
1 cup chopped nuts

Cream shortening and sugar together. Add eggs. Beat till fluffy. Sift flour and measure. Add soda, salt and spices. Sift again. Add dry ingredients to cream mixture. Mix thoroughly. Add mincemeat, and nuts. Drop by teaspoon on greased baking sheet. Bake at 350°.

TOLL-HOUSE COOKIES

Mix together:
 1 cup shortening
 3/4 cup brown sugar
 3/4 cup white sugar
Sift and add:
 1 1/2 cups sifted flour
 1 tsp. soda
Add:
 2 cups oatmeal
 1 cup chopped nuts

2 eggs, beaten
1 tsp. hot water
1 tsp. vanilla

1 tsp. salt

1 pkg. Toll-house chocolate
chips or butterscotch chips

Drop by teaspoon on cookie sheet. Bake at 350° for 10 to 15 minutes.

COCONUT KRISPIES

1 cup butter or 3/4 cup oil
1 cup raw sugar
1/2 cup honey
2 eggs
1 tsp. vanilla
2 cups whole wheat flour
1/2 cup wheat germ

1/2 tsp. soda
1/4 tsp. salt
1/2 tsp. baking powder
1 cup coconut (unsweetened)
2 cups rolled oats
1 cup bran flakes (optional)

Mix in order given, adding bran flakes last. Form in ball size of a walnut. Place on greased cookie sheet. Bake at 350° for 10 to 12 minutes.

SNITZ COOKIES

1 cup lard	4 cups flour
2 cups brown sugar	2 tsp. baking powder
2 eggs	2 tsp. soda
1 cup cooked snitz	1 tsp. salt
1/2 cup raisins	1 tsp. cinnamon

Mix: lard and sugar; add eggs and cooked snitz. Sift together dry ingredients and stir in. Add raisins just before baking.

COCONUT COOKIES

Sift:

2 cups all-purpose flour	2 tsp. baking powder
1 tsp. salt	

Add:

3/4 cup sugar	2 tsp. vanilla
1/2 cup melted shortening	1 cup shredded coconut
2 eggs	

Blend sugar and shortening. Add eggs and stir well. Stir in vanilla and coconut. Add dry ingredients. Make into roll and chill. Slice and bake in 375 degree oven.

COCONUT OATMEAL GEMS

1/2 cup vegetable oil	1 cup raw sugar
1 cup honey, or maple syrup	3 eggs
1 tsp. soda	1/2 cup chopped dates or raisins
1/2 tsp. baking powder	3 cups whole wheat flour
3 cups rolled oats	1 cup ground oatmeal or
1 cup unsweetened coconut	wheat germ
1/2 cup hickory nuts	1/2 tsp. salt

Cream sugar, honey and oil until light and fluffy. Add beaten eggs and dates, beating thoroughly. Add dry ingredients, oatmeal, coconut, and nuts mixing well after each addition. Drop on cookie sheet with spoon, then flatten with fork. Bake at 350°.

PEANUT BUTTER OATMEAL COOKIES

Cream together:

1 cup shortening	2 tsp. vanilla
1 cup peanut butter	

Add gradually:
  2 cups sugar

Cream until light and fluffy. Beat in 4 eggs.
Sift together:

3 cups flour	2 tsp. cinnamon
2 tbsp. baking powder	1/2 tsp. cloves
1 tsp. salt	1/2 tsp. nutmeg

Add:
4 cups quick cooking oats, (or 5 cups wheat flake cereal).

Stir into creamed mixture alternately with 2/3 cup milk and blend in 1 cup chopped nuts (if desired). Spoon onto greased cookie sheets. Bake in 375⁰ oven 12-15 minutes. Makes 6 dozen cookies.

Variations:
* Substitute 1 cup molasses or honey for 1 cup of the sugar.
* Stir in 2 cups raisins, or 2 cups chopped dates, prunes or apricots (uncooked) when adding nuts.

PEANUT SURPRISES

1 cup shortening (part butter for flavor)	1 cup wheaties
	1/2 tsp. salt
2 cups brown sugar, packed in cup	1 tsp. soda
	2 cups quick cooking oatmeal
2 eggs	1 cup coarsely chopped salted peanuts
2 cups flour	
1 tsp. baking powder	

Mix then drop by teaspoonful on a lightly greased baking sheet. Flatten out each cookie with a fork dipped in flour. Bake 10 to 12 minutes in a moderate oven.

OATMEAL MOLASSES COOKIES

1/2 cup sugar	1 tsp. cloves
1/2 cup molasses	1 tsp. soda
3/4 cup shortening	2 cups flour
2 eggs	1 cup raisins
1/4 cup sweet milk	2 cups oatmeal
2 tsp. cinnamon	

Mix ingredients in order given. Drop by teaspoons on greased cookie sheets. Bake at 380⁰.

SOFT OATMEAL DROP COOKIES

3/4 cup melted Crisco	1/8 tsp. salt
2 beaten whole eggs	2 tsp. soda
3/4 cup buttermilk	1/2 cup brown sugar

4 cups oatmeal
1 1/2 cups raisins or
1/2 cup shredded coconut
1/4 cup corn oil

1/2 cup raw sugar
1/2 cup honey
2 cups flour
1 tsp. baking powder

Mix all ingredients. Grease fingers to press the cookies flat and to make a nice edge. Bake at 350°. Makes 42 cookies.

BANANA OATMEAL COOKIES

1 1/2 cups sifted flour
1 cup sugar
1/2 tsp. soda
1/2 tsp. nutmeg
3/4 tsp. cinnamon

3/4 cup shortening
1 egg, well beaten
1 cup mashed bananas
1 3/4 cups rolled oats
Nuts

Sift dry ingredients. Cut in shortening. Add eggs, bananas, oats, and nuts. Beat thoroughly until blended. Drop by teaspoon about 1 1/2 inch apart on greased cookie sheets. Bake at 400° for about 15 minutes. Makes 3 1/2 dozen.

PEANUT BUTTER COOKIES

1/2 cup shortening
1/2 cup peanut butter
1/2 cup granulated sugar
1/2 cup brown sugar
1 well-beaten egg

1 tsp. vanilla
1 1/4 cups flour
1/4 tsp. salt
1/2 tsp. baking powder
3/4 tsp. soda

Thoroughly cream shortening, peanut butter, and sugar. Add eggs and vanilla. Beat well. Add sifted dry ingredients and mix thoroughly. Chill dough well. Then form in small balls on cookie sheet and flatten with fork. Bake in moderate oven, 375° for 10 to 15 minutes. Makes 3 to 4 dozen.

CHOCOLATE PEANUT BUTTER COOKIES

Preheat oven to 375 degrees.
Sift together:
  2 cups sifted all-purpose flour
  1/2 tsp. double-acting
       baking powder

1/4 tsp. baking soda
1/4 tsp. salt

Cream together:
  1/2 cup shortening

1/2 cup peanut butter

Blend in:
  1/2 cup sugar

1/2 cup firmly packed
       brown sugar

Add 1 well-beaten egg and mix thoroughly. Stir in flour mixture alternately with 1/2 cup milk: mix well. Fold in 1 cup (6 oz.) Hershey's Semi-Sweet Dainties. Drop by small **spoonsful** onto ungreased baking sheet. Bake about 12 minutes. Yield about 3 dozen cookies.

CHERRY COOKIES

Sift together:
 2 1/4 cups flour   1/2 tsp. soda
 1 tsp. baking powder   1/2 tsp. salt
Combine:
 3/4 cup shortening   1 cup sugar
Blend in: 2 eggs
Add:
 2 tbsp. milk   1 tsp. almond extract
                                      1 tsp. vanilla
Blend in sifted dry ingredients, mix well.
Add:
 1 cup chopped pecans   1 cup chopped dates
 1/3 cup chopped maraschino cherries

Mix well. Shape into balls using 1 level tablespoon for each cookie. Crush 2 1/2 cups corn flakes and roll each ball of dough in corn flakes. Place on greased cookie sheet and top each with 1/4 cherry. Bake at 375°. Do not stack until cold.

NUT COOKIES

Cream:
 1/2 cup shortening   1 1/2 cup sugar
Blend in:
 4 egg yolks, beaten   1 tsp. vanilla
Sift:
 1 3/4 cup flour   1/4 tsp. salt
 1/2 tsp. baking powder

Mix all ingredients together. Roll dough in tiny balls, then dip in a mixture of: 3/4 cup nuts and 2 tsp. cinnamon. Bake in moderate oven.

APPLESAUCE NUT COOKIES

1/2 cup shortening   1/2 tsp. cinnamon
1 cup sugar   1/4 tsp. cloves
1 egg   1 cup thick unsweetened
2 cups flour   applesauce

3 tsp. baking powder
1/2 tsp. salt

1/2 cup raisins
1/2 cup nuts

Cream shortening, add sugar, egg. Add applesauce and dry ingredients. Fold in raisins and nuts. Place on cookie sheet 2 inches apart and bake in 350⁰ oven for 15 to 20 minutes.

APPLESAUCE DROP COOKIES

2 cups flour
1 tsp. soda
1/4 tsp. salt
1 tsp. cinnamon
1/2 tsp. nutmeg
1/2 cup butter
1/2 cup sugar (white)

1/2 cup brown sugar, packed
1 egg
1 cup applesauce
1 cup rolled oats
1/2 cup raisins
1/2 cup chopped nuts
1/2 cup chocolate chips

Sift together first five ingredients. Set aside. Mix butter, sugar, and add egg and blend. Add applesauce and dry ingredients. Add the rest and mix well. Drop by teaspoon on ungreased cookie sheet. Bake 8 minutes at 375⁰.

PINEAPPLE COOKIES

1 cup brown sugar
1 cup granulated sugar
1 cup shortening
2 eggs
1 cup crushed pineapple

1 tsp. pineapple flavor
1/2 tsp. salt
1 1/2 tsp. soda
1/2 tsp. baking powder
4 cups flour or more if
   pineapple are not drained

Combine in order given. Drop on tins and bake at 350° for 20 minutes.

PINEAPPLE DROP COOKIES

3/4 cup Crisco
3/4 cup butter
1 cup sugar
1 egg
1/2 cup sour cream

1/2 cup pineapple juice
3 1/2 cups flour
1/8 tsp. salt
1 tsp. baking powder
1 tsp. soda

Measure and sift dry ingredients together in bowl. Cut in shortening as for pie crust. Add beaten egg, pineapple juice and sour cream. Stir only enough to blend. Drop on greased cookie sheet. Press small piece of pineapple into each cookie. Bake at 400⁰ for 12 minutes or until light brown.

BROWN SUGAR COOKIES

4 eggs, beaten
1 cup butter
1 cup Crisco or lard
2 cups granulated sugar
2 cups brown sugar
1 tsp. baking soda

1 tbsp. vanilla
3 tsp. baking powder
1 cup milk
1 cup cream
1 tbsp. vinegar
7 cups pastry flour

Drop and bake in 400° oven. Store in lard can or similar container (between sheets of Saran Wrap) while still slightly warm. Cover. This will keep cookies nice and soft.

MARY'S SUGAR COOKIES

2 eggs
1 1/2 cups granulated sugar
1 cup lard
1 cup sweet milk
1 tsp. vanilla

4 cups flour
2 tsp. baking powder
2 tsp. cream of tartar
2 tsp. soda, scant

Beat eggs 1 minute. Add sugar and shortening and beat 1 minute. Add vanilla and milk. Sift dry ingredients and combine with first mixture. Drop by spoon onto cookie sheet and bake. When cool, spread the following icing on top: 6 tablespoons butter (room temperature), 2 teaspoons vanilla, 1/8 teaspoon salt, 1 lb. powdered sugar, 4 to 5 tablespoons milk.

Put all ingredients in bowl and beat for 1 minute. Divide icing into several parts and color with food coloring. Make variety out of one batch of cookies.

JUBILEE JUMBLES

1/2 cup soft shortening
1/2 cup white sugar
1 tsp. vanilla
1/2 tsp. soda
2 eggs
1 cup brown sugar

1 cup undiluted evaporated milk
3 cups flour (scant)
1 tsp. salt
1/2 cup nuts
1/2 cup coconut
1 pkg. chocolate chips

Mix shortening, sugar and eggs thoroughly. Stir in evaporated milk and vanilla. Sift together; flour, soda, salt and stir in. Blend in nuts, coconut and chocolate chips. Chill 1 hour, drop on greased baking sheet and bake 8 - 12 minutes in 375° oven. While warm frost with creamy fudge frosting.

LEMON CRISPS

1 3/4 cups shortening	2 tsp. grated lemon rind
1 cup granulated sugar	5 1/2 cups all-purpose flour
1 cup brown sugar	1/2 tsp. salt
2 tbsp. lemon juice	1/2 tsp. baking soda
2 eggs	

Mix well, form into small balls and place on cookie sheet; then flatten. Bake at 350° 10 to 12 minutes.

* Orange Crisps: Substitute oranges for lemons.

SNICKERS

1/2 cup white sugar	2 3/4 cups flour
1 cup brown sugar	1 tsp. soda
1 cup shortening	2 tsp. cream of tartar
2 eggs	1/4 tsp. salt

Mix well. Chill dough overnight, form into balls.
Mix 1/2 cup brown sugar and 1 teaspoon cinnamon. Roll balls in the mixture and bake.

GRAHAM GEMS

2 cups dark brown sugar	1 tsp. soda
2 eggs	5 tbsp. sour cream
1/2 cup butter or lard	1/4 tsp. salt
1/2 cup raisins (optional)	1 tsp. vanilla
4 cups whole wheat flour or part white	

Mix the above ingredients together, then drop by teaspoons on a greased cookie sheet. Bake at 400°. The raisins add a better flavor if a little water is added and cooked a few minutes first. Add raisins and water to the dough. More flour may then be needed.

WHOLE WHEAT COOKIES

Measure:

2 1/4 cups whole wheat flour	1 1/2 tsp. soda
1 1/2 cups sifted white flour	1 1/2 tsp. salt
1 1/2 cups brown sugar	

Mix together then make a well and add:

1 1/2 cups sour milk	1/4 cup molasses
2 eggs	1 1/2 tsp. vanilla
1/2 cup melted butter	

Beat well, then stir in: 1 cup chocolate bits. Drop on cookie sheet and bake.

Variation: Omit vanilla and chocolate bits and add 1 1/2 teaspoon cinnamon and 1 cup raisins.

MICHIGAN ROCKS

1 1/2 cups brown sugar
3/4 cup shortening
4 eggs
3 cups flour (scant)
1 tsp. soda

1 lb. dates, chopped fine
1 1/2 cups nut meats
1 tsp. vanilla
1/4 tsp. salt

Mix then drop by teaspoons on cookie sheet and bake.

NO-BAKE COOKIES

2 cups white sugar
3 tbsp. cocoa

1/4 cup butter
1/2 cup milk

Boil one minute. Remove from heat. Add:

3 cups oatmeal (crumbled fine)   1 tsp. vanilla
1/2 cup peanut butter

Drop quickly on wax paper by teaspoonful.

Variations: coconut, nuts, chocolate chips may be used instead of peanut butter.

Here is an easy recipe for little girls.

NUTTY FINGERS

1/2 cup margarine
1/4 cup, plus 1 tbsp.
    powdered sugar
1 tsp. vanilla

1 cup enriched flour
1 cup finely chopped nuts

Cream margarine; add powdered sugar and vanilla; add flour gradually, then add nuts. Form cookies the size of a little finger. Bake at 375° for 8 to 10 minutes or until lightly browned. When cool, roll in powdered sugar.

BUSHEL OF COOKIES

5 lb. sugar
2 1/2 lb. lard
12 eggs

1 cup maple syrup
    (or 1 pt. syrup)
2 oz. or 3 tbsp. soda

1 lb. salted peanuts &
1 lb. raisins
   ground coarsely together
2 lb. quick oats

2 oz. or 3 tbsp. baking powder
1 qt. sweet milk
6 lb. flour

Mix all ingredients. Grind coarsely peanuts and raisins before adding. Bake at 350°.

Bushel of Cookies (1/2 recipe - in cup measures)

7 cups sugar
2 1/2 cups lard
1/2 lb. peanuts
1/2 lb. raisins
2 tbsp. soda
2 cups milk

6 eggs
4 3/4 cups oatmeal
1 cup syrup
2 tbsp. baking powder
12 cups flour

Drop with a spoon on cookie sheet.

CHOCOLATE REVEL BARS

1 cup butter or oleo
2 cups white sugar
2 eggs
2 tsp. vanilla

2 1/2 cups flour
1 tsp. soda
1 tsp. salt
3 cups oatmeal

Spread 2/3 inch in pan, then top with filling. Save some crumbs to put on top.

Filling:

Melt together in double boiler 12 oz. chocolate chips, 1 can Eagle Brand milk, 2 tablespoons butter, 1/2 teaspoon salt. Bake at 350° 25 to 30 minutes. 1 cup nuts may be added.

TOLL-HOUSE MARBLE SQUARES

1 cup flour plus 2 tbsp.
1/2 tsp. soda
1/2 tsp. salt
1/2 cup soft butter
6 tbsp. white sugar
1 egg

6 tbsp. brown sugar
1/2 tsp. vanilla
1/4 tsp. water
16 oz. pkg. chocolate morsels
1/2 cup chopped nuts

Sift flour, soda and salt. Blend together butter, sugar, vanilla and water. Beat in egg. Mix in flour mixture. Spread in greased pan 13 x 9 x 2 inch pan. Sprinkle chocolate morsels over dough. Place in oven 1 minute. Run knife through dough to marbleize. Bake at 375° 12 to 14 minutes. Cool, cut into 24 squares.

*Important: Use bread flour to make these cookies.

WALNUT SQUARES

Beat 1 egg until foamy.
Beat in:
1 cup brown sugar   1/2 tsp. vanilla
Sift together and stir in:
1/2 cup sifted flour   1/8 tsp. soda
1/2 tsp. salt

Mix in 1 cup cut-up walnuts. Spread in well greased 8 inch square pan. Bake until top has a dull crust. Cut in squares while warm. Cool, then remove from pan.

CHOCOLATE CHIP BARS

2 cups flour   1 1/2 tsp. salt
2 cups sugar   1/2 cup butter, melted
2 tsp. baking powder   1 tsp. vanilla
2 cups chocolate chips
4 eggs, beat if you want a glossy top.

Mix together then spread on cookie sheet. Bake for 25 minutes in 350° oven. (Don't over bake.)

DATE BARS

Filling: Dough Part:
1 lb. pitted dates   2 1/2 cups flour
1/2 cup granulated sugar   1 tsp. soda
3/4 cup light corn syrup   1 tsp. salt
1/4 cup orange juice   1 cup brown sugar
2 tsp. grated orange rind   1 cup soft shortening
1/4 tsp. salt   1/2 cup water
Combine and cook until thick   2 1/2 cups oatmeal
Cool.   (uncooked)

Sift together flour, soda, and salt into a bowl. Add brown sugar, shortening, and water. Beat until smooth. Fold in oatmeal. Spread half of the dough over greased 12 x 15 inch baking sheet. Cover with date filling.

Roll remaining dough and place between 2 sheets of waxed paper. Chill. Remove top sheet of paper. Place dough over filling, remove other sheet of waxed paper. Bake in a moderate oven (350°) 30-35 minutes. Cool and cut into bars.

MARSHMALLOW BARS

1/2 cup oleo	1/4 cup cocoa
1 cup brown sugar	2 cups flour
1 egg	1/2 tsp. soda
1 tsp. vanilla	1/2 tsp. salt
	1/2 cup milk

Combine sugar, oleo, egg and vanilla. Add dry ingredients. Spread on greased cookie sheet. Bake at 375° for 8 minutes. Remove from oven. Sprinkle a few miniature marshmallows over the top. Return to oven 1 minute.

Icing:

1/3 cup butter	2 tbsp. cocoa
1 cup brown sugar	1/4 cup milk

Combine. Boil till it forms large bubbles. Cool and add powdered sugar to thicken. Spread thinly over cookies.

OLD-FASHIONED RAISIN BARS

1 cup seedless raisins	1 tsp. cinnamon
1 cup water	1/4 tsp. salt
1/2 cup salad oil or shortening	1 tsp. soda
(oleo may be used)	1 tsp. nutmeg
1 cup sugar	1 tsp. allspice
1 slightly beaten egg	1/2 tsp. cloves
1 3/4 cups sifted flour	1/2 cup chopped nuts (optional)

Combine raisins and water. Bring to boiling. Remove from heat. Stir in shortening. Cool to lukewarm. Stir in sugar and egg. Sift together dry ingredients. Beat into raisin mixture. Stir in nuts. Pour into greased 13 x 9 x 2 inch pan. Bake in 375° oven 20 minutes or until done. When cool, cut in bars. Dust with confectioners' sugar.

For thin brownie size cookies, bake in greased 15 1/2 inch jelly-roll pan 12 minutes, or till done.

RAISIN BARS

Mix like pie crumbs:

3 1/2 lb. bread flour	1 lb. shortening
2 lb. white sugar	1 tsp. salt

Cook 2 pounds raisins in as little water as possible and cool. Then mix to crumbs.

Add:

5 eggs, beaten   3 tbsp. soda
1 pt. mild Brer Rabbit   Pour 1/2 cup boiling
    molasses   water over soda

Mix in a large container. Mix dough and let stand overnight or longer. Make in long rolls about 1/2 inch thick. Garnish top with beaten egg, add a little water to egg. Bake at 350⁰ to 375⁰ ; take out of oven. Let set a little, then cut.

ORANGE RAISIN BARS

Stew 1 cup raisins in 1 1/2 cups water. If not enough juice to fill 1 cup, add water to make 1 cup. Add 2 tablespoons Crisco and cool. Sift and add:

1 cup sugar   1 tsp. soda
2 cups flour   1/2 tsp. nutmeg
1 tsp. baking powder

Spread on a large greased pan. Bake 18 to 20 minutes in 375⁰ oven.

Mix:

1 cup powdered sugar   1 tbsp. butter
Orange juice

Spread this over the top while hot and cut in bars.

LEMON BARS

1 cup sifted flour   1/4 cup powdered sugar
1/2 cup butter or margarine

Mix together, put into 8 x 8 inch pan. Bake 15 minutes at 350⁰ .

2 eggs, beaten   2 tbsp. flour
2 tbsp. lemon juice   1/2 tsp. baking powder
1 cup sugar   1/2 tsp. lemon flavoring

Combine ingredients in order given, pour on top of crust. Bake for 25 minutes. Cut when cool.

SUNNY GRAHAM CHEWIES

1 2/3 cups graham cracker   1/2 cup nuts
       crumbs   1/4 tsp. baking powder
2 tbsp. flour   2 eggs
1/2 cup butter or oleo   1 tsp. vanilla
1 1/2 cups brown sugar, packed

Combine 1 1/3 cups crumbs, flour, and butter in a bowl. Blend till particles form like rice. Pack into greased 9-inch square cake pan. Bake 20 minutes at 350º. Combine sugar, remaining crumbs, nuts, salt and baking powder. Blend. Add beaten eggs, and vanilla with brown sugar mixture. Blend well. When crust has baked, pour brown sugar mixture onto the crust. Return to oven and bake 20 minutes or more. Cool and cut into bars.

PEANUT BUTTER BROWNIES

6 eggs	1 tbsp. vanilla
2 cups sugar	4 cups flour (pastry)
1 1/2 cups brown sugar	1 1/2 tbsp. baking powder
1 cup peanut butter	1 1/2 tsp. salt
1/2 cup shortening	1/2 cup nuts

Cream sugar, shortening, peanut butter. Add eggs and vanilla, then add dry ingredients and mix well. Press into 2 cookie sheets. Bake 30 minutes. Cut bars while warm.

YUM YUM BROWNIES

2 cups gran. sugar	4 eggs, beaten
3/4 cup butter and lard combined	1 tsp. vanilla
1 cup all-purpose flour	1/2 cup cocoa
1/2 tsp. salt	1/2 cup chopped nuts

Cream sugar and shortening well. Add eggs, vanilla, and nuts. Sift together flour, salt and cocoa; add to sugar mixture and stir well. Bake in greased and floured 8 x 14 inch pan in a 350º oven, until it shrinks from edges of pan. Let cool and cut into squares.

BUTTERSCOTCH BROWNIES

1/4 cup butter	1 cup flour
1 cup brown sugar	1 tsp. vanilla
1 egg	1/2 tsp. salt
1 tsp. baking powder	1/2 cup nuts

Melt butter in pan then stir in sugar. Heat until sugar has melted. Cool, then add beaten egg, flour, vanilla, salt and baking powder. Add nuts last. Bake at 350º for 30 minutes. Cut in squares while hot. Sprinkle with 10 x sugar.

GRANOLIES

1 1/2 cups granola cereal	1/2 cup chopped nuts
3/4 cup unsifted all-purpose flour	1/2 cup butter, softened
1 tsp. baking powder	1/2 cup sugar
1/4 tsp. baking soda	1/4 cup molasses
1/4 tsp. salt	1 egg
1/2 cup chopped dates	1/2 tsp. vanilla

Measure cereal, flour, baking powder, soda, and salt onto waxed paper; stir to blend thoroughly. Mix in dates and nuts. Cream butter. Beat in sugar, molasses, egg, and vanilla. Stir in cereal-date and nut mixture and mix well. Spread in ungreased 9-inch square pan. Bake in preheated 350° oven 25 to 30 minutes or until done. Cool and cut into squares. Makes 16 to 20 squares.

CHOCOLATE SANDWICH WAFERS

Combine:

1 1/4 cups sugar	1/2 cup butter
2 eggs	3 envelopes* Chocobake or equivalent
1 tsp. vanilla	

Beat creamy, then gradually add:

2 cups flour	1 1/2 tsp. baking powder
1/2 tsp. soda	1/2 tsp. salt

Chill well. Roll 1/8 inch thick and cut in rounds. Put on ungreased cookie sheets and bake at 350° for 8-10 minutes. Cool. Put together with your favorite frosting.
* 1 envelope equals 1 square chocolate.

CREAM WAFERS

2 cups lard and oleo	10 1/2 cups flour
8 eggs, beaten	4 tsp. cinnamon
4 tsp. cream	Vanilla
6 tsp. soda	Salt
4 cups brown sugar	

Mix and roll out with cookie cutter or put through cookie press. Bake at 350°. When done spread with your favorite frosting. Place another cookie on top.

PIES

PIE CRUSTS

MOON PIES

TARTS

PIE HINTS

* *Add a tablespoon vinegar to the pie dough and a bit of sugar to keep it from drying out when storing for later use. Store in a plastic bag or covered dish in a cool place.*

* *When pie crust shrinks, rinse the pan in cold water before putting the crust in.*

* *For STREUSEL PIES, mix 1/3 cup peanut butter and 3/4 cup powdered sugar. Spread this on the bottom of a baked pie shell. Top it with your favorite cream pie recipe. Top with meringue or whipped cream.*

* *For best results, pie dough should be worked very lightly after the water has been added.*

* *Pie crusts will have a browner crust when milk is used in the dough. Milk can also be brushed over the top before baking.*

* *To glaze pies or cookies brush the top with beaten egg, or egg white.*

* *When making fruit pies, put in the sugar when the pan is half full instead of on top- the pastry will be lighter.*

* *Do you have trouble baking custard pies? Try heating the milk to the boiling point before mixing it with the eggs. This also helps keep the undercrust crisp.*

BUTTERSCOTCH PIE

2 tbsp. butter   2/3 cup hot water
1 cup brown sugar

Put butter in a heavy saucepan and brown. Add brown sugar and stir until sugar is melted. Add the hot water and cook slowly until all the lumps disappear.
Mix:
2 tbsp. flour   2 egg yolks
3 tbsp. cornstarch   2 cups milk
1/2 tsp. salt

Stir slowly into hot syrup. Boil until it thickens. Add 1 tea-spoon vanilla. Pour into baked pie shell and top with meringue.

* If you wish to use this as a butterscotch pudding or sauce, add 1/2 cup more milk.

MOM'S CARAMEL PIE

Boil the following until brown:
3 tbsp. butter   1/2 tsp. soda
1/2 cup hot water   1 1/2 cups brown sugar

Then add: 2 1/2 cups cold water. Bring to a boil, then add a thickening made of the following:
4 tbsp. flour   1/2 cup sugar
2 egg yolks   **1/2 tsp. salt**

Bring to a boil then add 1/2 teaspoon vanilla. Beat the 2 egg whites for meringue. (Two pies)

BOB ANDY PIE

2 cups brown or white sugar   1 tbsp. butter
4 tbsp. flour   3 eggs, beaten separately
1/2 tsp. cloves   2 cups milk
1 tsp. cinnamon

Mix the dry ingredients then add butter, beaten egg yolks, and milk. Fold in the egg whites. Pour into 2 unbaked pie crusts and bake at 400° for ten minutes, then reduce heat to 350° and bake until done.

MOTHER'S PUMPKIN PIE

1 egg   1/4 tsp. ginger
2/3 cup sugar   1/4 tsp. cinnamon
1 tbsp. flour (heaping)   1 1/2 cup milk

1/2 cup stewed pumpkin (more   2 or 3 drops of vanilla
 if stronger flavor is preferred)   1/2 tsp. salt
1 tbsp. melted butter

Beat thoroughly the sugar, butter and spiced pumpkin and yolk of egg. Add vanilla and milk. Beat the white of egg and fold into the mixture. Pour into unbaked crust and bake slowly as for custard.

PUMPKIN PIE (Betty's)

1 1/2 cup brown sugar   1/2 tsp. nutmeg
1 cup mashed pumpkin   1/2 tsp. allspice
1 tbsp. flour   sprinkle of cloves
1 tsp. cinnamon   5 eggs, separated
3 cups milk

Mix as for custard pie, beating the egg whites and fold them in last. For extra rich pie, use partly condensed milk. Bake at 400° at first then reduce to about 350°. Makes two pies.

PUMPKIN CHIFFON PIE

1 envelope unflavored gelatine   1/2 cup milk
3/4 cup brown sugar   1/4 cup cold water
1/2 tsp. salt   3 egg yolks
1/2 tsp. nutmeg   1 cup cooked pumpkin
1 tsp. cinnamon

Dissolve gelatine in water. Mix all the other ingredients, including gelatine, except the egg whites and put into saucepan over medium heat for 10 minutes, stirring constantly. Remove from heat and cool until mixture is partially set. Beat egg whites until stiff. Add 1/4 cup sugar and beat into pumpkin mixture. Pour into 9-inch baked pie shell. Top with whipped cream before serving.

BASIC CREAM PIE

2 cups milk   2 eggs, separated
1/2 cup sugar   1 tbsp. butter
2 tbsp. flour   1/2 tsp. salt
2 tbsp. cornstarch   1 tsp. vanilla

Scald 1 1/2 cups milk in top of double boiler. Combine sugar, flour, salt. Stir in remaining 1/2 cup milk and egg yolks. Stir this flour mixture into hot milk and cook until thickened. Remove from heat. Add butter and vanilla. Let cool a little and pour into baked pie shell. Cover with meringue.

VARIATIONS:

Coconut Pie - Add 3/4 cup coconut to the Cream Pie filling. Top with whipped cream and sprinkled coconut.

Chocolate Pie - Add 2 to 4 teaspoons cocoa to the thickening of the Cream Pie recipe.

Banana Pie- Cover bottom of baked pie shell with sliced bananas before adding Cream Pie filling.

Streusel Pie- Mix 1/3 cup peanut butter with 3/4 cup powdered sugar. Sprinkle on the bottom of a baked pie shell, saving some crumbs to put on top. Pour in the Cream Pie filling and top with whipped cream. Sprinkle crumbs on top of cream.

Graham Cracker Pie- Pour filling into graham cracker pie crust.

Raisin Cream Pie- Add 1/3 cup raisins and 1/2 tsp. allspice (optional) to Cream filling.

COCONUT CUSTARD PIE

2 eggs, beaten	1/2 cup sugar
1 cup molasses (white or dark)	1 tbsp. flour
1 cup milk	2 tbsp. melted butter
1 tsp. vanilla	1 cup coconut

Mix all ingredients. Pour into unbaked pie shell. Then bake at 450° for 15 minutes. Reduce heat to 350° and bake 20 to 30 minutes longer.

SUSIECUE PIE

Mix:

1 cup brown sugar	1 tbsp. flour
1/2 cup white sugar	

Add:

2 beaten eggs	2 tbsp. milk
1 tsp. vanilla	1/2 cup butter

Beat until thick. Bake at 375° for 20 minutes then sprinkle 1 cup nuts (pecan or hickory nuts) over the top. Continue baking until the filling has set.

KENTUCKY PECAN PIE

1 cup white corn syrup	1/3 tsp. salt
1/2 cup brown sugar	3 eggs, slightly beaten
1/3 cup melted butter or oleo	1 cup pecans
1 tsp. vanilla	

Combine syrup, sugar, salt, butter and vanilla and mix well. Add eggs. Pour into 9-inch pie shell. Sprinkle pecans over all. Bake in heated oven 350° for about 45 minutes.

* This recipe may also be used for tarts.

* English walnuts may be used instead of pecans.

* OATMEAL PIE - Use 2/3 cup quick oatmeal instead of nuts.

* KRISPIE PIE - 1 cup rice krispies instead of nuts.

* COCONUT PIE - Use coconut instead of pecans.

The above variations may also be used with the Southern Pie, omitting the Grapenuts.

PECAN PIE

2 eggs, beaten	1 cup milk
1/4 tsp salt	1 tsp. vanilla
1/2 cup sugar	2 tbsp. melted butter
1 cup molasses (white or dark)	1 cup chopped pecans,
1 tbsp. flour	peanuts or coconut

Mix then pour in unbaked pie shell. Bake 45 minutes at 350°.

SOUTHERN PIE

3/4 cup Post Grapenuts cereal	3 tbsp. dark corn syrup
1/2 cup warm water	3 tbsp. butter, melted
3 eggs, well beaten	1 tsp. vanilla
3/4 cup sugar	1/8 tsp. salt

Combine cereal and water; let stand until water is absorbed. Meanwhile, blend eggs with sugar; add syrup, butter, vanilla, and salt. Fold in softened cereal. Pour into a 9-inch unbaked pie shell. Bake at 350° for 50 minutes or until filling is puffed completely across the top. Cool. Garnish with whipped topping. Sprinkle with additional cereal, if desired.

CHOCOLATE MOCHA PIE

Soak: 1 tbsp. gelatine in 1/4 cup cold water.
Combine in saucepan:

1 tbsp. cocoa   3/4 cup sugar
1/8 tsp. salt   1 tsp. instant coffee
1 1/4 cups milk

Bring to a boil. Stir constantly. Remove from heat and add gelatine. Cool until slightly thickened. Stir in 1 cup whipped cream, and 1 teaspoon vanilla. Pour into pie crust and top with chopped nuts. (Graham cracker pie crust may be used.)

* Dream whip may be substituted for whipped cream.

MAPLE NUT PIE

Heat 1/2 cup milk and 1 cup maple syrup (or maple flavored syrup). Add 2 slightly beaten egg yolks. Cook a little, then add 1 tablespoon gelatine, which has been softened in a little cold water. Add 1 teaspoon maple flavor and chill until the mixture begins to thicken. Fold in 2 stiffly beaten egg whites. Add 1 cup whipped cream and 1/2 cup chopped nut meats. Pour into baked pie shell. If you double this recipe, it makes three 8-inch pies. (This tastes like maple nut ice cream.)

VANILLA PIE

Cook together:
1 cup molasses or maple syrup   2 cups hot water
1 cup brown sugar   1 egg beaten

Second part:
1 cup granulated sugar   2 cups flour
1/2 cup lard   1/2 tsp. soda
1 egg   2 tsp. baking powder
1 cup sour milk or cream

Mix second part like you would mix a cake. Divide batter into four unbaked pie shells. Pour syrup over the batter and bake at 400° about 10 minutes then reduce heat to 350° and bake until done. Cake will rise to the top during baking.

VANILLA CRUMB PIE

1 cup brown sugar   2 cups water
1 cup King syrup   2 tbsp. flour
Boil together 1 minute and set aside.
Into a large bowl, beat:
  1 egg   1/2 tsp. cream of tartar
  1 tsp. vanilla   1 tsp. baking soda

Add to the above syrup mixture, then divide equally into 3 unbaked pie shells. Top with crumbs made of:

2 cups pastry flour	1/2 tsp. baking soda
1 cup brown sugar	1 tsp. cream of tartar
1/2 cup lard	

Bake 45 minutes in 350-375° oven.

MONTGOMERY PIE

Bottom part:

1 egg	3 tbsp. flour
1 lemon	1 cup white syrup
1 cup sugar	1 pt. water

Boil together and cool. Divide into 3 unbaked pie shells.

Top part:

2 eggs	1 cup milk
2 cups sugar	2 1/2 cups flour
1 cup butter	2 tsp. baking powder

Mix top part as cake batter then pour on top of syrup in pie shells. Bake in hot oven (450°) for about 10 minutes, then reduce heat to 350° and bake till done.

UNION PIE

2 cups sugar (scant)	2 cups molasses
2 cups sour cream	2 cups buttermilk
4 tbsp. flour	4 eggs, beaten
1 tsp. soda	3/4 tsp. nutmeg

Mix all ingredients then pour into 4 unbaked pie shells. Bake at 400° for 10 minutes, then at 325° for 20 to 25 minutes or until knife comes out clean.

OATMEAL PIE

3 eggs, beaten	2/3 cup oatmeal
2/3 cup white sugar	2/3 cup coconut (optional)
1 cup brown sugar	2/3 cup milk
2 tsp. oleo, softened	1 tsp. vanilla

Blend together, pour into unbaked pie shell. Bake 30 to 35 minutes at 350°.

* Variation: 1/2 tsp. cinnamon and 1/2 tsp. cloves may be added.

LEMON SPONGE PIE

1 cup sugar	2 eggs
2 tbsp. flour	1 tbsp. butter
juice and grated rind of 1 lemon	1 cup milk

Sift flour and sugar together, then cream in butter, add milk with egg yolks stirred in, add lemon and well-beaten **egg whites last.** Put in unbaked pie crust. Bake in moderate (375-400°) oven. This makes one good sized pie. Lemon sponge may be made without crust. Set in a pan of hot water to bake.

LEMON PIE

3 tbsp. cornstarch	3 eggs
1 1/2 cups sugar	1 1/4 cups boiling water
juice and grated rind of 1 lemon	

Mix cornstarch and sugar. Cover with lemon juice. (Boil the rind in the hot water.) Add beaten yolks of eggs, then the boiling water with lemon rind removed and cook in double boiler. Put in baked crust. Beat egg whites until stiff, add 6 tablespoons of sugar to the 3 egg whites, spread over pie and brown.

SHOO-FLY PIE

Syrup:	Crumbs:
2 cups molasses,	5 cups all-purpose flour
2 cups hot water	2 cups light brown sugar
1 cup light brown sugar	1 cup shortening (scant)
1 tsp. soda (scant)	1/2 tsp. soda
Mix ingredients until dissolved	1/2 tsp. cream of tartar
	Mix to crumb consistency

Use a cup or more of syrup for a 9-inch pie shell. Pour syrup into unbaked crusts and divide the crumbs on top. Bake 10 minutes at 450°, plus 30 minutes at 375°, then 30 minutes at 350°. The temperature may vary with different ovens. Makes four pies. (2 teaspoons nutmeg and 3 teaspoons cinnamon may be added to crumbs.)

GOOEY SHOO-FLY PIE

Crumbs:	1/3 cup lard or butter
2 cups flour	1/2 tsp. nutmeg (optional)
3/4 cup brown sugar	1 tsp. cinnamon (optional)

Syrup:

1 cup molasses
1/2 cup brown sugar
2 eggs

1 cup hot water
1 tsp. soda, dissolved in
   hot water

Put half of syrup in pie crust, then add half of crumbs. Add remaining syrup and other half of crumbs. Bake 10 minutes at 400°. Reduce to 350° for 50 minutes. Makes 2 pies.

LEMON SAUCE FOR SHOO-FLY PIE

2 tbsp. cornstarch
1/2 cup sugar
1/4 tsp. salt
1/4 cup butter or margarine

2 cups boiling water
3 tsp. lemon juice
1 tbsp. grated lemon rind

Mix together cornstarch, sugar and salt in saucepan. Gradually stir in boiling water. Cook, stirring constantly, until mixture boils and is thickened and clear. Remove from heat; stir in remaining ingredients. Serve warm over Shoo-fly pie. Yield: 2 1/4 cups.

CREAM CUSTARD PIE

1 cup brown sugar
1 cup cream

3 eggs
1 tsp. vanilla

Beat eggs. Add brown sugar, cream and vanilla. Pour in unbaked pie shell. Bake in hot oven (450°) for 15 minutes. Reduce heat to 300° and bake 30 to 35 minutes longer. Filling should appear slightly less set in center than around edge.

VELVETY CUSTARD PIE

Thoroughly mix:
4 slightly beaten eggs
1/2 cup sugar

1/4 tsp. salt
1 tsp. vanilla

Slowly stir into this, 2 1/2 cups hot (scalded) milk. Pour at once into unbaked pastry shell. Bake at 475° for five minutes, reduce heat to 425° and bake 30 minutes longer or until knife inserted halfway between center and edge comes out clean.

RAISIN CUSTARD PIE

Mix:
3 eggs, beaten
1 cup raisins

1 tbsp. butter
1 tsp. vanilla

1 cup molasses

Bake in unbaked pie shell at 400° for 10 minutes. Then reduce heat to 350°. Bake 1/2 hour. Walnuts may be used instead of raisins.

FILLED RAISIN PIE

2 cups raisins	2 cups water
4 tbsp. flour	1 tsp. vinegar
2 cups sugar	1 tsp. salt
2 eggs	

Stew raisins until soft. Add flour, sugar, egg yolks, water, vinegar and salt. Let come to a boil and keep stirring. Cool and pour into baked crust. Top with meringue.

FRUIT CRUMB PIE

Prepare your favorite fruit pie filling. (Cherry, blueberry, raspberry, elderberry or raisin may be used.) Pour into unbaked pie shell, top with crumbs. Bake at 425° for 25-30 minutes or until filling boils and the crumbs are nicely browned.

Crumbs:

3/4 cup flour	1/2 tsp. soda
3/4 cup oatmeal	1/4 tsp. salt
2/3 cup brown sugar	1 tsp. cinnamon
1/2 cup melted butter	

Mix dry ingredients together in bowl, add melted butter and mix thoroughly until all the dry ingredients are moistened. This makes enough crumbs for approximately 3 pies.

OHIO STATE RHUBARB PIE

2 cups rhubarb	1 tbsp. flour
1 cup sugar	1/2 tsp. salt
1 egg	1 tsp. lemon juice

Mix sugar, flour, salt and slightly beaten egg. Add rhubarb and lemon juice. Bake between rich crusts, at 425° for 15 minutes; reduce heat to 350° and bake 25-30 minutes longer.

FRENCH RHUBARB PIE

Topping:

3/4 cup flour	1/3 cup margarine
1/2 cup brown sugar	

Mix together: 1 tsp. vanilla
1 egg   2 cups diced rhubarb
1 cup sugar   2 tbsp. flour

Put rhubarb mixture into an unbaked pie shell. Cover with topping. Bake at 400° for 10 minutes. Continue baking at 350° for 30 minutes or until done.

RHUBARB CUSTARD PIE

1 large cup rhubarb   1 tbsp. flour
3/4 cup sugar   1 tbsp. butter
1 cup milk   1/4 tsp. salt
2 eggs

Cut rhubarb fine. Mix sugar, flour, salt and beaten egg yolks, milk and melted butter. Pour over rhubarb which has been placed in unbaked pie shell. Bake until firm. Cover with meringue made of beaten egg whites and 2 tablespoons sugar. Brown.

RHUBARB CREAM PIE

2 1/2 cups cut rhubarb   1 cup sugar
2 tbsp. flour   1 tbsp. melted butter
2 eggs, separated   2 tbsp. sugar

Beat egg yolks with 3 tablespoons water. Add sugar mixed with flour and melted butter. Stir until smooth. Arrange rhubarb in unbaked pie shell and add the sugar mixture mixing it with the fruit. Bake in a hot oven of 450° for 15 minutes. Then reduce the heat to 350° to finish baking. Add meringue made of the egg whites and 2 tablespoons sugar. Brown.

RHUBARB PIE

Melt 2 tablespoons butter, add 2 cups rhubarb and 1/2 cup water (or 1 pint canned rhubarb with no extra water), 1 cup sugar. Cook slowly until tender.

Combine 1/4 cup sugar, 2 tablespoons cornstarch, 1/8 teaspoon salt, 2 egg yolks, beaten and 1/4 cup cream or rich milk. Add to rhubarb and cook until thick. Put in baked pie crust. Use egg whites for meringue.

* This may be used as a pudding. Fold in the beaten egg whites when rhubarb is taken from the stove. Chill.

MOTHER'S ELDERBERRY PIE

Mix 1 cup sugar with yolks of 2 eggs. Add 1 cup sour cream, 2 cups uncooked elderberries, 2 tablespoons cornstarch. Cook on stove until thick. Pour into baked pie shell. Top with meringue of the two egg whites and brown in the oven.

ELDERBERRY PIE

2 1/2 cups elderberries	1/8 tsp. salt
1 cup sugar	2 tbsp. flour
3 tsp. lemon juice or vinegar	

Pour washed elderberries into unbaked pie crust. Mix other ingredients and pour over the berries. Cover with top crust. Bake at 425° for 10 minutes then reduce temperature to 350° and bake 30 minutes longer.

ELDERBERRY CUSTARD PIE

1 cup elderberry juice	1/4 tsp. salt
4 tbsp. flour	1 egg, separated
1 cup sugar	1 cup milk

Bring juice to a boil. Combine flour, sugar and salt. Gradually add the egg yolk and milk. Add this mixture to the boiling juice and stir till thickened. Fold in stiffly beaten egg whites. Pour into unbaked pie shell. Bake at 350° for 20 to 30 minutes.

PINEAPPLE COCONUT PIE

3 eggs	1/2 cup light corn syrup
1 cup sugar	1/4 cup shredded coconut
1 level tbsp. cornstarch	1/4 cup melted butter
1/2 cup drained crushed pineapple	

Beat eggs slightly; add all remaining ingredients. Blend well. Pour into a 9-inch unbaked pie shell. Bake at 350° for 45 or 50 minutes or until slightly set.

HAWAII FOOD PIE

1 cup crushed pineapple	1/8 tsp. salt
1 cup cold water	3 tbsp. cornstarch
1/2 cup sugar	2 eggs

Cook all together until thick. Fold in beaten egg whites while hot. Pour into baked pie crust.

STRAWBERRY PIE

1 1/2 qt. fresh strawberries   1/2 cup cornstarch
2 cups sugar

   Combine strawberries and sugar and let stand 2 hours. Drain off juice and add water to make 2 cups. Blend in cornstarch and cook over low heat until thickened. Mix with strawberries. Cool. Put into baked pie crust or graham cracker crust and serve with whipped cream.

* Pie filling like this may be prepared according to directions and canned. Cold pack only a few minutes.

JELLO-STRAWBERRY PIE

Boil together:
1 cup sugar	2 rounded tbsp. strawberry
1 cup water	jello
2 even tbsp. Clear-Jel	1/4 tsp. salt

   Cool and add 1 pint fresh strawberries. Top with whipped cream.

An ideal pie if you have only a cup of strawberries.

STRAWBERRY PUDDING PIE

   Wash and stem berries then slice them into a pie pan. Prepare half a small box of strawberry jello, dissolved in 1 cup and 2 tablespoons boiling water. Pour over strawberries. Let set until it jells. Make 2 cups of the basic vanilla pudding (page 187). Cool, and then pour into a baked pie crust. Put the bottom of the pie pan with the thickened jello into a pan of hot water for a moment until the jello loosens. Slide it off on the pudding in the crust. Top with whipped cream.

* RASPBERRY PIES or other berry pies may be made with this method, using the same pudding but jello flavors accordingly.

FRESH STRAWBERRY CHIFFON PIE

   Mix one 3-ounce package of your favorite instant strawberry pudding or pie filling and blend in 1 1/4 cups of crushed strawberries. Pour into graham cracker pie crust and chill until firm. Spread with whipped cream and serve.

STRAWBERRY CHIFFON PIE

Beat 3 egg yolks, slightly. Add 1/4 cup sugar. Put in top of double boiler and cook, stirring constantly until thickened. Soak 1 **pkg.** gelatine in 4 tablespoons cold water and add to the mixture. Remove from heat.

Add and mix well, 1 1/2 cup crushed fresh strawberries and chill until it begins to thicken.

Beat 3 egg whites until it holds soft peaks. Add 1/4 cup sugar; beat stiff. Mix this with the strawberry mixture. Fill a baked pie shell. Chill and serve with whipped cream. (3/4 cup raspberry juice may be used instead of strawberries.)

CHERRY PIE FILLING

Mix and bring to a boil:

4 cups red sweet cherries	1 1/2 cups water
2 cups sugar	

Mix 2 heaping tablespoons clear jel with water, enough to make a thin paste. Slowly add this to the boiling cherry mixture, stirring constantly until it comes to a boil. Add 1 teaspoon almond flavor, a few drops of red coloring if desired and cool. Makes 2 pies.

CHERRY PIE

2 tbsp. tapioca	1/2 cup cherry juice
1/8 tsp. salt	1/4 tsp. almond extract
1 cup sugar	Red coloring, if desired
3 cups drained sour cherries	

Mix together and let stand 15 minutes. Pour into 9-inch pie shell; dot with 1 tablespoon butter. Add top crust. Bake at 425° for 50 minutes.
Note:

A scant measure of cornstarch may be used for recipes requiring clear-jell.

PEACH CRUMB PIE

Mix:	Crumb Topping:
2 1/2 tbsp. tapioca	1/3 cup packed brown sugar
3/4 cup sugar	1/4 cup flour
1/4 tsp. salt	1/2 tsp. cinnamon
4 cups sliced peaches	2 1/2 tbsp. soft butter

Let set 5 minutes then pour into unbaked 9-inch pie shell.

Mix crumb topping and put on top of fruit. Oven temperature 425° for 45 to 50 minutes. Other fruits may also be used, especially good with apples.

FRESH PEACH PIE

Arrange in an unbaked pie shell:
One layer of fresh peach halves
Pour over this:

1 cup sugar   3 partly beaten eggs
2 tbsp. butter

Bake at 350° until crust is baked.

PEACH - PINEAPPLE PIE

1 qt. canned sliced peaches   2 cups sugar
1 small can crushed pineapple   1/2 tsp. salt
3 tbsp. clear-jel

Cook till thick. Bake between 2 crusts at 400° until crust is brown. Makes 2 pies.

EMMA'S PEACH PIE

Filling:
1/2 cup sugar   3 tbsp. flour
1/2 tsp. salt   3 tbsp. cornstarch
2 cups milk

Cook and then let cool. Add 1 teaspoon vanilla and 1/4 cup whipped cream. Make glaze with the following: Mash 3 peaches; add 1/4 cup water. Boil 2 minutes. Strain. Add sugar to taste, cook slightly again and thicken with clear jel. Put filling into a baked pie shell. Cover this with peach slices and top with the glaze.

DOUBLE TREAT PEACH PIE

1 cup sugar   3 tbsp. cornstarch or tapioca
1/2 cup water   6 large peaches
1 tbsp. butter
1 baked 9-inch pie shell

Mix together sugar and cornstarch; add water and butter and bring to a boil. Dice 3 of the peaches and add to syrup; simmer 5 minutes or until thick. Cool. Slice remaining peaches into **baked** pie shell and pour the cool peach and syrup mixture over it. Top with whipped cream.

PLAIN APPLE PIE

2 tbsp. flour
6 medium apples, sliced
1 cup sugar

1/4 tsp. cinnamon
1 tsp. butter
1 tbsp. water

Mix flour, apples, sugar and cinnamon. Pour into an unbaked pie shell. Add the water than dot the center with butter. Place 1/2 inch strips of dough over the apples, connecting the strips to the sides of the pie shell. Bake at 400° until the apples are done.

PAPER BAG APPLE PIE

6 cups coarsely sliced or
   chopped apples
1/2 cup sugar
1/2 tsp. nutmeg

2 tbsp. flour
2 tbsp. lemon juice

Measure apples in bowl; mix with 1/2 cup sugar, flour, nutmeg and lemon juice. Turn into unbaked pie shell. Pat down evenly.

Topping:

1/2 cup butter, 1/2 cup flour, 1/2 cup brown or white sugar. Measure the butter, sugar and flour. Cut butter in with pastry blender until crumbs are the size of peas. Sprinkle this over the apples evenly and pat down around the edges. Slide the pie into a brown paper bag, fold end under pie. Put on a cookie sheet for easy handling. Bake at 425° for 50 minutes. Dividends: No scorched rim, no under-baked apples, no boiling over in your lovely clean oven, no grief!

APPLE CREAM PIE

3 cups finely cut apples
1 cup brown or white sugar
2/3 cup cream or top milk

1/4 tsp. salt
1 rounded tbsp. flour

Mix together and put in an unbaked pie shell. Sprinkle top with cinnamon. Bake in a hot oven 450° for 15 minutes. Then reduce heat to 325° and bake 30 to 40 minutes longer. When pie is about half done, take a knife and push top apples down to soften.

* Variation: Elderberries or other fruit may be used instead of
        apples.

DUTCH APPLE PIE

3 cups sliced apples	1 cup light cream
1 cup sugar	1 tsp. vanilla
3 tbsp. flour	1/2 cup chopped nuts
1/2 tsp. cinnamon	1 tbsp. butter
1 beaten egg	1 unbaked 9-inch pie shell

Place apples in pie shell. Mix sugar, flour and cinnamon. Combine egg, cream, and vanilla; add sugar mixture and mix well; pour over apples; sprinkle with nuts and dot with butter. Bake in moderate oven (350°) 45 to 50 minutes till apples are tender.

GREEN TOMATO PIE

Fill unbaked pie shell with very thin-sliced peeled green tomatoes. Remove seeds, if you wish. Mix 1 1/2 cups sugar (1 cup white, 1/2 cup brown), 2 tbsp. flour, 4 tbsp. vinegar, 1 tbsp. butter and 1 tsp. cinnamon, then pour over tomatoes. Put top crust on tomatoes and bake at 425° for 15 minutes, then at 350° for 30-40 minutes.

KATIE'S MINCE PIES

6 cups apples	2 cups sugar
1 pt. hamburger	1 tsp. cinnamon
1 cup raisins	1 tsp. allspice
3 tbsp. vinegar	Salt to taste
1 tbsp. butter, melted	

Mix all ingredients, then pour into 2 unbaked pie shells. Bake at 350° for 25-35 minutes.

HALF MOON PIES

1 quart dried apple snitz boiled in 1 1/2 cup water, until soft and no water remains. Put through colander and add:

1 qt. applesauce	1/2 tsp. cinnamon
1 1/2 cups brown sugar	1/2 tsp. salt

Make pie dough, then shape dough to the size of a large egg. Roll out thin as pie dough. Fold over to make a crease through center. Fold back and make 2 holes in top part of the dough. On the other half place 1/2 cup of the filling. Wet edges and fold over. Press edges together. Cut off remaining dough with pie crimper. Brush top with buttermilk or beaten egg. Bake at 450° until brown.

SNITZ PIE - Put 2 or 2 1/2 cups of this filling into an unbaked pie shell. Place another crust on top and bake at 400° until crust is baked.

APPLE FRITTERS

1 cup flour
2 tbsp. sugar
1/2 cup milk
5 or 6 apples

1 1/2 tsp. baking powder
1/2 tsp. salt
1 egg

Core and peel apples. Slice and put in the batter. Drop by spoonsful in 1 inch fat or oil in frying pan. Drain on paper towel or in colander. Sprinkle with powdered sugar or eat with syrup. Jag with fork when frying to test if apples are soft. Makes about 4 skillets full of fritters.

FRIED APPLE TURNOVERS

2/3 cup granulated sugar
1/2 tsp. cinnamon
1/4 cup butter or margarine

2 cups sliced, pared, tart apples
1 pkg. refrigerator biscuits
Powdered sugar

Combine granulated sugar, cinnamon, butter and apples in a sauce pan; simmer, stirring occasionally until apples are tender. Separate biscuits and roll each to an oval shape, about 5 inches long. Place 1 tablespoon of apple filling on half of oval, fold dough over filling and seal edges with a fork. (Be sure they are sealed or filling will leak out.) Fry in 375° deep hot fat, turning once, for about 1 minute or until golden brown. Drain and sprinkle with powdered sugar. Serve warm. Makes 10 turnovers. (Biscuit Mix may be used.)

PIE DOUGH

3 qt. flour
2 tbsp. vinegar

4 cups lard
2 cups water (approx.)
2 tsp. salt

Mix into crumbs. Wet with 2 tablespoons vinegar and water as needed. This will be enough for top and bottom crusts for 6 pies, (more or less depending on size of pies or how thin it is rolled out). If crumbs are not needed all at once, they may be stored in a tight container for future use.

PIE CRUST

3 cups sifted flour
1 cup shortening
1/2 tsp. salt

1 egg
5 tbsp. water
1 tsp. vinegar

Mix flour, shortening and salt. Beat egg, add water and vinegar then add to flour mixture, enough to make soft dough. Makes 1 double-crust pie or 2 single-crust pies.

NEVER FAIL PIE CRUST

6 cups flour
2 cups lard
1 egg in cup, filled up with water

3 tsp. baking powder
1 tsp. salt

Mix flour, lard, salt and baking powder until crumbly. Add egg with water. Mix. Sometimes it takes more water. This dough will keep for awhile.

PAN PIE DOUGH

1 1/2 cups flour
1 1/2 tbsp. gran. sugar

1 tsp. salt

Mix in pie pan. Add not quite 1/2 cup cooking oil in which 2 tablespoons milk has been stirred in. Blend with dry ingredients, then press on bottom of pan and sides.

SPOON PIE DOUGH

To one cup lard add 1/2 cup boiling water. Stir until the lard is melted. Add 3 cups flour, 1 teaspoon baking powder, and 1 teaspoon salt. Stir with a spoon then chill dough in the ice box for a few hours.

FLAKY PIE CRUST

2 cups sifted whole wheat flour
1 tsp. salt
2 tbsp. wheat germ

3/4 cup margarine
4 - 5 tbsp. ice water

Sift flour with salt into medium bowl; add wheat germ. With pastry blender cut in shortening. Sprinkle ice water over pastry and mix with fork. Pastry should be just moist enough to hold together. This dough handles just like any dough using white flour and is far more nutritious.

WHOLE WHEAT PIE CRUST

2 cups whole wheat flour	1/2 tsp. salt
1 cup ground oatmeal	1/2 cup water
1/3 cup vegetable oil	

GRAHAM CRACKER CRUST

1 cup graham crackers	1/4 cup melted butter
3 tbsp. brown sugar	

Crush graham crackers to fine crumbs. Add sugar, melted butter, and mix thoroughly. Press firmly in an even layer around bottom and sides of a 9-inch pie plate. Bake 5 to 8 minutes. Cool.

NO BAKE GRAHAM CRACKER CRUST

1 cup (1/4 pkg. or lb.)	3 tbsp. powdered sugar
graham crackers	1/4 tsp. plain gelatine
1/4 cup melted butter	

Make graham crackers fine. Add sugar and gelatine and butter and mix thoroughly. Save 2 tablespoons mixture for the top. Press the rest firmly in 9-inch pie pan. Chill 15 minutes.

OATMEAL PIE CRUST

Combine:

1 cup quick-cooking oats	1/3 cup brown sugar
1/3 cup sifted flour	1/2 tsp. salt

Cut in 1/3 cup butter till crumbly. Press firmly on bottom and sides of 9-inch pie plate. Bake in a moderate oven (375°) about 15 minutes. Cool crust completely and fill with any desired cream filling.

EGG WHITE PIE CRUST

3/4 cup graham cracker	3 egg whites
crumbs	1/3 cup sugar
1/3 cup sugar	1 tsp. vanilla
1/2 cup pecans	

Mix crumbs, 1/3 cup sugar and pecans. Beat egg whites until stiff, gradually adding the other 1/3 cup sugar and vanilla. Add to crumb mixture. Pour into greased pie pan and bake at 350° for 30 minutes. When cool, mash down to shape of pan. Fill with ice cream and freeze.   Thaw slightly before serving.   Top with favorite fruit, or fill with favorite filling.

MERINGUE FOR PIE

2 egg whites   1/4 tsp. cream of tartar

   Beat until soft peaks.   Add 4 tablespoons granulated sugar to which 1/2 teaspoon cornstarch has been added, 1 teaspoon vanilla; beat until stiff.

SUNSHINE PIE

A pound of patience, you must find
Mixed well with loving words, so kind
Drop in two pounds of helpful deeds
And thoughts of other people's deeds.

A pack of smiles, to make the crust,
Then stir and bake it well you must.
And now, I ask that you may try,
The recipe of this Sunshine Pie.

                                        -Submitted

DESSERTS

PUDDINGS, FRUIT, PIES, CAKES, COOKIES, some so-called salads... all these can be classed as desserts. Dessert is the food we all so dearly love and which makes a meal lavish. It is often the most tempting part of the meal... and the most calorie-laden. In some homes it is not uncommon to find four or five desserts in a meal prepared for company. Yet in Grandmother's day, desserts consisted often of two kinds of pies—take your choice. One may have been a nutmeg pie, and the other a snitz pie.

I remember Mother making only one kind of pudding when I was a child. It was a plain vanilla pudding, with bananas and broken white crackers added. We all loved it. It was no wonder, for bananas were a very rare item, as were oranges and grapefruit.

During the 1974 sugar shortage, we discovered that many of these recipes can take 1/4th to 1/3rd less sugar than what the recipe calls for; this does not make the food less tasty.

If we want to be simple folks... Let's have simple meals... And not just cook for honor... Merely food that appeals... To the taste—for we must eat... Each day life to sustain... The simpler that we eat and live ... The more we stand to gain... Christ fed the multitude on fish... The bread He did not spare... Simple food for hunger's sake... To show His love and care... We thank Him for the lavish meal... And gorge down all the frills... We pay the price—our sacrifice in ruined health... And all the doctor bills.

BASIC VANILLA PUDDING

3 1/2 cups milk, scalded   1 tbsp. butter
3/4 cup sugar   1 tsp. vanilla
1/3 cup cornstarch   2 egg yolks
1/2 tsp. salt   1/2 cup milk

Make thickening with dry ingredients, beaten egg yolks, and 1/2 cup cold milk. Pour into hot milk and stir until it thickens. Add 1 tsp. vanilla and 1 tbsp. butter. Fold in whipped cream or beaten egg whites, or top with meringue.

COCONUT PUDDING

Use basic vanilla pudding and add 1 cup coconut. Top with meringue and coconut.

GRAHAM CRACKER PUDDING

Make alternate layers in a serving dish of basic Vanilla Pudding, then graham cracker crumbs; on this add sliced bananas and nuts (optional). Continue until the dish is full. Top with whipped cream. Sprinkle crumbs over this and banana slices.

* Various desserts may be made by adding pineapple chunks, orange slices, strawberries or other fruit, or grapenuts and whipped cream.

The following custard recipe may be expanded to suit one's needs.

BASIC CUSTARD RECIPE

1 cup scalded milk   1 beaten egg
1 tbsp. sugar   1 tsp. vanilla
1/4 tsp. salt   a dash of nutmeg, if desired

Mix together and set in pan of hot water to bake. Bake at 350° until done. To test, insert knife in center of custard. If knife comes out clean, custard is done. Do not let custard boil.

* Add chocolate (not cocoa) to the custard recipe for chocolate custard.

* Use no-calorie sweetener and skimmed milk for low-calorie custard.

* Use lemon flavoring instead of vanilla.

* Use brown sugar instead of white for carmel taste.

DATE PUDDING

1 cup chopped dates	1 tsp. butter
1 cup boiling water	1 tsp. vanilla
1 cup sugar	1 egg
1 1/2 cups flour	2 tsp. soda
1/2 cup chopped nuts	1/2 tsp. salt

Put dates in bowl. Pour boiling water over them. Let set to cool a little. Then add the other ingredients. Bake at 325° for 30-40 minutes. When cold, chop up before serving and mix whipped cream through it.

RICH DATE PUDDING

18 graham crackers, crushed	12 marshmallows (chopped)
3/4 cup chopped dates	1/4 cup cream
3/4 cup chopped nuts	

Mix well and pack in dish or make into a roll. Let set 12 hours. Slice and serve with whipped cream.

RAISIN-NUT PUDDING

Syrup:	Batter:
1 cup brown sugar	1/2 cup sugar
2 cups hot water	2 tbsp. butter
2 tsp. butter	1 cup milk
1 tbsp. cornstarch	1 cup flour
Boil together 5 minutes then	2 tsp. baking powder
pour into cake pan.	1/2 tsp. salt
	1/2 cup raisins
	1/4 cup nuts

Mix second part as you would mix a cake. Put batter on syrup. Bake until knife inserted comes out clean. Serve warm with milk or whipped cream.

DEPRESSION PUDDING

Batter:	Syrup:
1/4 cup butter or margarine	1 cup brown sugar
1 cup sugar	1 tbsp. butter or oleo
2 cups flour	1 1/2 cup raisins
1 cup milk	4 cups boiling water
4 tsp. baking powder	2 tsp. vanilla
	1/2 cup nuts (optional)

Combine syrup ingredients and boil 5 minutes. Pour into a greased loaf pan. Dab tablespoons of the batter over the syrup and raisins. Bake 30-35 minutes at 350°. Serve with whipped cream or milk.

CINNAMON PUDDING - Omit raisins and add 1 teaspoon cinnamon to the batter. Pour batter into greased pan and pour syrup on top.

CHEESE CAKE

Combine:

3/4 cup graham crackers	1/4 cup margarine
1/2 cup sugar	

Line bottom of pan with crumbs (9 x 9).

Beat 2 eggs
Add 16 oz. cream cheese
Whip until smooth
Add: 1 teaspoon vanilla and 1 cup sugar. Pour on top of crumbs. Bake 15-20 minutes. Top with your favorite fruit pie filling; cherry, blueberry, raspberry, strawberry, or any other fruit desired. Refrigerate several hours.

LEMON CHEESE CAKE

1 large can Pet milk or	30 graham crackers
1 cup cream	1 stick oleo (1/2 cup)
1 tsp. vanilla	1 8 oz. pkg. cream cheese
1 cup hot water	1 cup sugar
1 box lemon Jello	

Dissolve Jello in hot water, let stand to thicken. Meanwhile crush graham crackers, then blend in butter. Line bottom of 2 8-inch cake pans, saving a few crumbs for the top.

Soften cream cheese and add the sugar and vanilla. Beat the cream until thick. Add the cheese mixture and whipped cream to the Jello which has thickened somewhat. Beat until fluffy. Pour into pans, top with remaining crumbs and cool.

MAPLE SPONGE

2 cups brown sugar	1/2 tsp. maple flavor
2 cups hot water	

Boil together 10 minutes. Soak 1 package gelatin in 1/2 cup cold water a few minutes, then mix with hot syrup. Let set till firm. Use your favorite vanilla pudding and 1 cup cream, whipped. Put spoonfuls of all 3 alternately in serving dish. Nuts or bananas may also be added.

VANILLA SOUFFLE

1/4 cup butter, melted	1/4 cup sugar
1/4 cup flour	3 eggs, separated
1 cup milk, scalded	1 tsp. vanilla

Make a white sauce of butter, flour, milk and sugar. Add beaten egg yolks and vanilla. Mix thoroughly. Fold in stiffly beaten egg whites. Pour into greased baking dish, set in pan of hot water and bake in moderate oven (350°) 40 to 45 minutes or until souffle is firm to the touch.

MISSISSIPPI MUD

1 1/2 cups brown sugar	3 egg yolks
2 1/2 cups milk	4 tbsp. flour
1/2 cup water	12 graham crackers
1 tsp. vanilla	1 tbsp. butter (heaping)

Melt butter and brown. Add sugar and water and boil until thick. Mix egg yolks, flour and milk, add to syrup and boil until thick. Add vanilla and put into dish. Roll graham crackers and spread on top. Spread with beaten egg whites and a few graham cracker crumbs. Brown slightly.

SODA CRACKER PUDDING

18 sq. soda biscuits (crushed)	2 tbsp. peanut butter
1/2 cup brown sugar	1/4 cup butter

Melt butter and peanut butter; add to sugar and cracker crumbs and mix well. Wet a bowl and press crumbs around side and bottom. Reserve 1/4 cup crumbs for top.
Filling:

3 cups milk	1 cup white sugar
2 eggs	1 tsp. vanilla
2 tbsp. cornstarch	1/2 cup coconut

Boil together first 4 ingredients until thick; add vanilla and coconut. Pour slowly on crumbs. When cooled sprinkle with remaining crumbs.

FLUFFY PUDDING

Separate 1 egg; beat white until foamy. Measure 1/3 cup sugar, gradually add 2 tablespoons to whites; beat to soft peaks. Mix rest of sugar, egg yolk, 3 tablespoons tapioca, 1/8 teaspoon salt and 2 cups milk. Bring to full boil. Very slowly add to the beaten white, stirring rapidly to blend. Add 3/4 teaspoon vanilla. Cool 20 minutes, then beat it well.

AUNT CLARA'S DESSERT

1 pkg raspberry gelatine	2 eggs, separated
1 cup boiling water	1/2 cup melted butter
1 cup pineapple juice	1/4 cup brown sugar
1/4 cup butter	16 graham crackers, crushed
1 1/2 cups powdered sugar	1 cup drained, crushed pineapple

Dissolve gelatine in boiling water. Add pineapple juice. Chill until mixture is slightly thickened. Cream 1/4 cup butter and powdered sugar. Blend in well beaten egg yolks. Beat egg whites until stiff, but not dry. Fold into creamed mixture. Combine melted butter and brown sugar with cracker crumbs. Put half of crumb mixture in bottom of buttered 9-inch square pan. Spread evenly with egg mixture. Spread pineapple over filling. Sprinkle on remaining crumbs. Pour gelatine over top. Chill until set. Cut in squares. Top each serving with whipped cream. Makes 9 servings.

EAGLE BRAND DESSERT

Put a can of Eagle Brand milk in your teakettle and boil it for 3 1/2 hours. Set it where it will get cold. When cold, open both ends. Push contents out and slice. Put each slice on top of Dole pineapple slices. Add a spoonful of whipped cream. Garnish with red maraschino cherry.

This is a handy dessert. You can boil as many as you wish and set on your pantry shelf for unexpected company.

BUTTERSCOTCH NUT TORTE

6 eggs, separated	1 tsp. almond extract
1 1/2 cups sugar	1 cup broken nuts
1 tsp. baking powder	2 cups graham cracker crumbs
2 tsp. vanilla	1 pt. whipping cream

Beat egg yolks well; add sugar, baking powder and flavoring.

Beat egg whites enough to hold a peak. Fold into yolks. Add crumbs, then nuts. Line two 9-inch layer pans with wax paper. Pour in cake batter. Bake at 325° for 30-35 minutes. Cool. Whip cream and sweeten with 3 tablespoons powdered sugar and put between layers on top and sides. Put the following sauce on top:

Sauce:

1 cup brown sugar	1/4 cup orange juice
1/4 cup butter	1 well-beaten egg
1/4 cup water	1/2 tsp. vanilla
1 tbsp. flour	

Mix well and boil until thick enough to pour. When cool, pour over whipped cream.

* This can be fixed like date pudding. Cut the cake in small pieces, and make alternate layers of sauce, whipped cream and cake.

GRAHAM CRACKER FLUFF

Filling:

Soak: 1 pkg. gelatine in 1/3 cup cold water
Mix: 1/2 cup sugar, 3/4 cup rich milk and 2 egg yolks

Cook for one minute in double boiler, stirring all the time. Remove from heat; add gelatine and 1 teaspoon vanilla. Chill until mixture begins to thicken. Then add 2 stiffly beaten egg whites and 1 cup cream, whipped.

Crumbs:

Melt 1 1/2 tablespoons butter and 3 tablespoons brown sugar together. Mix with 12 crushed graham crackers.

Line the bottom of a dish with 1/2 of the crumbs and pour in pudding. Put remaining crumbs on top. Set in a cool place to chill.

GRAHAM CRACKER CUSTARD

18 graham crackers	1/2 cup butter
1/4 cup sugar	

Crush crackers. Add butter and sugar. Line a dish with these crumbs saving a few to put on top.

Custard:

3/4 cup milk	1 pkg. lemon or orange jello
3 egg yolks	1/2 cup sugar

Bring milk to a boil. Add eggs and sugar. Remove from heat and add jello. Allow to cool and partly set, then fold in 3 egg whites beaten stiff, and 1/2 to 3/4 cup cream (whipped). Pour in dish lined with crumbs. Sprinkle with remaining crumbs and chill.

WEDDING TAPIOCA

9 cups water
1/2 tsp. salt
1 1/2 cups tapioca (baby pearl)
1 cup sugar

2 small boxes pineapple jello
1 small box orange jello
1 small box lemon jello
Pineapples as desired

Bring the water and 1/2 teaspoon salt to boiling point. Add tapioca. Boil till tapioca is clear. Keep stirring while it boils. Remove from heat; add sugar and the jello. Chill. Whipped cream may be added if desired. Also nuts or other fruit, such as bananas or orange slices.

FRUIT TAPIOCA

1 small pkg. jello (any flavor)
1/4 cup minute tapioca
2 1/2 cups water, fruit juice,
  or syrup from canned fruit

1/4 tsp. salt
1/2 to 3/4 cup sugar

Mix and let stand 5 minutes. Bring to a boil over medium heat, stirring often. Cool 20 minutes. Add any fruit desired. Makes 6 servings. Adding a package of orange Kool-Aid makes a delicious pudding and goes well with peaches, pineapple, or pears. This recipe helps stretch the fruit supply.

STEAMED CHOCOLATE PUDDING

3 tbsp. melted butter
2/3 cup sugar
1 egg
1 1/8 cup flour
2 tsp. baking powder

1/8 tsp. salt
3/4 cup milk
4 tbsp. cocoa
1 tsp. vanilla

Mix in order given, then pour into buttered double boiler. Steam for 2 hours.

CHOCOLATE FUDGE PUDDING

Cream together:
  3 tbsp. shortening   3/4 cup sugar
Sift together:
  1 cup flour   1/2 tsp. salt

1 1/2 tsp. baking powder

Add alternately with 1/2 cup milk to the creamed mixture. Fold in 1/2 cup nuts. Put in ungreased pan.
Mix:

1 cup brown sugar   1/4 tsp. salt
1/4 cup cocoa

Sprinkle this mixture over the top of the batter. Do not stir in. Pour 1 1/4 cup boiling water over the top of the batter and all. Do not stir. Bake at 350° for 40 to 45 minutes. Serve with whipped cream.

CHOCOLATE PUDDING

1 cup shortening   3 cups flour
2 cups sugar   2 tsp. soda
2 eggs   1 tsp. salt
1 tsp. vanilla   2/3 cup cocoa
1 cup buttermilk or sour milk

Mix together until smooth, then add 1 cup hot water. Pour into a 13 x 9 inch pan.
Mix together: 1 1/2 cups sugar
               2 tbsp. cocoa
               3/4 to 1 cup hot water

Pour over cake batter. Bake in a 350° oven for 50-60 minutes. Good with ice cream.

STEAMED GRAHAM PUDDING

1 egg   1 cup whole wheat flour
1 cup sugar   1 tsp. soda
1 cup sour milk   1 tsp. cinnamon
1 cup white flour   2 tbsp. molasses
1/2 cup raisins   1/2 tsp. salt

Steam on top of stove, preferably using an angel food cake pan, set in a large covered kettle. Simmer 1 to 1 1/2 hours. Serve warm with milk. Very good and economically made.

TWO-EGG BOSTON CREAM PIE

1 cup sugar   1 3/4 cups flour
1 egg   1 tsp. soda
1/2 cup sour cream   2 tsp. baking powder
1/2 cup milk

Bake at 350° in 2 layer cake pans. When **cool, split the layers** and fill with the following filling:

3/4 cup sugar   1 pt. milk
1 egg yolk   1 tbsp. flour
1 tbsp. cornstarch   vanilla

Cover with brown sugar frosting. (1 1/2 teaspoon grated lemon peel, lemon extract, or 4 1/2 teaspoons lemon juice may be added to the filling.)

PEACH PETZ

1 cup flour   Filling:
1/2 tsp. baking powder   2 tbsp. butter
1/4 tsp. salt   3/4 cup sugar
1/3 cup shortening   1/3 cup flour
3-5 tbsp. cold water   **14 peach halves (canned)**

Combine flour with other dry ingredients. Cut shortening into the flour mixture. Add water slowly and mix using only enough water to hold the dough together. Chill. Roll out the dough a little thicker than pie dough. Put in a large pie plate or cake pan.

Mix butter, sugar and flour for filling. Sprinkle half of this mixture over the crust. Place peaches (halves down) on crust and cover with remaining crumbs. Pour peach juice over top. Bake at 375° for 35 minutes or until crust is brown. Serve with milk.

RASPBERRIES WITH KNEPP

2 cups whole raspberries   Mix:
      or juice   1 cup flour
3/4 cup sugar   5 tsp. baking powder
2 cups water   3 tsp. sugar
Bring to a boil   1/4 tsp. salt
                                   1 cup milk

Mix 3 level tablespoons cornstarch with **enough water** to make a smooth sauce. Stir into the hot raspberry mixture and bring to a boil.

Drop the dough part by spoonfuls into the boiling raspberry mixture. Cover with a tight lid and let boil slowly for 20 minutes. Do not uncover during the boiling period. Serve with milk. Elderberries or other fruit may be used.

OATMEAL BROWN BETTY

2 1/2 cups sliced apples
1 cup whole wheat flour
1/2 tsp. salt
1/2 cup brown sugar

1/2 cup shortening, scant
1/4 cup raisins
1/2 tsp. soda
1 cup rolled oats

Mix dry ingredients. Cut in shortening till mixture is crumbly. Spread half of mixture into baking dish. Cover with apples and raisins. Put the remainder of the crumbs on the top, covering the apples and the raisins. Dot with butter. Drip 1/2 cup of corn syrup or honey over the top. Bake in a moderate oven, 35 minutes or until the apples are soft. Serve with milk. Other fruit may be used.

CROW NEST PUDDING

Make cake batter with cake mix (page 254) or Handy Made Cake (page 115). Pour 1 quart peaches into a buttered baking dish. Sprinkle 1 tablespoon flour over them. Top with the cake batter and bake at 350° for 30 to 40 minutes. Serve warm with top milk. Other fruit may also be used.

APPLE RICE BETTY

4 large apples
1 cup cooked brown rice
1/2 cup chopped walnuts
1/2 cup honey

1/4 tsp. cloves
1 tsp. salt
1/4 tsp. cinnamon
2 tbsp. oil

Mix honey with spices. Grease baking dish and place a thin layer of rice in dish; add a layer of thinly sliced apples, and sprinkle with honey, spices and nuts. Repeat layers until all ingredients are used, saving some honey, spices and nuts for the top. Pour oil over top. Bake in 350° oven until apples are soft. Serve hot or cold.

SARAH SCHWARTZ'S RHUBARB ROLLS

2 cups flour
2 tsp. baking powder
7/8 cup sweet milk
1 tsp. salt
2 1/2 tbsp. lard

Sweet Sauce:
1 cup sugar
1 heaping tbsp. flour
1/4 tsp. salt
1 cup hot water
Small lump of butter
Dash of nutmeg
Boil 3 minutes

Sift flour, salt and baking powder. Cut lard into this, add milk and mix well. Roll dough out 1/4 inch thick, spread thick with soft butter, granulated sugar and finely cut rhubarb. Sprinkle with nutmeg. Roll as you would cinnamon rolls and cut in 1 1/2 to 2 inch slices. Place in pan, pour sweet sauce over and around them. Bake at 350° until brown. Diced apples may be used in place of rhubarb.

APPLE GOODIE

Delicious & Crunchy "9"

Top part:

1/2 cup sugar	1 cup oatmeal
2 tbsp. flour	1 cup brown sugar
1/4 tsp. salt	1 cup flour
1 tsp. cinnamon	1/4 tsp. soda
1 1/2 qt. apples, sliced	1/3 tsp. baking powder
	2/3 cup butter ← *didn't use all*

Mix sugar, flour, salt and cinnamon. Add to apples and mix. Put on the bottom of a greased pan.

Mix the ingredients of top part until crumbly, then put on apples and pat firmly. Bake at 350° until brown and crust is formed. Serve with milk or cream.

RHUBARB CRUNCH

Use the above recipe but substitute 3 cups diced rhubarb and 1 extra cup sugar, with 1 tsp. nutmeg.

RHUBARB CRUNCH

1 cup whole wheat flour	3/4 cup oatmeal
1 cup brown sugar	1/2 cup melted butter
1 tsp. cinnamon	

Mix until crumbly. Put 1/2 of crumbs into greased 9-inch pan and cover with 4 cups diced rhubarb.
Combine:

1 cup sugar	1 cup water
2 tbsp. cornstarch	1 tsp. vanilla

Cook until clear and pour over rhubarb. Top with remaining crumbs. Bake at 350° for 45 minutes or until the rhubarb is tender.

SPICED APPLE DESSERT

4 large apples (cube or slice)
1 cup brown sugar
1 cup flour
1/2 tsp. soda
1 tsp. cinnamon

1/2 tsp. baking powder
1 tsp. nutmeg
1 tsp. cloves
1/2 tsp. salt
4 tbsp. butter
2 eggs, beaten

Put dry ingredients together then add apples, eggs and butter. Bake 45 minutes at 350°. Eat with milk and sugar when cooled.

APPLE-RHUBARB CRISP

2 cups finely cut apples
2 cups finely cut rhubarb
1 cup flour
1 egg, beaten

3/4 cup white sugar
1/4 tsp. nutmeg
1/2 cup butter or oleo
1 cup brown sugar

Mix apples, rhubarb, egg, sugar and nutmeg together. Place in glass baking dish. Combine butter, flour, and brown sugar to crumby consistency. Pack over apple-rhubarb mixture. Bake in 375° oven, 30 minutes. Serve with sweetened milk or whipped cream.

* 4 cups apples may be used, omitting the rhubarb. Add 1/2 cup nuts, if desired.

APPLE DUMPLINGS

Dough:
2 cups flour
2 1/2 tsp. baking powder
1/2 tsp. salt
2/3 cup shortening
1/2 cup milk

Sauce:
2 cups brown sugar
2 cups water
1/4 cup butter
1/2 tsp. cinnamon

6 apples, peeled and cut in halves

Roll out the dough, cut in squares. Place one apple half on each square. Wet edges of dough and press into a ball around the apple. Set dumplings in a pan. Pour sauce over dumplings and bake.

RAW APPLE PUDDING

Mix several cups diced apples, about 1/4 cup chocolate shavings (or chips), nuts, broken homemade graham crackers with whipped cream.

APPLE SURPRISE

1 pkg. jello (flavor desired)	1/2 cup diced apples
1/2 cup chopped celery	1 cup drained pineapples
1/2 cup chopped dates	1/4 cup chopped nuts
1/2 cup whipping cream	

Prepare jello and cool. When slightly thickened, fold in fruit and other ingredients. Add whipped cream last. Put in molds. To serve garnish with mayonnaise.

MY OWN APPLE DESSERT

Wash and slice enough apples to make 4 quarts. Put in a large kettle. Add 1 cup raisins, 1 teaspoon cinnamon, 1 1/2 cups sugar, and enough water to almost cover the fruit. Bring to a boil.

Take 2 tablespoons cornstarch. Mix with a little water. Add to fruit, then boil until it thickens. Cool. Slice 5 or 6 bananas and add to cooled mixture. This is best with solid cooking apples.

RHUBARB TAPIOCA

1 cup tapioca (pearl)	2 cups cold water
3 cups hot water	2 cups sugar
2 cups rhubarb	1 can crushed pineapple

Soak tapioca in cold water overnight or a couple of hours. Cinnamon may be added, if desired. Add remaining ingredients and cook, stirring constantly, until tapioca is clear, or nearly clear. (When cooking tarty fruit, such as rhubarb, apricots, grapes, cherries or red raspberries, add a generous amount of cinnamon for added flavor.)

RHUBARB PUDDING

Mix: 1 egg, 1 cup sugar, 2 cups flour, 1 cup milk, 2 teaspoons baking powder, vanilla. Put this in bottom of cake pan. Mix: 4 cups rhubarb, 2 cups sugar and 2 cups boiling water. Pour this mixture over the dough. Bake at 350-375° for 40 minutes or until done.

APPLE-CRANBERRY DUMPLINGS

Syrup:

2 cups water

2 cups sugar

1/2 tsp. cinnamon

1/2 tsp. cloves

1/2 cup butter

Combine first four ingredients and boil together for 5 minutes. Remove from heat and add butter.

Biscuit dough:

2 cups sifted flour

1 tsp. salt

1/2 cup shortening

1 tbsp. baking powder

2 tbsp. sugar

3/4 cup milk

Sift together dry ingredients and cut in shortening. Gradually add milk, tossing to make a soft dough. Roll out on floured board to form rectangle 18 x 12".

Filling:

4 cups grated, peeled apples

1 cup drained, cooked, whole cranberries, or canned, whole cranberry sauce

1/2 cup black walnuts, chopped

Spread with apples, cranberries and nuts. Roll up like jelly roll. Cut in 1 inch slices and place in 13 x 9 x 2 pan. Pour hot syrup over all and bake in hot oven (425°) for 40 minutes. Serve warm.

CHERRY PUDDING

3 cups cherries

1 1/2 cups water

1/4 cup sugar

2 tbsp. flour

Boil mixture together

Dough part:

3 cups flour

9 level tbsp. butter

9 tbsp. sugar

1 tsp. salt

3 tsp. baking powder

Work like pie crumbs, then add 1 1/2 cups milk and 1 teaspoon vanilla. Pour cherry mixture in pan and put dough on top. Bake about 1 hour or until done. Serve hot with milk. Other fruit may also be used instead of cherries. Dough may be omitted and biscuit mix from page 257 used instead.

BAKED CHERRY ROLL

Use a good biscuit recipe and roll the dough 1/2 inch thick. Cover with sugared, pitted sweet cherries. Roll as for cinnamon roll and slice 1 inch thick. Set the pieces on end in an oblong baking dish. Bake 40 minutes at 375°. Make a syrup of 1/2 cup sugar, 1 tablespoon butter and 1/2 cup water. When rolls are almost done pour sauce over them and bake 10 minutes more.

Sliced, sugared apples sprinkled with cinnamon may be used instead of cherries.

CHERRY ROLLS

1 egg	2 1/2 tsp. baking powder
3/4 cup sour cream	2 tbsp. butter
2 cups flour	2 cups drained cherries
3/4 tsp. salt	2 tbsp. sugar
1/4 tsp. soda	1 tsp. cinnamon

Beat egg and add sour cream. Sift flour, measure and add salt, soda and baking powder. Sift again. Add sifted dry ingredients to egg mixture and stir well. Toss onto a slightly floured board and roll in an oblong piece 1/4 inch thick. Spread lightly with soft butter and cover with cherries. Sprinkle with sugar and cinnamon. Roll up like a jelly roll and cut in cross wise slices 1 1/4 inch thick. Place slices close together, cut side turned up in a greased baking pan. Pour over them the following sauce:

1/3 cup brown sugar	1 1/2 cups cherry juice
1/3 cup white sugar	a few drops red coloring
1 1/2 tbsp. cornstarch	1/2 tsp. almond flavor
1 1/2 tbsp. butter	

Combine dry ingredients, add liquid, coloring and flavor. Bring to a boil. When slightly thickened, add butter and pour over rolls. Bake at 375° for 25 minutes. Makes 12 rolls.

BAKED BERRY PUDDING

1 tbsp. butter	1/2 cup sugar
1/2 cup milk	1 cup flour
1 tsp. baking powder	

Mix, then spread in a greased, deep baking dish. Pour 1 cup sweetened berries and 1 cup boiling water over the dough. Bake at 400° until cake part is baked.

SUDDEN COMPANY DESSERT

Pour 3 cups canned, thickened cherries into a graham cracker crust. Top with Dream Whip or whipped cream mixed with Phila- delphia Cream Cheese. Sprinkle graham cracker crumbs on top of cheese mixture.

CHERRY CRISP

2 tbsp. flour
1 cup sugar
2 cups drained, unsweetened
    cherries

1 tsp. grated lemon rind
            (optional)
1/2 cup juice

Mix flour, sugar, lemon rind, and juice. Add this to cherries and put into buttered baking dish. Mix lightly the following in- gredients into a crumbly mass and spread over cherries.

1 cup sugar
3/4 cup flour

7 tbsp. butter
1/4 tsp. nutmeg

Bake about 30 minutes in medium hot oven (375°). Serve with whipped cream or sweet milk. (Other fruit may be used.)

STEAMED BANANA PUDDING

1 1/4 cups sugar
1 egg
1/4 cup shortening
2 tbsp. molasses
2 cups pastry flour
2 cups mashed bananas

1 tsp. baking powder
1/2 tsp. soda
1/4 cup milk
cloves, cinnamon,
    ginger and nutmeg

Mix all ingredients together and steam 2 hours in a covered dish. Set in hot water to steam.

COTTAGE PUDDING

2/3 cup sugar
1/4 cup butter
1 egg
1 tsp. vanilla

1 cup milk
2 1/2 cups flour
4 tsp. baking powder
1/2 tsp. salt

Cream the butter and sugar and add the well-beaten egg and vanilla. Mix well. Sift the dry ingredients and add alternately with the milk to the first mixture. Pour into a well greased cake pan and bake in a moderate oven 350° for 35 minutes. Serve with fruit and milk.

QUICK SYRUP KNEPP

In a cooker, approximately 10 inches wide, bring to a boil:

1 cup brown sugar or maple syrup	1 tbsp. butter
2 1/2 cups water	1 tsp. vanilla

Make a dough of:

2 cups flour	4 tsp. baking powder
1/2 cup brown sugar	1/2 tsp. salt
3 tbsp. lard	1 egg
3/4 cup milk	

Mix as for biscuits or pie dough, stirring lightly. Add by spoonful to syrup. Cover and let simmer 20 minutes. Do not remove lid at any time during the cooking process. Serve with milk.

* Cocoa may be added to syrup or dough or both.

* Add sliced apples to syrup.

* Peaches are good in the syrup when cocoa is put in the dough.

* Omit the sugar in the dough and use to make Sauerkraut Knepp.

* Drop dough minus sugar on hot stewed fruit. Follow with same directions.

CORN PONE

1 cup corn meal	2 eggs
1/4 cup flour	4 tbsp. sugar
1 1/2 tsp. baking powder	1/2 cup milk
1/2 tsp. salt	4 tbsp. shortening, melted

Mix and sift dry ingredients, except sugar. Beat the eggs, then stir in sugar and milk. Add dry ingredients and shortening. Bake in well greased (9 x 12 inch) pan for 25 minutes at 425°.

JOHNNY CAKE

1 cup corn meal	1 egg
1 cup sifted flour	1 cup milk
1/2 tsp. salt	1/4 cup oil or shortening
4 tsp. baking powder	

(When using sour milk or buttermilk use 1 teaspoon soda and 3 teaspoons baking powder.)

Mix and bake in greased round cake pan. Serve hot with fruit and milk.

This whole wheat corn bread is delicious with fresh strawberries.

WHOLE WHEAT CORN BREAD

Dissolve 1 package or 1 tablespoon yeast in 1 cup lukewarm water. Let set then mix the following:

3 cups corn meal	3/4 cup soft homemade butter
2 cups whole wheat flour	6 unbeaten eggs
2 cups white flour	1/4 cup baking molasses
1/2 tsp. soda	3/4 cup honey
1 tsp. salt	3/4 cup grapefruit juice or 1/4 cup
1 cup sweet milk	sweet pickle juice

(When sweet pickle juice is used, add water - approximately 1 1/2 cup - instead of milk to make a medium thick cake batter.) Mix all ingredients then pour into two greased 2 x 9 x 13 inch cake pans. Bake at 350° for about 30 minutes or until done.

* Serve with strawberries or honey.

* This corn bread can be baked, then frozen.

Rolled oats pone may be used as a cobbler on top of fruit. Omit the sugar when used for this purpose.

ROLLED OATS PONE

1 pt. rolled oats	3/4 cup brown sugar
1 pt. whole wheat flour	2 tsp. soda

1 pint buttermilk and cream. Add a little extra if you do not like it very dry. Bake like Johnny Cake. Can be served with black cherries and top milk.

WHOLEWHEAT SHORTCAKE

1 lb. granulated sugar	1 tsp. vanilla
1 lb. whole wheat flour	2 tbsp. melted butter
1 lb. pastry flour	1 tbsp. soda
1 tsp. salt	1 qt. buttermilk or sour milk

Put dry ingredients in bowl, except soda, which should be added to the milk before adding the milk to the dry ingredients. Add flavoring and butter last. Mix well. Dough should not be too thick. Bake in 350° oven until done. Serve with milk.

SHORT CAKE

Make crumbs from:

2 cups flour	1 tbsp. sugar
4 tsp. baking powder	1/3 cup shortening
3/4 tsp. salt	

Add 2/3 cup milk and 1 beaten egg to crumbs and pour into small cake pan. Make the topping below and spread on top of batter and bake at 350°. Serve with fresh fruit and milk.

Topping: 1/2 cup sugar, 1/2 cup flour, 3 tablespoons oleo or butter.

DANNISH FRUIT DESSERT SAUCE

1 1/2 tbsp. cornstarch	1/4 cup jello (any flavor)
1 1/2 cups juice or water	1/3 cup sugar (white)
1/4 tsp. salt	

Heat to boiling 1 cup liquid. Combine jello, sugar and cornstarch. Make a paste of it with remaining 1/2 cup liquid. Stir into boiling juice until thick and clear. Cook about 1 minute. Pour over mixture of drained, canned fruit and chill well.

VANILLA TOPPING

Beat 2 egg whites, 1 teaspoon vanilla. Gradually add 3/4 cup white Karo syrup while beating. Beat until stiff and holds peaks. This may be used on pies and desserts as a substitute for whipped cream.

CREAMY VANILLA SAUCE (makes 1 1/3 cup)

Combine:

1/4 cup sugar,1/8 tsp. salt **and 1 teaspoon flour.** Stir in 1 beaten egg. Gradually stir in 1 cup light cream or top milk. Cook over medium heat, stirring constantly until mixture thickens and coats a spoon. Remove from heat and stir in 1/2 teaspoon vanilla.

DESSERT HINTS

* When cooking tart fruit such as rhubarb, apricots, grapes or red raspberries, add a generous amount of cinnamon. For grapes add vanilla too, for a different flavor.

* In a custard recipe calling for several eggs, one or more may be left out if 1/2 tablespoon cornstarch is added for each egg omitted.

* Lucky Whip makes twice as much as the directions say if the amount of milk is doubled. But make sure the bowl, egg beater and milk are very cold before starting.

* Have the children put graham crackers through the meat grinder. It is convenient to keep crumbs on hand for those busy days.

* Keep Tang in a salt shaker then sprinkle on applesauce to give a change in taste.

ICE CREAM

TOPPINGS

ICE CREAM (6 qt.)

4 qt. rich milk	2 tbsp. flour
4 cups sugar (brown or white)	2 tbsp. cornstarch
3/4 tsp. salt	4 eggs, beaten
2 tbsp. vanilla	Cream or canned milk may be added.

Heat milk, sugar and salt. Mix the flour, cornstarch and eggs with milk, enough to make a smooth sauce, stir into the milk and bring to a boil. Add vanilla and cool.

DAIRY QUEEN

Soak: 2 envelopes Knox gelatine in 1/2 cup cold water.
Heat: 4 cups whole milk until hot but not boiling. Remove from heat.
Add: Gelatine   2 tsp. vanilla
     2 cups sugar   1 tsp. salt
Cool and add: 3 cups cream

Put in ice box to chill 5 or 6 hours before freezing. Makes 1 gallon. Ingredients may be varied to suit taste.

* Gelatine can be bought by the pound at some health stores. This is much cheaper.

VANILLA ICE CREAM

1 qt. milk	4 egg yolks
2 cups sugar	1 qt. thick cream
1/2 cup cornstarch	1 tsp. vanilla
1/4 tsp. salt	4 egg whites, beaten
1 pkg. Knox gelatine	

Scald milk, and add sugar, cornstarch and salt which has been blended in 1 cup cold milk. Cook until thick. Add the egg yolks which have been mixed with 2 tablespoons of milk. Cook 1 minute. Add gelatine mixture which has been soaked in 3 teaspoons of cold milk. Remove cooked custard from stove and let cool. Then add the cream, vanilla and well-beaten egg whites. Freeze. This makes 1 gallon.

CHOCOLATE ICE CREAM

Chocolate can be made by adding 1/2 cup Hershey's cocoa. Mix cocoa with a little boiling water and add before freezing.
Crushed fruit may be added instead of cocoa.

JUNKET ICE CREAM

5 eggs, well beaten   2 tbsp. vanilla
2 cups sugar

Heat 1 quart cream or 1 pint cream and 1 pint top milk and 18 large marshmallows together until the marshmallows are melted. Do not boil. Then add the eggs and sugar mixture to this. Next add 1/2 gallon of milk and 1/2 teaspoon salt. Put 6 junket tablets in 1/4 cup lukewarm water. Add this after you have poured the ice cream into the can. Let set about 20 minutes before freezing. Two boxes of Junket mix or instant pudding may be used instead of the Junket tablets.

SIMPLE JUNKET ICE CREAM

1 junket tablet   1/4 cup sugar
1 pt. milk   1/4 tsp. vanilla

Heat milk to lukewarm. Stir in sugar and vanilla. Dissolve junket tablet in a little water and stir in. Let mixture stand 10 minutes. Cover, and freeze. This tastes delicious made with powdered milk. If put in a freezing unit, beat real well when half frozen. Put back into freezer and when about half frozen again, beat the second time, and it's ready to eat!

FROZEN CUSTARD

Put 1 quart milk in double boiler, add 6 to 8 egg yolks, well beaten (not whites) and 1 cup white sugar, 1 cup brown sugar, 1/2 tsp. salt. Cook till it coats spoon. In another pan heat 1 pint milk; add 1 cup sugar and 1 package Knox gelatine that has been soaked in 1/2 cup of cold water. Mix and add 1 can Pet milk and 1 pint cream. Freeze.

PERFECT DAIRY WHIP

1 quart prepared powdered milk (use only powdered milk)
1 can evaporated milk
2 cups white sugar
2 teaspoons imitation vanilla

This is for a four-quart freezer. One package of pudding mix (instant) may be added. We like this very well. It is delicious without adding the pudding mix. All ingredients are easy to keep on hand at all times. This will not come out right if cow's milk and cream are used.

JELLO ICE CREAM (4 qt.)

2 1/2 cups sugar
5 eggs (2 whole, 3 separated)
2 cups heavy cream

2 pkg. gelatine
1 cup cold water
2 tbsp. vanilla

Heat 4 cups milk to boiling. Beat the eggs together, add 2 tbsp. flour and 1/2 cup sugar. Stir this into the boiling milk and cook for 1 minute, stirring constantly. Pour over remaining sugar which has been measured into large bowl. Dissolve gelatine in cold water, pour into egg mixture. Add cream and vanilla and enough milk to fill 1 gallon freezer to within 2 inches of the top.

Variation: Eggs may be omitted and 2 more cups of cream added. Or make without any cream at all, for ice cream which isn't so rich. Any flavor Jello may be used instead of the gelatine. (Use 1 box Jello for 1 pkg. gelatine).

ORANGE-PINEAPPLE ICE CREAM (6 qt.)

9 eggs, beaten (fewer
  eggs may be used)

3 3/4 cups white sugar

Beat eggs and sugar together thoroughly. Add: 1/2 package orange Kool-Aid and 1 13oz. can crushed pineapple or juice. Pour into freezer. Heat one quart rich milk. Pour into freezer. Add cream or milk until the freezer is several inches from the top. Add 3 dissolved junket tablets. Stir. Let set 15 minutes, then freeze. (Variations: Omit pineapple and Kool-Aid and use vanilla or lemon flavoring. Brown sugar may also be used instead of white.)

CHOCOLATE CHIP ICE CREAM

2 tsp. melted butter
2 sq. Baker's Sweet Chocolate
2 tsp. sugar

Mix all ingredients together in saucepan. Put over medium heat and stir until chocolate is melted. After ice cream is frozen, open can and, with a long spoon make several holes on each side of the dasher as far down as you can. Dripple in chocolate mixture and quickly close the freezer again giving it a few turns. Just enough to turn the chocolate back into chips. Makes 1 1/2 gal.

CHOCOLATE TOPPING

4 tbsp. Nestles Quik	1 tsp. vanilla
1 tbsp. hot water	1 1/2 cups white Karo

Mix Quik with hot water and vanilla. Then add Karo and mix well.

CHOCOLATE TOPPING

1 cup Nestles Quik	1 tsp. vanilla
1/3 cup milk	1 tbsp. butter

Mix Nestles Quik and milk. Cook over medium heat until boiling. Boil 3 minutes, stirring constantly. Remove from heat, add vanilla and butter. Cool.

BUTTERSCOTCH TOPPING

1 cup brown sugar	1/4 cup rich milk
2 tbsp. Karo syrup	3 tbsp. butter

Combine all ingredients. Stir until boiling and simmer for 3 minutes.

STRAWBERRY TOPPING

1 qt. mashed strawberries
1 qt. sugar

Stir together until sugar is melted. Dissolve 1 pkg. Sure-Jell in 1 cup boiling water. Bring to a boil and immediately stir into berries. Stir for 5 minutes. Put in jars and freeze.

HOT CHOCOLATE SAUCE

1 cup white sugar	1 cup water
3 tbsp. cocoa	3 1/2 level tbsp. flour
1/2 tsp. salt	1 tsp. vanilla

Cook 3 minutes. Add vanilla.

HOT FUDGE SAUCE

1 1/2 cups evaporated milk	1/2 tsp. salt
2 cups sugar	1/4 cup butter
4 sq. unsweetened chocolate	1 tsp. vanilla
or cocoa, or less, as desired	

Heat milk and sugar to rolling boil, stirring constantly. Boil 1 minute. Add chocolate and salt, stir until chocolate is melted. Then beat with rotary beater until smooth. Remove from heat and stir in butter and vanilla. Serve hot on ice cream or chill if desired. Makes about 3 cups.

BREAKFAST TREATS

COFFEE CAKE

CEREALS

GRIDDLE CAKES

1 1/3 cups flour
2 tbsp. sugar
3 tsp. baking powder
3 tbsp. melted shortening or oil

1 egg
3/4 tsp. salt
1 1/4 cups milk

Combine all ingredients and mix well. Grease skillet lightly for first pancakes only. Fry until puffy and bubbly. Serve hot with butter and maple syrup. Yield: 10 - 6 inch pancakes.

TASTY PANCAKES

2 beaten eggs
2 cups sour milk
1 tsp. soda
2 1/4 cups flour

2 tsp. baking powder
1 tsp. salt
4 tbsp. melted butter
2 tsp. sugar

If sweet milk is used, omit soda and increase the baking powder to 3 teaspoons.
Whole wheat flour may be substituted for some of the white flour.
Beat eggs until light. Add milk. Sift flour with baking powder, salt and sugar. Beat flour mixture into egg and milk mixture. Add melted butter. Beat until smooth.

CORNMEAL PANCAKES

2 cups flour
1/2 cup corn meal
1/2 cup whole wheat flour

1 tsp. soda
1/2 tsp. salt
2 eggs, beaten

Add buttermilk or sour milk for desired batter. More milk for thinner cakes; less for fat cakes.
Syrup: 2 parts brown sugar to 1 part water. Bring to a boil. Add maple flavor. Use syrup while warm.

OATMEAL PANCAKES

2 cups white flour
2 cups whole wheat flour
2 cups quick oats
1 tbsp. each of baking powder, soda, salt

3 eggs, separated
1/2 cup cooking oil
about 1 1/2 qt. sweet milk

Mix dry ingredients thoroughly. Add egg yolks, oil, and milk that is warmed to lukewarm and mix. Fold in beaten egg whites. Bake on ungreased griddle, turning once.

WHOLE WHEAT PANCAKES

1 1/2 cup whole wheat flour	1 tsp. soda
1/2 tbsp. baking powder	3 tbsp. brown sugar
3/4 tsp. salt	1 1/2 cups buttermilk
2 beaten eggs	3 tbsp. melted shortening

Thoroughly mix dry ingredients. Combine the eggs, milk and shortening, add to dry ingredients; mix till smooth. Fry on hot, lightly-greased griddle.

GRAHAM CAKES (with yeast)

Dissolve 1 yeast cake in 2 cups warm milk with 2 teaspoons brown sugar or molasses. Stir together the yolks of 3 eggs, 3 tablespoons shortening and 1 1/4 cups whole wheat flour. Add yeast mixture. Set in warm place to rise, for 2 hours. Fold in the beaten egg whites just before frying.

YEAST BUCKWHEAT CAKES

1 cake yeast	1 pt. sifted Buckwheat flour
About 1 qt. lukewarm water	1 pt. sifted wheat flour
2 tsp. salt	2 tbsp. melted shortening
2 tbsp. sugar or molasses	1/2 tsp. baking soda

Dissolve the yeast in 1 cup warm water, add 1 teaspoon sugar and let set about 5 minutes. Dissolve the salt and sugar in remaining water, add shortening, dry ingredients, and yeast mixture. Beat until smooth. Let rise in a warm place until light and full of bubbles. This will take about an hour or more depending on the temperature. Then dissolve the soda in 2 tablespoons warm water and stir into batter. Bake thoroughly on a heated griddle. Serve with butter and syrup.

If the cakes are wanted for breakfast prepare the batter in the evening, using only 1/2 cake yeast. Do not keep too warm. Add the soda and 2 tablespoons warm water in the morning before baking.

BUCKWHEAT CAKES

2 cups buckwheat flour	1/8 tsp. salt
2 eggs, beaten	1 1/2 cup milk
2 tsp. sugar	1/2 cup water
2 tsp. baking powder	

Mix, and bake in a hot griddle.

EASY PANCAKES

2 cups self-rising flour
1/2 cup buttermilk
2 eggs

2 tbsp. sugar
1 tbsp. melted shortening

Enough milk to make batter to right consistency.

WAFFLES (cornmeal, rye, and wholewheat)

Ingredients	Cornmeal	Rye	Whole wheat
white flour	1 1/2 cups	1 cup	
other flour	1 1/2 cups cornmeal	2 cups rye	2 cups whole wheat
baking powder	1 tbsp.	1 tbsp.	2 tsp.
salt	1 1/2 tsp.	1 1/2 tsp.	1 tsp.
oil	1/3 cup	1/3 cup	1/4 cup
eggs	5	5	4
milk	3 cups	3 cups	2 cups

Separate the eggs. Add yolks to the batter. Beat whites until stiff. Fold into batter. Bake. Use a little less liquid for pancakes.

PANCAKE SYRUP

1 1/4 cups brown sugar   3/4 cup white sugar
1/3 cup molasses or Karo syrup (light)
1 cup water

Bring to a boil, stirring constantly. Simmer on low heat for five minutes. Remove from heat, and add 1 tsp. vanilla.
Maple flavoring may be added.

BREAKFAST CRUNCH

1 cup rolled oats
1 cup corn meal
3 cups whole wheat flour
1/2 cup sugar
2 tsp. baking powder

1 tsp. soda
2 tsp. salt
3/4 cup molasses
1 1/2 cup milk

Mix the dry ingredients together. Heat the milk and add molasses. Mix with dry ingredients. Bake in shallow pan in moderate oven. Cool and slice in strips. When dry, grind fine.

KALONA GRAPENUTS

5 cups flour	6 cups graham flour
2 cups sugar	2 1/2 cups cane molasses
3 tsp. salt	3 tsp. soda
3 cups sour milk	

Dough should be thick and hard to stir. Bake in 250° oven for 1 1/2 to 2 hours. Hint: Put in plastic bag then you won't have hard crusts.

TOBES' GRAPENUTS

5 lbs. brown sugar	3/4 lb. oleo (melted)
8 lbs. whole wheat flour	1 1/2 tsp. maple flavor
1 1/4 tbsp. salt	2 tbsp. vanilla
2 tbsp. soda	2 1/2 qt. buttermilk or sour milk

Put dry ingredients in bowl, except soda which should be added to milk just before adding the milk to the dry ingredients. Last add oleo and flavorings. Mix well. The thickness varies a little with your own whole wheat flour, or store bought flour. The dough should be fairly thick. If it is too thick I add a little more milk and if not thick enough add more wheat flour until the right consistency. Put in pans and spread even with spoon or spatula. Bake in 350° oven until done. (Makes approx. 15 lbs.)

SIEVE (to crumble grapenuts)

Make a strong rigid frame, approximately 14 x 14 inches. Over the top of this stretch a 1/4 inch wire mesh. Tack it in place. Place the frame over a large pan. Cut the grapenuts in small pieces and rub through as soon as cooled. Spread the crumbs in pans. Put in a slow oven and toast to a golden brown, stirring occasionally. An inverted deep-fat fry basket will also do the trick.

* A crumbling sieve is also handy to clean shelled peas. Roll the peas over the screen and the dirt will fall through.

DANNER BREAKFAST CEREAL

5 cups oatmeal	1 cup wheat germ
1 cup brown sugar	1 cup fine coconut or
1/2 to 2/3 cup white corn syrup	raisins (optional)
1/2 tsp. salt	1/4 tsp. cinnamon
	2 tsp. vanilla

Toast in shallow pans. 150° for 20-30 minutes.

GRANOLA

10 cups oatmeal	1/2 cup vegetable oil
2 cups wheat germ	1/2 cup honey
2 cups coconut	2 tsp. vanilla
1 to 2 cups brown sugar	1 tsp. salt
1 small pk. almonds	

Mix together, pour into pans, and toast at 270° until a golden brown, stirring occasionally. (30 to 40 minutes.)

* Some prefer to add nuts, wheat germ, and coconut after the granola has toasted.

* There's no end of ideas on how the granola recipe can be altered. Each mother changes it according to her family's taste. Following are a few suggestions:
1) For PEANUT BUTTER GRANOLA, heat the oil and honey to lukewarm; then stir in 1/3 to 1/2 cup peanut butter.
2) Add nuts (walnuts, pecans or whatever you prefer), or coconut after granola has been toasted.
3) Add about 1 1/2 cups water before toasting. Mix.
4) Omit wet ingredients.
5) Add any of the following: whole wheat flour, sesame seeds, sunflower seeds, or 1 to 2 tsp. cinnamon.
6) Coarse rolled oats makes Granola more crunchy.
7) Raisins and dates may be added.

COOKED GRAHAM

Sort untreated wheat kernels. Grind in small food grinder. Into a pan measure 4 cups boiling water, 1 teaspoon salt, and 1 cup cracked whole wheat kernels. Boil for 15 minutes to half an hour, stirring occasionally. Remove from heat, cover. Let stand until ready to serve. Continue cooking if the desired texture has not been reached. Serve hot with sugar and milk.

* GRAHAM MEAL is also delicious, the flavor greatly improved when using freshly ground whole wheat flour. This need not be cooked so thoroughly. Follow the above directions.

* Some people prefer the WHOLE KERNEL WHEAT CEREAL. This takes longer to cook but is an old-fashioned, chewy breakfast cereal.

* Cooking the brown sugar with the cereal, gives a carmel flavor.

CREAMY OATMEAL

Heat water in bottom of double boiler to boiling. In top part put 2 cups coarse oatmeal, 1/2 teaspoon salt, 1 quart cold milk. Put top part over the boiling water and forget it for 30 minutes. May be stirred once or twice, if wished.

QUICK COCOA

Take twice as much sugar as cocoa and mix thoroughly. Stir in hot water until it's the right consistency and the sugar is melted. Add hot or cold milk.

COFFEE CAKE

1/2 cup very warm, but not hot, water. Add 1 tsp. sugar. Stir. Then add 1 tablespoon yeast. Let set in warm place while beating 2 eggs. Add 1 teaspoon salt, 1 cup milk, 1 cup lukewarm water, 3/4 cup oil or other shortening, and 1 cup white sugar. Stir in yeast, then pour in the egg mixture. Mix in 3 cups flour. Slowly add more until mixture is smooth and elastic. Let rise until double. Punch down. Let rise again then cut and put in 4 round pans. Bake at 350° for 20-30 minutes.

*Variation: Brown sugar, cinnamon or nutmeg may be sprinkled on top.

FRENCH TOAST

Beat 2 eggs, add 3/4 cup milk. Dip pieces of bread in the mixture. Melt and lightly brown butter in a pan. Put in the bread pieces and sprinkle with salt. Fry until brown on both sides. Serve with syrup or jam.

EGG ON TOAST

Put 1 tablespoon butter into a small hot frying pan. Spread the butter over the bottom of the pan. In this lay a piece of bread. Break an egg on top. With a fork break the yolk and spread the egg over the bread. Sprinkle with salt and pepper. When bread has toasted, turn and fry the egg side, for 1 or 2 minutes.

This is good served at lunch with mayonnaise and lettuce on top of the egg.

GOLDEN EGG

Make a medium white sauce (page 49) while 4 pieces of bread are toasting. When sauce is done slice in 4 hardboiled eggs, reserving 1 yolk. Serve over the toast on individual plates. Press the remaining yolk through a strainer, sprinkling the yolk over the sauce for garnishing.

*Chipped beef or ham may be added to the sauce.

PARTY SNACK

7 oz. cheerios   7 oz. rice chex
7 oz. wheat chex
Mix with:
2 cups salad oil   2 tbsp. Worchestershire sauce
2 tbsp. savory salt

Put in oven at 250° for 1 hour, stirring occasionally. Then add 7 oz. thin pretzels. Roast for 15 minutes. Then add 2 lb. peanuts and roast for 15 minutes more.

CANDIES

MARSHMALLOW CREME

MARSHMALLOWS

I WISH WE COULD HAVE SOME HEALTHFUL, nourishing recipes for candy in this book, but that seems to be almost impossible. There are such unrefined sweets as maple cream, maple taffy (Spotza), and maple sugar cakes (Scheuflin), which are made from boiled down maple syrup and need no recipe. But there are many different kinds of snacks or treats for children that are more nourishing and cheaper than candy. To name but a few, there are the dried fruits such as prunes, apples, raisins, peaches, and even sweetened and creamed dried corn is good. Then there are the home-raised peanuts and popcorn, carrot sticks, cabbage slices, party treat, roasted soybeans, nuts, sunflower seeds and many other between-meal foods for children to munch on.

Candy as a whole is an expensive food, for sugar—its chief ingredient—is also expensive. Someone once said, "We pay twice for sweets: once for the sugar and again for the dentist bill!" So, although we aren't too enthusiastic about candy, here are a few recipes for those who want them, and who hopefully, already have false teeth!

IDA'S FONDANT CANDY

(No. 1)
3 cups sugar
1 cup Karo
1/2 cup hot water

(No. 2)
1 cup sugar
1/2 cup hot water

Combine (No. 1) in a saucepan and boil until it spins a thread.
Combine (No. 2) in a saucepan and boil until it also spins a thread.

Whip 2 egg whites until stiff. Then slowly beat into the whites the (No. 2) first and beat until stiff. Add (No. 1) to that mixture and beat until cool.

It may then be divided into parts, adding different flavors, as desired. Then form into shapes and dip in melted chocolate.

CARAMELS

Combine:
1 cup white sugar
1/2 cup brown sugar
  (firmly packed)
1/2 cup light corn syrup

1/2 cup cream
1 cup milk
1/4 cup butter

Cook over low heat to 246°, stirring constantly. Add 2 teaspoons vanilla and pour into an 8 inch square greased cake pan. Cool. Then turn out and cut in squares. Wrap each piece in wax paper.

OPERA CREAMS

1 1/2 cups sugar
1/2 cup cream

2 tbsp. butter
2 tbsp. chocolate

Boil and test in cold water to soft ball (236°). Take from heat. Add 1 teaspoon vanilla. Let cool without stirring. Beat when cool, until light in color. Drop on waxed paper.

MINT CANDY

2 cups sugar
1/4 cup butter

2/3 cup cold water

Boil to 267 or 270 degrees. Pour on buttered marble. Pull like taffy. Roll it in powdered sugar which was put on brown paper. Cut in squares. Put in jars. The candy will mellow in a day or two. The candy can be made in different flavors -- anise, wintergreen, peppermint, etc. and coloring added according to the flavor.

HARD TACK CANDY

1 3/4 lb. white sugar   1 cup white karo
1 cup water

Cook all together until 280°, then add coloring. Leave on stove until it reaches 290°. Remove and add chosen flavor (1/8 oz.), peppermint, spearmint, wintergreen, thyme, anise, cinnamon, etc. (Make each flavor a different color.) Pour at once on greased cookie sheet or marble slab. As soon as it is cool enough to work with, cut with scissors into strips and various size pieces. You can begin cutting on edges almost immediately. Flavoring can be bought at drug store.

GOLDEN CRACKER JACK

1/2 cup corn syrup   2 tbsp. water
1/2 cup baking molasses (dark)   1 tbsp. butter
1 cup sugar   1/4 tsp. soda
1 tsp. vinegar   5 qt. popped corn
                                         1 cup peanuts

Mix sugar, molasses, syrup, butter, water and vinegar. Cook until it forms a hard ball when dropped in cold water (265°). Stir frequently during last part of cooking to prevent scorching. Remove from heat and add soda. Stir lightly. While it still foams, pour over popcorn and peanuts and mix. Pour into a flat buttered pan. When cool, crumble into small pieces.

POPCORN BALLS

1 cup sugar   1/3 cup water
1/2 cup white or dark   3/4 tsp. salt
  corn syrup   3/4 tsp. vanilla
1/4 cup butter   3 qt. popped corn

Keep popcorn hot in slow oven. Stir and cook sugar, corn syrup, water, butter and salt until sugar is dissolved. Continue **cooking without stirring until syrup forms a soft ball (236°). Add** vanilla, pour syrup slowly over popped corn. Mix well to coat **every kernel.** Grease hands with butter before shaping. Makes 12 **medium-sized balls.**

* *When popcorn doesn't pop good, place the popcorn*
  where it's cold and damp.

CRACKER JACK

	For 2 gallons popped corn:
1 qt. syrup	2 cups syrup
3 cups white sugar	1 1/2 cup sugar
2 cups brown sugar	1 cup brown sugar
1/2 lb. butter	1/4 lb. butter
1 tsp. cream of tartar	1/2 tsp. cream of tartar
salt to suit taste	1 tsp. salt

Boil till hard crack, pour over a lard can of popped corn and stir. May also be made into balls. Grease hands well with butter or margarine and shape into balls immediately before popcorn cools.

CARMEL CORN

2 cups white sugar	2 tbsp. water
3/4 cup white syrup or sorghum	1/4 tsp. salt
2 tbsp. vinegar	1 cup peanuts (whole or chopped)
1 tsp. soda	5 qt. popped corn

Melt and lightly brown the sugar. Place over low heat when almost finished to prevent scorching. Then add syrup, vinegar, water and salt. Boil to a very hard ball when tested in cold water so that it can be snapped into pieces.

Remove from heat, add soda and peanuts, stirring well. Pour immediately over popped corn (have popcorn warm). Stir a few minutes until it is all coated, then stir occasionally until cold.

EASY CARMEL CORN

Fill 1/3 cup with popcorn, then add just enough water to cover the corn. Pour grease, popcorn and water and 1/3 cup white sugar into the popper. Stir constantly. Reduce heat when it starts popping.

Redhot popcorn: Place the usual amount of grease and popcorn into popper and add a spoonful of redhots.

Buttered popcorn: Pour melted butter over popped popcorn.

HIRES CANDY KISSES

3 cups brown sugar	1 egg white
1/2 cup water	Pinch of salt
1 1/2 tsp. Hires Rootbeer extract	

Cook sugar, water and salt until it spins a thread when dropped from spoon. Add extract and pour over stiffly beaten egg white, beating while pouring. Continue to beat until mixture is quite stiff, then drop by teaspoonsful on wax paper. Instead of 3 cups brown sugar, 2 cups of maple sugar and 1 cup of brown sugar may be used.

PEANUT BRITTLE

In a 4 qt. saucepan combine:
1 1/2 cups sugar   2/3 cup water
1/2 cup white corn syrup

   Cook to soft ball stage (238 degrees). Stir only until sugar is dissolved.
Add:
1 1/2 cup raw peanuts   1/2 tsp. salt
   Cook to hard crack stage (290 degrees). Remove from heat.
Add:
2 tbsp. butter   1 tsp. vanilla
1 tsp. soda

   Stir thoroughly and pour at once on well buttered sheet or slab. Spread thinly and let cool. Break in pieces.

OH HENRY CANDY

2 cups white sugar   1 cup water
1 cup Karo

   Cook this until it forms a hard ball in cold water. Let stand until cool, add 3/4 cup peanut Butter. Stir until cold. Shape into rolls as thick as your thumb and 2" long.
                    Part 2
1 cup Karo   1/2 cup brown sugar

   Cook until it forms a hard ball in cold water, then dip first part into this and roll in ground peanuts while hot. Coat with chocolate. Takes 2 lb. peanuts.

CHOCOLATE PEANUT CLUSTERS

1/2 lb. sweet chocolate   1 cup peanuts
2/3 cup (1/2 15 oz. can) Eagle Brand sweetened condensed milk

   Melt chocolate in top of double boiler over boiling water. Remove from heat, add Eagle Brand, sweetened condensed milk and peanuts; mix well. Drop by teaspoons onto waxed paper.

CHOCOLATE BALLS

1 can Eagle Brand milk	12 to 18 graham crackers,
1 oz. unsweetened chocolate	crushed
or 3 tbsp. cocoa and 1 tbsp. butter	

Melt in double **boiler, milk and chocolate.** Remove from stove and add crushed **crackers.** Form into balls. Roll in coconut.

FUDGE MELTWAYS

1/2 cup butter	1 egg, beaten
1 sq. unsweetened	2 cups graham cracker crumbs
chocolate (1 oz.)	1 cup coconut
1/4 cup sugar	1/2 cup chopped nuts
1 tsp. vanilla	

Filling:

1/4 cup butter	1 tsp. vanilla
1 tbsp. milk or cream	1 1/2 sq. melted unsweetened
2 cups sifted powdered sugar	chocolate (1 1/2 oz.)

Melt 1/2 cup butter and 1 square chocolate in saucepan. Blend sugar, 1 teaspoon vanilla, egg, graham cracker crumbs, coconut and nuts into butter-chocolate mixture. Mix thoroughly and press into 11 1/2 x 7 1/2 x 1 1/2 baking dish or square 9 x 9. Refrigerate while making filling.

Cream: butter, milk, powdered sugar, and 1 teaspoon vanilla. Mix and spread over crumb mixture. Chill in refrigerator. Pour 1 1/2 sq. melted chocolate over chilled mixture and spread evenly.

CREAMY-SURE FUDGE

2/3 cup (1 small can)	1/4 tsp. salt
evaporated milk	2 cups semi-sweet
16 marshmallows, or about	chocolate pieces
1 **cup marshmallow creme**	1 tsp. vanilla
1 1/3 **cups sugar**	1 cup coarsely chopped walnuts
1/4 cup butter or oleo	

Mix first 5 ingredients in saucepan, stirring constantly. Heat to boiling and boil 5 minutes only. Remove from heat; add chocolate. Stir until melted. Stir in vanilla and walnuts. Spread in 8 inch pan. Cool until firm. Makes about 2 pounds.

SNOWY FUDGE

1 1/2 cup Peanut Butter   1 cup marshmallow cream
2 cups sugar   1 tsp. vanilla
2/3 cup milk

Cook sugar and milk to 234 degrees or until syrup forms a soft ball which flattens when removed from water. Add other ingredients. Mix well. Pour into buttered pan, 8 x 6 x 2.

This candy can be stored away for months and still remain soft and eatable.

STORE-AWAY FUDGE

4 1/2 cups sugar   1 can condensed milk
1/2 cup (1 cube) oleo or butter

Bring to boil and boil 7 minutes or until soft ball stage. Remove from heat and add 2 large Hershey bars cut in small pieces and two packages chocolate chips, 1 pint marshmallows, cut in pieces, 1 teaspoon vanilla, 1/2 teaspoon black walnut flavoring, if desired, 1/2 cup chopped nuts (optional). Beat until smooth and pour into pan as regular fudge.

CHOCOLATE CANDY

3 cups sugar   1 tbsp. butter
3 cups milk   1 tsp. vanilla
5 tbsp. cocoa

Boil sugar, milk, and cocoa and stir while on stove. Boil to soft ball stage. Remove from stove and add flavoring and butter. Stir until it is creamy. Pour on buttered plate and cut in squares when cool.

MACAROONS

2/3 cup Eagle Brand sweetened condensed milk
3 cups shredded coconut
1 tsp. vanilla

Mix Eagle Brand sweetened condensed milk and coconut. Add vanilla. Drop by spoonsful on greased baking sheet about 1 inch apart. Bake in moderate oven (350 degrees) 10 minutes or until a delicate brown. Remove from pan at once. Makes 30.

TAFFY

1 qt. white sugar	1 tbsp. paraffin
1 pt. cream	1 pt. light Karo
1 tbsp. gelatin dissolved in 1/4 cup cold water	

Combine all ingredients and boil until it forms a hard ball in cold water when dropped from a tablespoon — 250° on candy thermometer. Pour onto a well greased cookie sheet. When cool enough to handle start pulling. When an ivory color is obtained pull into a long thin "rope" and cut with kitchen scissors.

ROCKY ROAD SQUARES

3 lb. milk chocolate	3 lb. walnuts (broken)
1/2 lb. soft butter	10 oz. miniature marshmallows

Melt chocolate, stir till smooth. Add butter and mix well (will be thick but warm). Set in cold place until it thickens around edges. Stir occasionally while cooling. Bring into warm room and stir 5 to 10 minutes until creamy and thinner. Add marshmallows and walnuts. Pour on wax paper lined cookie sheet. Press 3/4 inch thick and cool. Cut in squares at room temperature.

YUMMY CHOCOLATE SQUARES

1 lb. marshmallows	3 tbsp. butter
1 tsp. vanilla	1/2 tsp. salt
1 pkg. semi-sweet chocolate bits	1 cup rice krispies
1 cup broken walnut meats	

Melt marshmallows, chocolate, and butter over low heat, stirring constantly, until melted. Mix in remaining ingredients. Spread in well-buttered 8-inch pan. Cut in squares after it sets.

CHEERIOS BARS

1/2 cup light corn syrup	1 tsp. vanilla
1 pkg. (6 oz.) semi-sweet chocolate pieces	4 cups cheerios

Heat syrup to boiling. Remove from heat. Add chocolate pieces and vanilla, stirring until chocolate is melted. Add cheerios. Stir until well coated. Put into buttered pan 9 x 9 x 2. Cool 1 hour. Makes 3 dozen.

BUCKEYES

1 lb. peanut butter   1 1/2 lb. powdered sugar

Mix like pie dough, then add **1 cup oleo.** Roll in balls and let chill thoroughly. Melt one 12 oz. package chocolate chips and 1/2 stick paraffin. Dip balls in this.

KRISPIE CANDY

1/4 cup butter
32 marshmallows

Melt in pan until it gets syrupy. Keep stirring it. Pour over 5 or 6 cups rice krispies.

CHOCOLATE-COVERED CHERRIES

1 cup sifted all-purpose flour   1/3 cup brown sugar
1/2 cup butter or margarine   1/4 t. salt
18 well-drained maraschino cherries, cut in halves
6 squares semi-sweet chocolate, melted

Combine flour and sugar. Cut butter into flour mixture until it resembles pie dough. Press into an 8 x 8 x 2 inch pan. Bake at 350° for 20 minutes. While warm, cut into 36 squares. Cool and place squares in a pan lined with wax paper. Place a cherry halve on each square. Cover cherries with spoonsful of melted chocolate. Chill for a few minutes until chocolate hardens.

MARSHMALLOWS

2 envelopes Knox Gelatine   2 cups sugar
1/2 cup cold water   1 tsp. vanilla
1/2 tsp. salt   3/4 cup boiling water

Boil sugar and water together until a thread forms when syrup drops from spoon. Remove from heat. Soften gelatine in cold water. Add to hot syrup and stir until dissolved. Let stand until partly cool; then add salt and flavoring. Beat until mixture becomes thick, fluffy and soft. Pour into pan about 8 x 4 inches, thickly covered with 10 x sugar. Have the mixture 1 inch in depth. Let stand in refrigerator until thoroughly chilled. With a sharp wet knife, loosen around edges of pan. Turn out on a board, lightly floured with 10 x sugar. Cut in squares and roll in 10 x sugar or chopped nuts or coconut.

MARSHMALLOW CREME

2 cups sugar   1 cup water
2 1/2 cups corn syrup

Cook to 242° (med. hard ball); while this is cooking, place the following in a mixing bowl: 1/2 cup warm karo,   3 or 4 egg whites. Beat slowly till mixed, then beat hard until light and fluffy. Pour the first mixture into this — in a fine stream. When all mixed, beat hard for 3 minutes. Add 1 teaspoon vanilla. Store in cans or jars. Don't cover until cold.

EAGLE BRAND MILK

Boil together one part sugar and two parts milk, until thickened. 225°, or "jelly" on a candy thermometer.

THE BEST COOKS

I used to think that the really good cooks
  were the ones who threw away all of the books,
And whipped up their dishes and specialties hot
  with a stir of the spoon in a large boiling pot.

The pies were the richest, the dumplings the thickest,
  and the comments from guests were the loudest and quickest.
The food tasted good with each bite they gulped down,
  and the family proclaimed her the best cook in town.

But now'days I've read what the books have to say —
  it's the pies and the dumplings they should throw away!
And the rest of the starches and pastries they eat,
  all the gooey and sticky cakes and candy so sweet.

Nutritionally speaking, the best cooks around
  serve you salads and fruits that are rich from the ground.
And foods whole and natural, prepared the right way,
  so their life-giving strength will be left in to stay.

DRINKS

WHEN I WAS A CHILD WE KNEW NOTHING OF POP, coke, pepsi and the many other drinks that are so common in the world today. At that time lemonade was one of those rare, too-expensive drinks, so we seldom had that to enjoy either.

Children today are fortunate to be able to enjoy the healthful drinks mothers make in their kitchen these days; such as, grape juice, root beer, iced teas, and vegetable V-8 drink.

The most delightful drink I ever tasted was given to me about 20 years ago by an aged grandfather who had a "sugar bush." When the syrup had become buddy, he went into the woods and gathered what he called "spice hecka," which I guessed could have been anise. These switches he tossed into the hot boiling syrup. When the desired flavor was obtained, the syrup was canned for a drink.

A cool, refreshing drink for men who work under the hot sun in the fields is peppermint water. This is made by dipping a toothpick in pure peppermint oil then swishing it off in sweetened, cold spring water. This is done several times until the desired strength is obtained.

SUMMER SPARKLE PUNCH

2 (3 oz.) pkg. strawberry jello   2 (12 oz.) cans frozen lemonade,
2 cups boiling water   slightly thawed
                        3 (28 oz.) bottles ginger ale

Dissolve jello in water. Stir in lemonade. Add ginger ale. Makes 1 gallon.

GOOD LUCK PUNCH

1 qt. rhubarb (about 2 doz. stalks)   juice of 6 lemons
water to cover   1 cup pineapple juice
3 cups sugar   Rhubarb juice
2 cups water   1 qt. ginger ale

Cut rhubarb in 1 inch pieces. Add water to cover. Cook until soft, about 10 minutes. Drain through cheesecloth bag. You should have approximately 3 quarts juice. Dissolve sugar in 2 cups water. Cook 10 minutes to make a syrup. Add lemon, pineapple and rhubarb juice. Pour over a chunk of ice in punch bowl. Just before serving add ginger ale. Makes 1 gallon punch.

GOLDEN PUNCH

7 packages orange Kool Aid, mix according to directions.
4 large cans frozen orange juice
5 large bottles Teem or Sprite
   Makes 5 gallons.

FRUIT PUNCH

Boil together 3 cups sugar and 3 quarts water. Let stand till cool. Add 4 cans frozen orange juice, 4 cans frozen lemon juice, 1 1/2 cups strong tea and 4 quarts ginger ale. Add water. This recipe makes enough for 75 people.

QUICK ROOT BEER

2 cups white sugar   4 tsp. root beer extract
1 gal. lukewarm water   1 tsp. dry yeast
Use some hot water to dissolve sugar

Put in jars. Cover and set in sun for 4 hours. Chill before serving. Ready to serve the next day. No need to bottle.

RHUBARB JUICE

Cut rhubarb coarsely. Cover with water and boil 2 minutes. Drain off juice. Cover the cooked rhubarb a second time with water. Bring to a boil and drain again. May be sweetened to can.

Rhubarb juice may be added to other fruit juices. Or add rhubarb juice and a little lemon juice to meadow tea for a delicious refreshing cold drink.

TOMATO COCKTAIL

1 peck tomatoes
2 bunches celery
2 green peppers

1 bunch parsley
6 small onions

Cook together until soft. Put through a sieve.
Add: 1 cup sugar, 1/4 cup salt, 1/2 tsp. pepper (scant). Put in jars. Cold pack a few minutes.

V-8 DRINK

2 qt. celery
2 to 4 red beets
6 carrots

4 onions
2 gal. tomato juice

Cook everything separate till real soft. Mash vegetables till real fine. Strain and add 3 lemons, rind and all. Add salt to taste. Cold pack 10 minutes.

GRAPE JUICE

5 lbs. grapes
1 lb. sugar

1 qt. water

Wash and stem grapes; add water and boil 10 minutes. Strain, but do not press. Add sugar, stirring until dissolved. Bring to a boil and bottle. Add water before serving, about half and half, juice and water. (Put the pulp through the sieve, add sugar to taste and can for grape sauce.) Concord or Fredonia grapes are best.

CONCORD GRAPE JUICE

Wash fully ripened Concord grapes and spoon into a qt. jar until it is 1/3 full. Add 1 cup sugar and water to fill the jar. Seal and boil for 10 minutes.

CANNING APPLE JUICE or PEAR JUICE

Heat juice, but do not boil. Remove scum with spoon. Fill bottles or jars and seal. Set in hot water and bring to boiling point, then remove from water immediately. When apple juice is not boiled, it retains its fresh flavor.

CHOCOLATE SYRUP

4 cups brown sugar
2 cups cocoa
1/2 cup corn syrup

4 cups white sugar
2 cups water

Mix in a 6-qt. kettle until all is blended. Add 2 more cups of water and stir again. Bring to a boil and boil for 5 minutes. (It is very apt to boil over). Add: 4 tbsp. or 1/4 cup vanilla. If not canned, put cover on until cool or a crust will form over the top. Makes approximately 3 quarts. This will keep from September to April (school months) if put boiling hot into jars and sealed.

INSTANT SPICED TEA

2 1/2 cups sugar
2 cups instant powdered
  orange drink
1/2 cup instant tea

2 tsp. cinnamon
2 tsp. cloves
2 large pkg. instant
  lemonade mix

Mix ingredients together. Store in tight containers. To use, place approximately 2 teaspoons of mix to each cup of boiling water.

This is sometimes called Russian Tea. You may add to or take away amount of spices and lemonade mix, according to family tastes.

ICED TEA SYRUP

4 cups boiling water

1 cup loose tea

Let steep for 15 minutes. Strain. Add 2 1/2 cups sugar. Boil for about 10 minutes. This will make a quart of syrup. Put 1 tbsp. syrup in a glass, then fill with water and ice. This should make 1 gallon of ice-tea depending on strength desired.

PEPPERMINT - ADE

Sweeten a pitcher of cold water. Dip a toothpick into the pepper-mint oil bottle, then swish it off in the water. Do this a few times until the right strength is obtained. Stir the water before tasting.

This is a healthy drink and good on hot days for the men in the fields. (Synthetic peppermint oil is not recommended.)

LEFTOVERS

Cut <u>LEFTOVER BREAD</u> from church into cubes and toast them in pans in the oven. Stir a few times. When toasted and dried out well, store in tight containers. Use them in soups, dressings, in tossed salads (adding them just before serving), etc.

<u>LEFTOVER BREAD</u> can be dried out **completely, over the stove** and stored in lard cans or jars. When ready to use, place the bread slices in the steamer and steam until heated through. Serve warm. If you have no steamer, use a colander over a pan of hot water. Keep covered.

Pour bacon grease over pieces of <u>LEFTOVER BREAD OR TOAST</u>. Let harden, then put a string through the center and tie it to a branch on a tree for the birds.

Use OLD BREAD to make <u>CHOCOLATE BREAD CUSTARD</u>

2 1 oz. sq. unsweetened chocolate	3/4 cup sugar
	1/4 tsp. salt
3 cups scalded milk	3 well beaten eggs
4 cups bread crumbs	

Combine chocolate and milk. Heat and stir until chocolate melts. Add bread, sugar, and salt. Slowly stir this into the beaten eggs. Pour into greased 10 x 6 x 2 inch pan. Set this in pan of hot water. Bake in moderate oven about 50 minutes or until knife inserted comes out clean. Serve warm with creamy vanilla sauce on page 205.

* OLD-FASHIONED BREAD CUSTARD

Omit the chocolate and add 1 teaspoon nutmeg. Less sugar may be used if desired (1/3 cup).

<u>HANS WASCHTLIN</u> are made with a small amount of LEFTOVER PIE DOUGH. Roll out thin. Spread with applebutter. Roll up like a jelly roll and cut in 1/2 inch slices. Lay them on a pie pan with cut side down and bake. A treat for the children.

For little <u>SUGAR PIES</u> from LEFTOVER PIE DOUGH. Roll the dough thin; then fit it into a small tin foil pan, or any little pan. Into the crust put 2 tablespoons brown sugar, 1 tablespoon flour, 1/2 cup water, and nutmeg to taste. A bit of cream may be added. Mix with finger or back of spoon and bake. (Recipe is for 4 to 6 inch pie pan.) This is a childhood treat.

BAKED, BROKEN PIE CRUSTS can be refreshed by putting in the oven for a few minutes. Add to applesauce just before serving. Stir in cream (whipped or unwhipped). Blend. Cinnamon may also be added.

Not enough LEFTOVER MACARONI? Toast bread cubes in butter, in the frying pan. Add the macaroni and enough milk to soak up the bread and so the macaroni won't burn. Heat.

LEFTOVER MACARONI may be added to vegetable soup, chili soup, potato salad, or to stews.

With 4 or 5 cups LEFTOVER MACARONI AND CHEESE: Beat 2 eggs and add a little salt and 1 1/2 cups milk. Pour this over the macaroni and bake at 350° until brown. Extra cheese may be sprinkled on top if desired.

LEFTOVER NOODLES may be added to vegetable soup.

* Put about 1 or 2 tablespoons grease into the frying pan. When melted, sprinkle in about 1 tablespoon flour with flour shaker. Cut the LEFTOVER NOODLES in slices and lay in the floury grease. Fry.

STALE CHEESE turns into a delicious spread when processed through the meat grinder with several chunks of onions.

LEFTOVER CHURCH CHEESE

Cut up cheese and put in top of double boiler. Add 2 tablespoons oleo or butter and 1 tablespoon water. Boil until cheese is melted. Pour into wide-mouthed jars and seal. Coldpack for 1/2 hour, or until cheese looks smooth. When ready to use, put the jar into warm water until the cheese is loose from the sides of jars so it will slide out easily. Slice and serve.

Stir milk into LEFTOVER COOKED CEREAL before storing. Serve as a dessert by adding whipped cream, apples, raisins or other raw fruit. An old LEFTOVER CAKE or APPLE ROLL may also be added.

LEFTOVER CREAM OF WHEAT or ROLLED OATS may be added to hamburger or sausage. Mix thoroughly. Make into patties or a loaf.

LEFTOVER RICE can be prepared like LEFTOVER CEREAL as
a dessert. Prepare the Basic Custard Recipe, (page 187) then add
LEFTOVER RICE and bake.

GLORIFIED RICE

2 cups boiled rice	24 marshmallows
1 cup pineapple (cubed	1 cup chopped apples
or crushed)	1 cup whipped cream
1/2 cup sugar	

   Cook the rice until soft, but not mushy, and cool. Mix all ingredients but the cream and let stand 1 hour. Fold whipped cream
into mixture just before serving. Garnish with candied cherries.
(Leftover rice can be used.)

LEFTOVER SQUASH may be added to a caramel pudding. Mash
the squash and add to the milk.

LEFTOVER SQUASH may be used for "pumpkin" pies, or may be
made into a custard, minus crust. Set casserole into a pan of hot
water to bake.

   Make large crumbs of LEFTOVER CAKE. Put into serving dish.
Make the following NUTMEG SAUCE:

2 cups water	3 tablespoons flour
1/4 cup sugar	

   Mix, then bring to a boil. Boil a few minutes, stirring constantly. Add 2 tablespoons butter and 1/8 teaspoon nutmeg. Cool,
then pour over broken pieces of cake. Sliced bananas or nuts may
be added.

   To use up LEFTOVER FRUIT SYRUP from canned fruit, add an
equal amount of water to the syrup and thicken with tapioca (3 tablespoons tapioca to 1 pint of liquid). A pinch of salt and a package
of jello adds to the taste. Whipped cream may also be blended into
the cooled tapioca.

   Put LEFTOVER FRUIT JUICE from canned fruit into a bottle,
filling half full. Tie string or ribbon on neck and hang on fruit
trees in the spring. You will be surprised to see how many bugs
crawl in and drown.

To use LEFTOVER FRUIT (canned or fresh) make the following
FRUIT CAKE:

Sift together:
1 1/2 cups brown sugar	2 cups flour
2 tsp. soda	1/2 tsp. salt

Make a well and add:
2 cups fruit, mashed	1/2 cup salad oil
2 eggs	

Mix, then bake at 350°. When done, top with the following icing
and return to oven for a few minutes.

Icing: 1/4 lb. butter, 1/4 cup evaporated milk, 3/4 cup brown
sugar. Cook for 1 minute, then add 3/4 cup nuts.

Save your LEFTOVER PICKLE JUICE and re-can. Use for making relish, sandwich spread in the fall, or to can red beets (adding
more vinegar, sugar, etc.), or to make salad dressings. When
you use the juice to make salad dressings, omit the vinegar and
sugar in the recipe.

Hardboiled eggs are good when left overnight in LEFTOVER
PICKLED BEET JUICE.

LEFTOVER COLESLAW is good cooked before serving. Add a
white sauce made with 1 tablespoon flour and 1/2 cup cream.

LEFTOVER POTATO DISHES

To make POTATO FILLING with LEFTOVER MASHED POTA-
TOES, cook the greenest part of 1 stalk celery and 1 chopped
onion. With juice and all, pour over the mashed potatoes and mix.
Add 2 eggs and milk according to the amount of potatoes used.
Then add 4 or 5 slices cubed bread which has been toasted in 2
tablespoons butter. Pour into buttered baking dish and bake about
an hour at 350°. LEFTOVER CORN, PEAS, or LIMA BEANS, or
DICED MEAT may be added.

To approximately 2 cups LEFTOVER MASHED POTATOES, add
3 eggs, 1/3 cup milk, 1 small chopped onion, 2 or 3 slices of
bread made into crumbs, salt and pepper to taste. Mix everything
together. Put into a hot, buttered skillet. Cover and heat slowly.

POTATO PUFFS

1 cup leftover mashed potatoes   1/4 to 1/2 cup flour
1 or 2 beaten eggs   1 tsp. baking powder
1/4 tsp. salt

Mix well and drop by 1/2 teaspoon in deep fat. Fry until brown on both sides.

FRIED POTATOES

Use fried, cooked, or mashed potatoes. Pour into hot greased frying pan. Chop. Beat an egg or two with fork and pour over the top. Fry. If there aren't enough potatoes, toast bread cubes in the pan first, then add the potatoes. 1 tablespoon flour blended with 1 beaten egg and 3/4 cup milk may be added instead of the 2 beaten eggs. Add salt and pepper.

POTATO CAKES

2 cups cooked potatoes, peeled and grated with medium salad grater.
2 eggs   1 medium onion, chopped
1/2 tsp. salt   dash of pepper
1/8 to 1/4 cup of LEFTOVER BOLOGNA or DRIED BEEF, (optional)

Mix the above ingredients, then fry like pancakes.

* Leftover mashed potatoes may be used in place of grated potatoes.

POTATO CHEESE PIE

Crust: Filling:
2 or 2 1/2 cups leftover   2 eggs
  mashed potatoes   1 cup cream
2 tbsp. flour   Salt and pepper
1 tsp. baking powder   3/4 cup grated Velveeta
1 egg   cheese
2 tbsp. melted butter
Salt and pepper

Mix the ingredients thoroughly and pat into a large greased pie plate as if dough.

Beat the eggs, stir in cream and seasonings. Pour this into the potato crust and sprinkle the top with cheese. Bake at 350° for 20 minutes or until a knife inserted in center comes out clean.

POTATO SOUP

Cook a small chopped onion until soft. Add milk, as desired.
When hot, mix some in with the LEFTOVER MASHED POTATOES
until blended. Pour all back into the remainder of the milk. Heat
to the boiling point. Add a chunk of butter and a bit of chopped
parsley, salt and pepper.

* Potato Salad may be made with leftover mashed potatoes, adding
  other ingredients the same as you do for salad made with diced
  potatoes.

* Many salty leftover dishes, vegetables, noodles, **macaroni,**
  soups, etc. can be tossed into dressing. Beat **eggs,** add milk
  and the leftovers, seasonings; thicken with toasted bread
  crumbs. Top with white sauce. Bake at 350° until heated
  through.

* NEVER use leftover sweet potatoes, red beets, or squash with
  a mix-up of other salty leftover dishes. Sweet potatoes and
  squash are best in sweet dishes.

LEFTOVER VEGETABLE/MEAT DISHES

Use your leftover meat, potatoes, gravy, vegetables by placing
them in layers in a pan or casserole. Add meat broth or tomato
juice, herbs or spices. Make a plain biscuit dough and drop by
spoonfuls into the mixture and bake. Serve with applesauce.

* Mix all leftovers together. Add beaten eggs, some milk, diced
  onions and season it well. Put in greased baking dish. Bake at
  350° until bubbly.

SHEPHERD'S PIE from leftover company dinner.

Into a greased baking dish, spread out the leftover meat. Top
with the leftover vegetables. Last, dot with the leftover mashed
potatoes. Pour the gravy over all. Bake until heated through.
Tomato juice, or 1/2 cup milk blended with 1 beaten egg may be
poured over the top before baking, instead of the gravy.

LEFTOVER CHICKEN

Cook macaroni until soft. Mix with diced leftover chicken and
gravy. Put in baking dish. Add milk to cover macaroni. Season
with salt and pepper. Top with bread crumbs. Bake about 20-30
minutes.

LEFTOVER ROAST BEEF

Prepare 1 package onion soup mix according to package directions; add peeled chopped carrots. Cook carrots until tender.   Thicken with flour and water paste. Add sliced, cooked roast beef. Pour into greased casserole. Top with MASHED POTATOES. Brush with butter. Brown in oven. Serve with crisp green salad and French bread.

LEFTOVER BEEF

Grind any LEFTOVER BEEF. Brown butter in a sauce pan; add a little milk. To this add the ground beef and enough milk to make the meat stick together. Stir in 1 tablespoon flour and an egg. Drop by tablespoons in cracker or bread crumbs. Coat well, then fry in hot fat.

LEFTOVER WEINERS

Cook sliced potatoes in water, adding salt to taste. Add sliced weiners for the last 5 or 10 minutes of cooking. When about finished add a small amount of cream.

* Smoked sliced PORK SAUSAGE are good instead of wieners.
  Cook the sausage with the potatoes.

LEFTOVER SOUP, which was made with hot milk and bread, may be mixed with eggs and more bread crumbs, if too thin, and fried in patties (like pancakes).

LEFTOVER MEAT, POTATOES, and VEGETABLES can be made into dressing by adding diced toast, eggs, milk and seasoning.

Cold SWEET POTATOES are good when sliced very thin, dipped into a beaten egg with a little salt added, then in flour. Brown quickly in skillet. Other potatoes may be made the same way.

STRING BEAN CASSEROLE

Take LEFTOVER BEEF and GRAVY, 1 quart string beans, cut small, 1 quart diced potatoes, and 1 or 2 diced carrots. Cook vegetables together until partly soft, then mix beef and gravy, seasoned salt, and salt to taste. Pour into casserole and bake at 350° for 45 minutes. Serve this with a salad and dessert.

Cook rice in LEFTOVER BOLOGNA or HAMBURGER BROTH.

Add canned hamburger to LEFTOVER GRAVY. Also add LEFT-OVER STRING BEANS. Put LEFTOVER POTATOES on top.
Sprinkle paprika over the potatoes. Bake until heated through.
LEFTOVER TOMATO GRAVY may be used instead of meat gravy.

* Cheese sauce goes well with most any kind of vegetable. Bake it with the vegetable, or pour it over the cooked vegetable when ready to serve.

OLD-FASHIONED POT PIE

Add 2 diced potatoes and 1 cup finely cut celery and 2 tbsp. minced onion (optional) to one quart LEFTOVER MEAT BROTH (ham, beef, or chicken). While this is boiling make a dough of 2 beaten eggs, 1/4 teaspoon salt, 1/2 cup milk, 1/4 teaspoon baking powder and enough flour to make a stiff dough, like biscuit dough. Roll thin and cut into squares. Drop into the meat broth and cook for 10 or 15 minutes. Add parsley before serving.

Dough may also be made as follows: 2 beaten eggs, 1/4 cup water and 1 tablespoon shortening, and enough flour to make a thick dough. Roll, cut in squares, then add to broth.

CORN BEEF PUDDING

1 cup diced, cooked beef	4 tbsp. flour, scant
(or any leftover cooked meat)	1/4 tsp. pepper
2 or 3 cups corn	2 tbsp. butter
(fresh, frozen, or canned)	1 tsp. salt
3 eggs, slightly beaten	2 cups rich milk

Add slightly beaten eggs to corn. Stir in flour and season as desired. Add milk and meat and pour into buttered baking dish and dot top with butter. Set baking dish in pan of warm water and bake in 350° oven about 35 minutes or until inserted knife comes out clean.

LEFTOVER CORN makes good CORN FRITTERS. Separate 2 eggs for each cup drained corn. Beat egg whites stiff. Add corn and yolks. Fry in butter.

Bits of LEFTOVER HAM can be ground and mixed with bread crumbs which had been soaked in a milk and egg mixture. Shape into patties and fry. Makes real hamburgers.

TRAMPS HASH

Cut up leftover sausage or beef. Cook 6 medium sized potatoes (amount according to family) and 2 sliced onions with the meat and meat stock until soft. Before serving, add enough bread crumbs to soak up the meat stock.

LEFTOVER TOMATO or MEAT GRAVY may be mixed with vegetable soup or stews.

LEFTOVER TOMATO GRAVY

Chunk 1 quart canned hamburger into a heavy skillet. Add left-over tomato gravy. If too thick, thin with milk or tomato juice, or a little cream. This is good with corn bread or hot biscuits, or with cooked navy beans and applesauce.

If you have but a small amount of fresh strawberries, mix them with the applesauce.

Pour a cup of fresh water into your LEFTOVER BUTTERMILK before storing. Pour off the water, which comes to the top, when you are ready to use the buttermilk again.

LEFTOVER HOME MADE CANDY (and candy that didn't turn out right) can be used for frosting on a cake. Add water or milk to the candy and place over a low heat to melt. Mix to the right consistency.

LEFTOVER TEA is good for the house flowers.

Dry celery leaves and add to soups, one-dish meals and sauces.
* Celery leaves may also be used in place of dandelion for dande-lion dish on page 46.

Don't throw out your LEFTOVER PANCAKE BATTER. Add a little milk to make it thinner then dip your hamburgers or other meat into the batter and fry in hot oil.

SCHOOL LUNCHES

Let nutrition be the key word when packing a lunch — not too many sweets, not too rich foods.

Beware of obesity in the child. A fat child is not as healthy or happy as those who appear overly thin. They are often teased, and may become sluggish. Heavy children are more apt to become diabetic.

To assure good teeth and strong bones, add bone meal powder in peanut butter and other foods. It is almost tasteless and not expensive. One-half teaspoon for each child daily is sufficient. Keep in a tight container where it's warm and dry.

Wheat germ is very good for growing children. This may also be mixed in with sandwich spread or a salad, or soups, or in bread. At times it may be bought much cheaper in large quantities at a feed mill. Keep in a cool place to retard spoilage.

Let your children help plan the school lunch. This can be an enjoyable family project, and educational.

* Don't cut lettuce wedges unless you want to use the remainder of the lettuce within a few hours. The edges of the cut lettuce will turn brown. With head lettuce use leaf by leaf and it keeps better.
* Be sure eggs are freshly cooked when putting them in the bucket. When hard-boiled eggs become too old, they may cause serious stomach disorders.

SANDWICH OR SALAD SUGGESTIONS

Following are various ideas on the different combinations of food that may be mixed with mayonnaise for a **sandwich** or salad:

1) 2 chopped, hardboiled eggs, 2 chopped pickles, a handful of peanuts, slightly crushed
2) Mashed cooked eggs (egg salad)
3) Flaked tuna, hardboiled eggs (tuna salad)
4) Ham, chicken, ground canned beef, liverworst, or any meat (may be diced)
   To ground meat may be added a variety of flavors. Suggestions: diced onion, dash of garlic, sprouts, pickles, (add some pickle juice) grated carrots, finely diced celery, lettuce, chopped cabbage.
   And spices, seasonings or herbs, parsley, dill, chives, Worcestershire sauce, sage.
5) Grind 1 tongue, chop 2 medium-sized sweet pickles, and 1 large sweet apple. Add salt to taste. (tongue salad)

6) 1/2 cup grated cheddar cheese, 1 tablespoon honey, 1/2 cup pitted, chopped dates. Mix with milk, cream or mayonnaise.

* Spread peanut butter on bread. Top with mayonnaise and lightly chopped or thinly sliced bananas.
* Put salad dressing in the sandwich and the lettuce in a plastic bag; let the child add the lettuce in school. It is crisper and better this way.
* Try softening a package of cream cheese and adding some chopped nuts. Spread on slices of date and nut loaf.
* For unusual flavor treats, try creaming one of your favorite seasonings into the butter. Mustard, horseradish, parsley, chives, curry powder, minced onion, celery salt, and even a light hint of garlic will bring a welcome note of flavor to the sandwiches.

ADDITIONAL SUGGESTIONS

* Ice cream in thermos, served with a piece of pie.
* Freezer cabbage slaw
  cabbage wedges (with or without peanut butter)
  carrot sticks
  grated carrots on buttered bread
  celery sticks (filled with peanut butter, or soft cheese)
  apple halves (filled with peanut butter)
  prunes (stuffed with cream cheese or nut paste)
  dates, raisins, figs, dried apples
  sliced radishes on buttered bread
  popcorn
  hotdogs, sliced lengthwise, in thermos. Have mustard or ketchup on the bread.
  Applesauce in strawberry jello
  cottage cheese, topped with applesauce
  cottage cheese with raisins and nuts
  soda crackers with peanut butter
  Custard or pumpkin custard made in custard cups (set in hot water to bake)
  Bake different kinds of breads for variety.
  Grind raisins, dates and nuts together. Mix with coconut.

Fill a week's supply of baby food jars with hot cooked carmel pudding or Dannish dessert. The baby food jars often seal, which keeps the pudding from spoiling.

DANNISH DESSERT

2 pint frozen strawberries or 1 quart canned; add 3 or 4 cups water and sugar to taste. Let this come to the boiling point. Add enough clear jel so that it's a little runny. Remove from heat and add 5 rounded tablespoons jello.

* Jello is cheaper when bought by the pound.

SCHOOL ICE CREAM

By the time it is below freezing most of the day, the scholars are tired of the same things in their bucket. A simple, yet delicious dessert can be made by cooking cornstarch (see Basic Vanilla Pudding, page 187). Cool, then add whipped cream. Spoon it into a tumbler with a lid. When the scholars get to school, they set the tumbler outside and let it freeze. Simple homemade ice cream!

Crunchy or smooth peanut butter mixed in with leftover frosting, milk, and powdered sugar, makes a very delicious snack. Put between graham crackers.

* Make a paste of powdered sugar and milk. Add peanut butter to taste. Spread between graham crackers.

* For a hot sandwich in tinfoil heated on the school stove, try the beanburger on **page 77**. Leftover heated pizza in tinfoil is delicious.

* Make the TEA SYRUP on **page 237**, then follow simple directions for a quick tea for school.

* Homemade cereal is good for school. Send a thermos with cold milk along.

THERMOS POTATO SOUP

Dice and cook potatoes with parsley and onions. While it is cooking, melt a few tablespoons margarine or butter in a pan. Add a heaping tablespoon of flour. Brown slowly. Add milk, stirring all the time. Let boil then pour over soft potatoes. Grated hardboiled eggs may be added.

* Variation: Fry bacon then use the grease to make the pan sauce. Proceed as before. Add bacon to soup.

MIXES

FEATHER-LIGHT PANCAKES

8 cups flour	2 tbsp. soda
1 cup sugar	2 tsp. salt

Mix and store in tight container.

To make pancakes: Beat 2 eggs well; add 1/4 cup vinegar, 2 cups milk and 1/4 cup soft shortening. Then add 2 1/4 cups mix, making the 1/4 cup quite full.

* When dry milk is added to the mix then water instead of milk is required in preparing the pancakes.

PANCAKE MIX

12 cups flour	2 tbsp. salt
3/4 cup sugar	3/4 cup baking powder
4 cups dry milk	

Mix well and store in tight container.

Method: 1 1/2 cup pancake mix, 1 beaten egg, 1 cup water, and 2 tablespoons salad oil.

* Buckwheat or whole wheat flour may be used for part of flour.

* Dry milk can be omitted if milk is used in place of the water.

PANCAKE AND WAFFLE MIX

4 cups white flour	2 cups buckwheat flour
2 cups cornmeal	1 cup raw wheat germ
3 tsp. salt	4 tsp. soda
4 tsp. baking powder	

2/3 cup liquid shortening (for pancakes only half of the shortening may be used)

Mix together thoroughly. This may be used immediately or stored away in a cool place for later use. When using take equal amounts of mixture and milk. (Sour milk is best.) For pancakes use 1 egg to 1 or 2 cups of mixture. For waffles, use 1 egg to each cup of mixture.

* Peanut oil does not become rancid as corn oil. Safflower oil is recommended also because of its nutritious value.

BASIC CAKE MIX

10 cups all purpose flour	5 tsp. salt
5 tbsp. double-acting	7 cups sugar
baking powder	2 1/2 cups shortening

1 cup dry milk

Sift dry ingredients together 3 times. Rub shortening into dry part until like cornmeal texture. Lift lightly into containers and store at room temperature. May be kept for 3 months. (Dry milk may be omitted if whole milk is used instead of water for the batter.) With this mixture you can make the following cakes:

PLAIN CAKE

4 1/2 cups mix   1 cup milk or water
2 tsp. vanilla   2 eggs

Bake 25-30 minutes at 375º.

For SPICE CAKE - Add to plain cake recipe: 2 teaspoons cinnamon, 1/2 teaspoon cloves, 1/2 teaspoon allspice.

For WHITE CAKE - Use plain cake recipe, only use 3 whites of eggs instead of 2 whole eggs.

For ORANGE CAKE - Add to plain cake recipe: 1 tablespoon rind and omit 1 cup of milk. Use 3/4 cup water and 1/4 cup orange juice.

For CHOCOLATE CAKE - Use recipe for plain cake. Add 1/4 cup cocoa before any liquid.

CHOCOLATE CHIP COOKIES

4 1/2 cups basic mix   2 eggs
2 tbsp. flour   1 small pkg. chocolate chips
3/4 cup brown sugar   nuts
1/3 cup cooking oil

Mix all ingredients. Bake at 375º for 10-12 minutes on ungreased cookie sheets.

CHOCOLATE CINNAMON BARS

4 1/2 cups basic mix   3 tsp. cinnamon
1 egg   1 egg yolk
1/2 cup oleo

Mix and press into greased 9" x 12" or 15" x 10" pan. Beat 1 egg white slightly. Brush over mixture. Sprinkle topping over top. Bake at 350º for 25 minutes. Cool. Cut in bars.

Topping: 1 tsp. cinnamon, 1/3 cup sugar, 1 cup chocolate chips and 1/2 cup nuts.

VARIATIONS WITH CAKE MIX

APPLESAUCE CAKE

Add to plain cake recipe:

3/4 cup brown sugar   1 tsp. soda
1/2 tsp. cloves   2 tsp. cinnamon
1/2 tsp. nutmeg   2 cups applesauce
raisins or nuts (optional)

<u>Omit</u> the liquid in the **plain cake recipe.**

APPLESAUCE RAISIN BARS

Use the Applesauce Cake ingredients, plus 1 stick margarine (1/2 cup). Add 4 eggs one at a time, after adding all other ingredients and beat well. Add as many raisins as desired, cut-up, whole or ground. Frost with a powdered sugar icing. This makes a large batch. Prepare two 2" x 13" x 9" pans.

BUTTERMILK CAKE

Use buttermilk in place of sweet milk in the **plain cake recipe and** add 1 teaspoon soda.

PINEAPPLE UPSIDE-DOWN CAKE

Syrup:

2/3 cup melted butter   1 cup brown sugar
1/4 cup nuts   6 tbsp. pineapple juice
1 tbsp. flour

Mix and pour in bottom of greased 9" x 12" pan. Arrange pineapple in bottom of pan. Pour the basic recipe cake batter over pineapple. Bake at 375⁰. Invert on large plate then serve with whipped cream or substitute.

DESSERT (from Cake Mix)

Put fruit pie filling in bottom of cake pan. Top with plain cake batter and bake at 375⁰. Use almond in the cake when cherry pie filling is used. Serve with whipped cream, top milk or ice cream.

BASIC COOKIE MIX

10 cups flour   4 tbsp. baking powder
7 1/2 cups sugar   4 1/2 tsp. salt
3 1/3 cups **shortening**

Measure flour into large bowl. Add sugar, baking powder and salt. Blend thoroughly. Add shortening and work into mixture until uniformly blended. Put into tight containers. Do not pack down. Cover. Store at room temperature.

MINCEMEAT BARS

3 cups cookie mix   1 cup mincemeat
1 large egg

Mix all ingredients thoroughly. Spread in greased 9" x 13" x 2" pan. Bake in 400° oven 30 minutes. If desired, while hot, sprinkle top with white sugar. Cool in pan. Yield: 36 (2-inch) bars.

ORANGE DATE NUT STICKS

3 cups cookie mix   2 eggs
1 tbsp. grated orange rind   1 cup chopped dates
1/4 cup orange juice   1 cup finely chopped nuts

Follow same directions as for Mincemeat Bars, but cut sticks about 1" x 2 1/2".

BANANA COCONUT BARS

3 cups cookie mix   1 cup mashed bananas
1 large egg   1/4 cup finely chopped
1/2 cup coconut   candied cherries
1 tsp. vanilla   2/3 cup chopped nuts

Follow Mincemeat Bar directions, but sprinkle part of the nuts on top.

BISCUIT MIX

8 cups flour   1/3 cup baking powder
8 tsp. sugar   2 tsp. cream of tartar
2 tsp. salt   1 cup powdered milk
1 3/4 cups shortening

Sift dry ingredients 3 times then cut in shortening. Pack loosely in airtight container.
Method: 1 cup mix, 1/3 cup water
Mix, then bake at 450° for 10-12 minutes. (Powdered milk may be omitted when milk is used instead of water when making the biscuits).

* This biscuit mix may be used with the cherry pudding, page 200, and the cherry roll on page 201.

* The pizza pie on **page** 80 may also be made with biscuit mix.

CUSTARD PIE with biscuit mix

1/2 cup biscuit mix   3 tbsp. butter
1/3 cup sugar   1 tsp. vanilla
4 eggs   1/2 cup coconut (optional)
2 cups milk

Beat the egg whites until stiff, then add the remaining ingredients and mix well again. Pour into buttered pie pan. Bake 25-30 minutes at 400⁰ or until pie is golden brown. The mix forms the crust.

SIX-WEEKS MUFFINS

6 cups bran (or all-bran cereal)   1 cup shortening
2 cups boiling water   3 cups sugar (scant)
4 eggs, beaten   5 cups flour
1 qt. buttermilk   2 tsp. salt
5 tsp. soda

Pour the boiling water over 2 cups bran and let stand. Mix in melted shortening. Mix rest of bran with sugar, eggs, and buttermilk. Sift flour with soda and salt. Combine all ingredients and bake as needed at 400⁰ for 20 minutes.

Mixture will keep 6 weeks or more in refrigerator. Makes 6 dozen. Dates, raisins or chopped apples may be added at baking time.

WHOLE WHEAT MUFFIN MIX

24 cups finely ground   8 tbsp. baking powder
   whole wheat flour   3 cups lard
3 tbsp. salt
3 cups sugar

Mix dry ingredients. Cut in lard until very fine like meal. Store in a cold place.
Method:
2 3/4 cups muffin mix   1 beaten egg
1 cup milk

Mix until moistened. Bake at 425⁰ for 20-25 minutes. Makes 12 medium sized muffins.

THREE-FLOUR MUFFIN MIX

12 cups fine whole wheat flour
6 cups sifted, white
  all-purpose flour
6 cups oatmeal

3 tbsp. salt
8 tsp. baking powder
3 cups sugar
3 cups lard

Mix as for whole wheat muffin mix. Use same muffin recipe for baking as whole wheat muffin mix.

Variations: add **raisins, carob flour,** and bake in oblong pan like corn bread.

GINGERBREAD MIX

8 cups flour
2 1/4 cups sugar
2 1/2 tsp. soda
2 tbsp. baking powder
3 tbsp. ginger

3 tbsp. cinnamon
1 tsp. cloves
1 tbsp. salt
2 1/4 cups shortening

Sift together all dry ingredients and cut in shortening. Store in gallon jar, tightly covered, in cold place. Will keep about 3 months.

Method for use: 2 cups mix, 1 beaten egg, 1/2 cup molasses, 1/2 cup boiling water. Put mix in bowl. Combine rest of ingredients and stir into mix. Blend until smooth. Pour into greased 8" x 8" pan. Bake at 350° for 35 minutes. Serve warm with whipped cream.

Maple Gingerbread:

Heat 2/3 cup maple syrup, combine with 1/3 cup sour cream and stir into 2 cups mix. Add 1 egg, well beaten. Pour into greased 8" x 8" pan. Bake at 350° for 40 minutes.

LYDIA'S PIE DOUGH MIX

9 lbs. flour
4 lbs. lard
1 cup cornstarch
1 tbsp. baking powder

2 cups sugar (confectioner's
  or brown, sifted)
1 tbsp. salt

Use about 1 1/2 cups for 1 pie crust. Wet with water or milk.

SHOO-FLY CRUMB MIX

4 lbs. flour
1 lb. lard

2 lbs. brown sugar

Mix like pie crust and store in tight container

SHOO-FLY CAKE

2 cups crumb mix	3/4 cup molasses
3/4 cup hot water	1 tsp. soda (scant)

Mix, then pour into greased 9" x 9" cake pan. Top with dry shoo-fly crumbs. Bake at 450° for 10 minutes, then about 40 minutes at 375° or until done.

SHOO-FLY PIE

For pie, pour into an unbaked pie shell. Bake as for shoo-fly cake.

PUDDING MIX

1/2 cup corn starch	1 1/2 cups sugar
1 cup flour	1 tsp. salt

Mix well and store in tight container.

VANILLA PUDDING

3/4 cup pudding mix	3 cups milk
2 eggs, beaten	2 tsp. vanilla
2 tbsp. butter	

Heat 2 1/2 cups milk. While milk is heating, make a paste of the pudding mix, 1/2 cup milk, and eggs. Add to hot milk. Cook 1 minute.

CHOCOLATE PUDDING

3/4 cup pudding mix	5 tbsp. cocoa
1/4 cup sugar	3 cups milk
2 eggs	2 tsp. vanilla
2 tbsp. butter	

Cook as with vanilla pudding.

BUTTERSCOTCH PUDDING

4 tbsp. butter	1/2 cup brown sugar
3 cups milk	3/4 cup pudding mix
2 eggs	1 tbsp. vanilla

Cook as with vanilla pudding. Top with nuts.

CRUNCH MIX

5 cups oatmeal	5 cups flour
5 cups brown sugar	1 1/2 tsp. soda
1 1/2 tsp. baking powder	1/2 tsp. salt
	2 tsp. cinnamon

Mix and store in tight container.

Method:

Put 1 quart **sweetened,** slightly thickened fruit in the bottom of a buttered baking dish. Mix 3 cups of the crunch mix and 2/3 cup butter. Pour over the top of the fruit. Pat down and bake at 350° for about 30-45 minutes. Serve with milk or cream.

ONE GALLON MUFFIN MIX

2 cups oatmeal	2 cups shredded wheat
2 cups all-bran	

Beat 4 eggs until fluffy then add 3 cups sugar (less sugar may be used if desired).

1 heaping cup shortening	5 tsp. soda
5 cups flour	1 qt. buttermilk or sour milk
2 tsp. salt	

Store at least one day in ice-box or cool place before baking, then bake only the amount needed. The remaining dough will keep for days or weeks. Keep refrigerated. Bake in muffin tins at 400° for 25 minutes or until done.

GARDEN HINTS

*Glass jugs may also be used as hot caps. Tie twine around the bottom of the jug. Light a match to it. As soon as the twine has burned and the jug is still hot, dip the bottom in cold water. The jug will break where the twine was. The sun will shine through glass jugs.

*To make flowers grow soak egg shells in warm water and use this to water the plants.

*Lay black plastic for eggplants, peppers, pickles, melons, canteloupes, sweet potatoes. Results: no weeds and yields double!

*Plant your cabbage in the onion row. By the time the cabbage plants need more room the onions are pulled for eating.

*Plant marigold seeds in the same hill as squash seeds to keep away the bugs. This may work for pickles also.

*Spray grapes twice during the summer with Captain — during the last 60 days before they ripen. Between the spraying, dust with sulphur four times for mildew.

*If you have trouble with birds picking tomatoes, or rabbits eating lettuce, dust them with talcum powder and they won't bother.

*Instead of buying hot caps for your early plants, use lightweight plastic milk jugs (gallon size). Cut off the bottom and place the top over your early plants. Leave the cap off. Push the jugs well into the ground to keep the wind from blowing them away.

*To ward off bugs and worms from watermelon, muskmelon and cucumber plants, put the seeds into kerosene before planting. Fish them out immediately with a spoon, then plant.

*Prune tomato vines by cutting off the long, wild, shooting vines and you'll have nicer and larger tomatoes.

*Bury large crocks in the garden to store carrots. They should be extended about two inches above the ground to keep out surface water. Wash the carrots and dry them before storing. Place a board or tight lid on top.

*Put some wood ashes on the ground where you planted radishes to keep away worms. Wood ashes and lime is also good for dusting cabbage.

CANNING

VEGETABLES

PUDDING

SOUPS

CREAM

CANNING HINTS

* Boric acid is poisonous and should never be added to food.

* While peeling apples, pears, or peaches, place the slices in slightly salted water. They will then retain their natural color. This also enriches the flavor.

* Don't peel your pumpkins (or squash). Wash them, take out the seeds, then put them in a pressure cooker with a very small amount of water (1/2 to 1 cup). Cook for 10 minutes, timing after cooking starts. The shell comes off easily and the pumpkin is ready to use.

* Use a melon ball tool or a measuring spoon to scoop out the centers of pears or apples.

* If you have a lot of peas to shell, place them in a bucket and pour boiling water over them. Cover, and let them stand for 10 to 15 minutes. They shell easier this way and will have a better flavor.

* Check cans to see if they are sealed while still warm. If any have not sealed, give them a few hard turns. This almost always eliminates the need to reheat the cans. Turning them upside down also helps.

* Boil used flats in water with a little soda added for 10 minutes to make them look like new. Be careful how cans are opened, then mark the lids. Use the ones you used for coldpacking for pressure canning the next year.

MARASCHINO CHERRIES

4 1/2 lb. seeded white cherries   Juice of 1 lemon
4 1/2 lb. sugar   1 oz. almond extract
3 cups water   1 oz. red coloring
Brine:
  2 tbsp. salt   1 tsp. alum
                                   Water to cover

Soak cherries over-night in brine. Next day drain and rinse cherries in water. Add water, juice, sugar and color. Heat to boiling point. Let set 24 hours. Bring to boil again the third day, add almond extract. Jar and seal.

COLD PACKING HUCKLEBERRIES

Make a syrup of:
  2 cups sugar   1 cup boiling water

Pack berries in jar. Add syrup. Place jars in water, until water starts to boil, then remove from heat and seal.

CANNED STRAWBERRIES

3 qts. strawberries, lightly mashed, if preferred
2 cups sugar
1/2 cup water

Boil 8 minutes. Put in **jars** while hot, and seal.

CANNING PRUNES WITH SODA

Take 2 tablespoons soda to 1 gallon of water. Bring to a boil then drop the prunes in — a handful at a time. As soon as they rise to the top, ladle them out into a clean jar. When the jar is full, fill with hot syrup, then seal.

RHUBARB

There are many variations in canning rhubarb by canning some with pineapple and some without, and some with different flavors of jello. Use 2 small boxes of jello to 6 qts. cooked rhubarb. On each can write what flavor it contains so you can decide which flavor your family enjoys the most. While boiling hot pour into jars and seal.

* Rhubarb may also be canned for pies by putting the raw, diced fruit in jars and filling with cold water. It need not be heated; the acid in the fruit keeps it from spoiling.

SPICED MELONS

2 cups sugar   3/4 tsp. salt
1/2 cup vinegar   1 tbsp. whole cloves
1 cup water

Boil 20 minutes to get the taste of the cloves. Put muskmelons in jars and pour the syrup over them. Cook 20 minutes. Do not can the cloves as they will color the muskmelons.

MUSKMELONS

Peel and wash melons. Pour over them 1 tbsp. salt and hot water to cover. Scald 5 minutes. Drain and add syrup:
4 cups sugar   3 cups water
1 cup vinegar   2 tsp. salt

Boil syrup and pour over melons in jars. Boil 1 hour. Makes 5 quart.

SIMPLE SAUERKRAUT

(A quick easy way to make Sauerkraut)
Shred the cabbage and pack into jars loosely. Make a hole down through the middle with a wooden spoon or similar utensil and put in a tablespoon of salt to each quart. Then fill with boiling water and seal your jars tightly, at once.
Will be ready to use in 4 to 6 weeks. More salt may be added if desired.

CROCK KRAUT

Measure 3 tablespoons pure granulated salt and sprinkle over 5 pounds shredded cabbage. Allow the salted cabbage to stand a few minutes to wilt slightly. Mix well, with clean hands or a spoon, to distribute salt uniformly. Pack the salted cabbage into a large crock. Press down firmly with potato masher, until the juices drawn out will just cover the shredded cabbage. Place a water filled plastic bag on top of the cabbage. This fits snugly against the cabbage and against the sides of the container and prevents exposure to air. Place crock in room with temperature of 68° to 72°.
Instead of covering the cabbage with a plastic bag you may cover it with a clean, thin, white cloth (such as muslin) and tuck the edges down against the inside of the container. Cover with a plate or round paraffined board that just fits inside the container

so that the cabbage is not exposed to the air. Put a weight on top of the cover so the brine comes to the cover but not over it. A glass jar filled with water makes a good weight.

When fermentation is complete, remove from crock and heat in kettle to simmering temperature. Pack hot sauerkraut into clean, hot jars; cover with hot juice, filling to 1/2 inch of top of jar. Adjust lids. Place jars in boiling water bath and process 15 minutes for pints and 20 minutes for quarts. Start to count the processing time as soon as hot jars are placed into the actively boiling water.

Remove jars from the canner and complete seals if necessary. Set jars upright, several inches apart, on wire rack to cool.

An off odor indicates that sauerkraut may be spoiled. It rots when it isn't covered sufficiently to keep out air.

SAUER KRAUT (short method)

For this it is well to use large bursted heads of cabbage. Shred and chop. Pack in jars. Add 1 teaspoon salt to each jar. Fill the jars with boiling water. Do not seal tightly. Let stand to ferment — about 10 days. Turn the lids tightly and store.

CANNED CORN

Cut off corn, cover with water and cook 5 minutes. Put corn and liquid in pint jars. Add to each pint: 1 tsp. salt, 1 tsp. sugar, 1 tsp. lemon juice. Boil in hot water bath for 3 hours.

This makes a delightful and colorful addition to your salad plate.
STUFFED LITTLE PEPPERS

Make your favorite cole slaw and stuff into the small green, red and yellow peppers. Pack into jars and cold pack for 3 hours.

GREEN PEPPERS

Dice and fry in butter. Put in small jelly jars. Cold pack until the boiling point, then remove from stove. Good for one-dish meals and casseroles.

Peppers for Casseroles may also be diced and packed in small jars, adding about 1/4 tsp. salt to 1 cup peppers. Fill with water. Cold pack. Bring to boiling point then remove from stove.

CANNED PEPPERS

Clean peppers (cut in strips if desired) and pack into jars. Add 1 teaspoon vegetable oil and 1 teaspoon salt to each quart jar.
Syrup:
1 pint vinegar
3 cups water
3 cups sugar

Mix, then pour over peppers while boiling hot. Seal. Cold pack until the boiling point.

WATERLESS STRING BEANS

Wash the beans and pack them in jars. Drain off all the water. Seal. Cold pack for 3 hours.

To use them, put a little butter in a sauce pan. Melt, then add the beans, and salt. There will be enough juice in the jars from the beans that no water need be added, when using.

This recipe is good if you like variety in canning. The vegetables resemble the frozen mixed vegetables we can buy in the stores. This is also delicious with meat broth for soup.

MIXED VEGETABLES

Cook separately — carrots (diced small), lima beans, string beans, corn, soup-beans, peas, potatoes (diced small), and green peppers (small amount). Salt each vegetable when cooking. Mix together. (Don't overcook.) Cold pack one hour.

QUICK STEPS FOR CANNING PUMPKIN

Wash pumpkins, take out the seeds, put into pressure cooker with a very small amount of water and cook for 10 minutes, timing after cooking starts. The shell comes off easily and the pumpkins are soft and ready for use. This eliminates the peeling and cubing and the pumpkins are nice in texture and not water soaked. If desired, pumpkins may be put through a foley mill. Put into jars and cold pack 1 hr.

TOMATO SAUCE FOR PIZZA PIE

1 peck tomatoes   3 onions
3 red peppers

Cook together until soft. Drain well. Put through a colander.

Add:

2 tbsp. salt	2 tsp. dried celery leaves
1/2 tsp. pepper	1/4 tsp. red pepper, if desired
1/2 cup vinegar	2 tsp. oregano may be added

Put in pint jars and seal. Boil 30 minutes.

PIZZA SAUCE

Cook 1/2 bushel tomatoes and 3 lbs. onions 2 1/2 to 3 hours. Put through sieve. Add the following:

4 hot peppers or 1 1/2	1 tbsp. Oregano
tsp. red pepper	1 1/2 cups white sugar
2 cups vegetable oil	1/2 cup salt
1 tbsp. Basil leaves	

Boil 1 hour, then add 4- 12 oz. cans tomato paste. Bring to boil. Pack into hot jars and seal. Makes 20 pints.

MARY'S TOMATO SOUP

1 peck ripe tomatoes	1 tsp. pepper
1/2 cup sugar	3 bunches celery
2 red peppers	10 small onions
5 sprigs parsley	1/2 cup butter
1/4 cup salt	1/2 cup flour

Cook tomatoes and sieve. Boil pulp down nearly half. Grind onions, parsley, celery and peppers through food chopper. Pour in with the tomatoes. Make thickening with flour and enough water to make it smooth. Stir into the pulp and tomato juice and boil 1/2 hour. Add butter before removing from heat. Can while hot. Makes 6 or 7 pints. To use, add milk, and heat.

VALLEY TOMATO SOUP

1 peck tomatoes	5 tbsp. sugar
8 onions fried in 2 tbsp. butter	4 cloves, 1 stick cinnamon
6 peppers, sweet	bark and 4 bay leaves
5 tsp. salt	2 qts. water

Boil all together and run through sieve. Put on stove again and bring to a boil. Add 5 teaspoons cornstarch mixed with 1/2 cup cold water. Boil 15 minutes. Can.

To serve: Heat soup and an equal amount of milk in separate pans, add 1/4 tsp. soda to 1 qt. of soup. Mix milk in soup and let come to a boil. Serve with crackers.

VEGETABLE SOUP WITH RICE

1 pt. potatoes (diced)	1 pt. corn
1 pt. peas	1 pt. carrots (diced)
1 pt. celery	1 pt. soup beans (cooked)
1/2 onion	1 tbsp. chili powder
1/4 cup sugar	salt to taste

Add 3 qts. strained tomatoes, 1 lb. lightly browned hamburger. Blanch vegetables separately. **Add 2 cups rice or alphabet noodles.** (optional) Cold pack 2 full hours.

VEGETABLE SOUP

10 carrots	6 bunches celery
2 heads cabbage	10 onions
10 peppers	3 lbs. hamburg or
1/2 gallon potatoes or macaroni	cut-up chicken
1/2 gallon navy beans	1 lb. butter
1/2 bushel **tomatoes, strained**	

Cook each separately. Fry the onions and hamburg in the butter and mix all together. Season with salt and pepper and sugar to taste. Cold pack 1 hour. 20 quarts.

CHILI SOUP

1 lb. hamburger	1 tbsp. salt
2 tbsp. butter	2 tbsp. prepared mustard
1 cup chopped onions	A little black pepper
2 pt. kidney beans	2 qt. tomato juice
1/2 tsp. chili powder	

Mix as you would other chili soup then cold pack 3 hours. Makes 3 quarts soup.

BYLERS' CHILI SOUP

8 lb. hamburger	6 qt. strained tomatoes
2 qt. red kidney beans	24 small onions
2 to 4 red peppers	1 1/2 tsp. chili powder

Cook each separate and then mix and put into jars and seal. Cold pack 2 hours.

CHICKEN SOUP

4 chickens   1 gal. noodles (cooked)
Salt to taste

1/2 gallon of each of the following: celery, carrots, and potatoes (all chopped). Cook each separately until nearly done. Cold pack 2 hours. 1 cup chopped onions may be added.

BAKED BEANS

8 lb. beans   1 1/2 lb. bacon or ham, cut fine
4 1/2 qt. tomato juice   8 tbsp. salt
1 lb. brown sugar   1 cup molasses
1/2 tsp. black pepper   1 tbsp. cinnamon
1 tbsp. ground mustard

Soak beans overnight. Cook until soft, then drain. Mix other ingredients together and cook a few minutes then add to the beans. Put in jars. Cold pack 1 1/2 or 2 hours. Makes 14 quarts.

* 3 lbs. wieners may be used instead of bacon. Slice and fry before adding.

* Tomato juice may be doubled, or part of the juice from cooking may be added.

CANNING POTATOES

Don't let the newly-dug small potatoes go to waste. Scrape them, pack them into a jar, and add 1 teaspoon salt. Coldpack for 3 hours. To use, drain off the water, and fry them in butter.

INSTANT PUDDING

Thicken any kind of fruit or fruit combinations such as, pears and pineapple, sour cherries and raspberries, apples and raisins, using tapioca or clear jel (tapioca should not be cooked until clear). As soon as the cooked fruit has reached the boiling point fill the jars, seal, and put them into the pressure cooker. Heat to 5 lb. pressure. Let steam out and then jars will seal. A hot water bath may also be used, or the jars may be placed in a hot oven a few minutes. Lemon jello may be used instead of lemon juice with some fruit. This thickened fruit may be used for puddings or pie filling when unexpected company arrives.

HOW TO MAKE HOMINY

In a large kettle bring 1 1/2 gallon water and 3 tbsp. lye to a boil. Then add 1 gallon clean corn. Simmer 10 minutes. (No need to stir.) Take off of heat and let set for 25 minutes.

Drain off lye water and add clean water. Wash and wash until black ends are all loose, changing water often. Soak overnight and follow "hominy canning" recipe. The corn can also be dried after the black ends are off and kept in a cool place.

HOMINY WITH SODA

Use 2 tablespoons soda and 2 quarts water for each quart of corn. Follow the same procedure as hominy made with lye (see the preceding recipe).

Household lime can also be used to remove hulls. Cook corn in lime water 2 hours or until hulls loosen.

HOMINY MAKING HINTS

* Always use stainless steel, iron, or enamelware for making hominy.
* Stir with a wooden spoon.
* The black ends may be removed by rubbing over a cloth on a washboard or by using a churn.
* It is delicious even if the hulls and centers aren't all removed.
* Hominy may be used in meat loaf.
* Do not inhale the steam from the lye water.

CANNING HOMINY

Boil hominy until about tender. Fill jars 3/4 full. Add 1 tsp. salt to each quart. Fill with boiling water. Process 3 hours in boiler, or 90 minutes in the pressure cooker.

CANNED NUTMEATS

Put nutmeats in cans with two piece lids on. Heat in oven to 250° on grate for 3/4 hour then turn off and let cool on grate.

CANNED CREAM

When there's an overabundance of cream during the summer months, can it and keep for the winter. First, cook the cream then seal it in pint or quart jars. Cold pack for 1 hour. This cream can be whipped and used same as fresh cream, and has a good flavor.

PRESERVED BUTTER

Form butter into patties, then place them in a crock with salty brine, so strong that an egg can be floated on the surface of the water. Keep in a cool place. In this way butter can be kept for several months.

HOW TO CAN SWEET CIDER

Never boil cider in a kettle to can. Pour the fresh apple juice in bottles or cans, filling it to the top. Place in canner with cold water that reaches to the neck of the cans. Leave the cans uncovered. Bring water to a boil. Remove scum that rises to the top, with a spoon or small ladle. Boil until no scum appears. Remove from water and seal.

QUEEN OF MY KITCHEN

Queen of my kitchen, I merrily sing,
While the dish pan foam rises high
As I happily wash and rinse, I bring
The sunshine into my sky;
And I pile the dishes into the rack
So sparkling clean to dry.

Some people wish from their hearts and souls
Sin stains could be washed away
And let soap and water by their magic make
Themselves as pure as they.
Much better it is to humble ourselves
And confess our sins of the day.

But the mothers who meekly follow their tasks—
The contrite who humbly pray,
Will find each hour is gloriously filled
As they toil for others each day;
The lowliest task to them is a joy
And the trials of the cross but a way.

S. M. W.

(With apologies to Louisa May Alcott)

RELISHES

RED BEETS

PICKLES

SOUR PICKLES

3 qt. water   3 tbsp. salt
1 qt. white vinegar   7 tbsp. sugar

Soak pickles in salt water overnight. Heat pickles in juice, not boiling. Pack in jars. Boil juice. Pour over pickles and seal.

EXCELLENT UNCOOKED PICKLES

Select good small cucumbers. Wash and dry. Pack into jars. Sweeten vinegar with saccharin to suit taste. Fill jars with vinegar. Seal as for cold packing. Put jars in a boiler in cold water and bring to a boil. When it starts to boil, take the jars out and tighten lid. Do not make the vinegar too sweet or the pickles will wrinkle. This makes a very crisp pickle.

ICICLE PICKLES

2 gal. large cucumbers   1 pt. salt
Water enough to cover

Mix cucumbers, salt and water. Let stand 4 days. Drain, and add boiling water. Let stand 24 hours. Drain, cut pickles in strips. Pour water over them again, adding a lump of alum, size of an egg. Let stand 24 hours. Drain, pour syrup over the pickles. Let stand 24 hours. Drain and pack. Bring syrup to a boil.
Syrup:
2 1/2 qt. vinegar   1 tbsp. salt
8 pt. sugar (less can be used) 1 scant handful mixed whole
Pour hot syrup over pickles in jars and seal.   spices

CHUNK PICKLES

1 gal. cucumber chunks   1 tsp. allspice
1/2 cup salt   1 tsp. dry mustard
Boiling water to cover   1 tsp. mustard seed
3 cups sugar   1 tsp. celery seed
3 cups vinegar   1/2 tsp. turmeric
1 cup water

Cut medium sized pickles into 1-inch chunks. Add salt and cover with boiling water. Let stand overnight and drain. Combine sugar, vinegar, 1 cup water, and spices. Bring to a boil and add pickles. Green cake color may be added if desired. Heat again to a boil, then can and seal.

SWEET DILLS

Fill jars with sliced pickles, adding 2 bunches dill and 3 or 4 garlic cloves to each quart. Pour the following liquid over the pickles:

1 quart weakened vinegar (1/2 water may be used)
1 pint water   4 cups sugar
1/4 cup salt

Bring to a boil. Fill cans, then put on the lids. Set cans in boiling water and bring to a boil, just long enough to seal.

OVERNIGHT DILL PICKLES

Wash 20 to 25 dill sized (about 4-inch) cucumbers. Put in pan of cold water and let stand overnight. Next morning pack in hot sterile jars.

Into each quart, measure 1/8 tsp. powdered alum. Add 2 heads dill (fresh with seed), 1 small hot red pepper. Combine 4 cups vinegar, 1 cup pure salt, 3 quarts water. Heat to boiling. Fill jars with liquid. Seal. Allow to stand for 6 weeks. A washed grape leaf or two can be put on the top for green color.

SEVEN DAY SWEET PICKLES

1st day - Wash 7 lbs. medium sized green cucumbers and cover with boiling water.
2nd day - Drain. Cover with fresh boiling water.
3rd day - Repeat second day.
4th day - Repeat second day.
5th day - Cut pickles into 1/4 inch rings.
Combine:

1 qt. white vinegar   2 tbsp. salt
8 cups granulated sugar   2 tbsp. mixed pickle spices

Bring to a full boil and pour over sliced pickles.
6th day - Drain brine from pickles, bring to a full boil and pour over pickles again.
7th day - Repeat same as 6th day. Jar and seal.

CLARA'S PICKLES

Chunk 1 gal. pickles. Add 1 cup salt and enough boiling water to cover. Let stand overnight. Next morning drain. Mix: 3 cups white sugar, 1 tsp. tumeric, 1 tsp. mustard seed, 1 quart vinegar, diluted. Pour over pickles and heat. Do not boil. Pack in jars and cover with syrup. Seal.

CRISP PICKLES

1 gallon cucumbers, sliced 1/8 inch thick
6 medium sized onions, sliced thin
Add 1/3 cup salt and cold water to the above. Let stand 3 hours
then drain. Pack in jars for cold packing.
Make a syrup of the following:
1 cup water, 2/3 cup strong vinegar, 1 3/4 cup raw sugar (scant),
1/2 tsp. turmeric, 1/2 tsp. celery seeds, 2 tsp. mustard seeds.
Tie turmeric, celery seeds, and mustard seeds in an organdy bag
and place it in the syrup. Cook syrup a few minutes then lift
out seed bag. Add 1/2 cup extra water and 1/8 cup more vinegar.
When syrup has cooled, pour it over the cucumbers and onions.
Cold pack 5 minutes, no longer. Use leftover syrup for the next
batch of cucumbers. Refrigerate syrup until used.

REFRIGERATOR PICKLES

4 cups vinegar	4 cups sugar
1 1/2 tsp. celery seeds	1 1/2 tsp. mustard seeds
1 1/2 tsp. turmeric	1/4 cup salt

This needs no boiling, just pour over pickles and put in ice box.
Will keep for months.

DOLLAR BREAD & BUTTER PICKLES

4 qts. sliced cucumbers (40-50)	1/2 cup salt
2 qts. sliced onions	1 qt. vinegar
4 cups sugar	1 tbsp. celery seed
2 tbsp. mustard	1 tbsp. ginger
1 tbsp. turmeric (optional)	

Gently stir salt into thinly sliced cucumbers. Cover with ice
cubes; let stand 2 or 3 hours until cucumbers are crisp and cold.
Add more ice if it melts; drain. Add onions. Combine remaining
ingredients. Bring quickly to a boil and boil 10 minutes. Add cucumber slices and onions and bring to boiling point. Pack at once
into hot jars. Process in boiling water bath 30 minutes. Remove
jars from canner and complete sealing. Makes 8 pts.

CHERRY PICKLES

1 1/2 gal cold water	1 qt. sweet cherry leaves
1 cup salt	

Mix the above ingredients and place the pickles in the solution and let stand for 8 days. Remove, wash, and cut in desired pieces. Heat in weak vinegar. Pack in jars and drain. Cook 4 cups sugar, 2 cups vinegar, 2 cups water, and 1 tbsp. mixed spices (all but little red peppers). Heat this well and pour over pickles in jars and seal.

MUSTARD PICKLES

Mix the following:

1 gal. vinegar	1 cup dry mustard
1 cup sugar (some saccharin	1 cup salt
may be used and less sugar)	1 tbsp. mixed pickling spices

Vinegar mixture should be boiled, then cooled. Lay pickles out on a cloth after washing and dry thoroughly or they will mold. Put about 2 gallon small cucumbers in a crock and cover with the brine. Put weight on to keep pickles in the brine. Cover the crock with a cloth.

LIME PICKLES

7 lbs. cucumbers, unpeeled and sliced into 1-inch chunks or thin-	
2 cups lime	ner, if desired
2 gallons cold water	1 tbsp. salt
9 cups sugar	1 tbsp. celery seeds
1 tsp. mixed spices	1 tbsp. whole cloves
2 quarts vinegar	

Mix lime and water and pour over the cucumbers. Let stand 24 hours. Wash out lime thoroughly. Cover with the sugar, vinegar, and spice mixture. Do not heat. Next morning simmer the cucumbers 40 minutes. Put in hot jars and seal. These stay good and crisp. Less sugar may be used.

POLISH PICKLES

Quarter 2 dozen cucumbers. Place in salted water (1 tbsp. salt to each quart of water) and let stand overnight. Drain, then heat (do not boil) in a weak vinegar solution. Drain, and pack in jars. Fill with the following syrup, which has been boiled for 3 minutes:

1 1/2 pt. vinegar	1/4 tsp. red pepper
1 1/2 pt. sugar	1/2 tsp. turmeric

Put 1/4 tsp. alum and a slice of onion on top of each jar and seal.

FROZEN CUCUMBERS

7 cups cucumbers, sliced thin   1 cup onions, diced
1 cup peppers, diced

    Mix, then add the following vinegar solution: 1 tbsp. salt, 1 tsp. celery seeds, 2 cups sugar, 1 cup white vinegar.
    Let stand in ice box 4 or 5 days. Stir every day. Freeze.

COLD PACKED PICKLES

    Pack pickles in jars. To each quart add 1/3 cup vinegar, 1 heaping tbsp. salt, 1/2 tsp. sugar. Fill with water. Seal jars and set in a boiler, in cold water. Heat until the color is completely changed or until it starts to boil.

SPICED RED BEETS

2 cups sugar (raw may be used)   3 cups water or beet juice
1 cup vinegar   Juice of 1 lemon
1/2 tsp. cinnamon   1/2 tsp. allspice
1/2 tsp. cloves

    Salt to taste. Mix liquid and pour over 1 gallon cooked beets. Simmer 15 minutes. Pack beets in jars. Heat liquid to a good boil. Pour over the beets and seal.

PICKLED BEETS

3 quarts small beets   4 cups sugar
3 cups vinegar   1 1/2 cups water
2 tbsp. salt   2 cinnamon sticks (optional)

    Cook beets. Put hot in jars and pour boiling syrup over them and seal. Cold pack them 10 to 15 minutes.

MIXED PICKLES

8 cups sliced cucumbers   2 cups sliced onions
4 green peppers   3/4 cup cooked carrots
About 1 1/2 qt. cooked lima beans   (more, if desired)

    Soak cucumbers, onions, and pepper separately in hot salt water, adding 1 cup salt to each gallon of hot water. Soak 1 hour. Drain, then add the following mixture:
1 tsp. turmeric   1 tsp. celery seed
2 cups vinegar   1 stick of cinnamon

2 to 3 cups sugar   Salt if needed
Boil vegetables and vinegar mixture together for 20 minutes.
Jar and seal while hot.

DELAWARE MIXED PICKLES

2 quarts of each of the following: carrots, corn, cabbage, celery,
beans, cucumbers   4 or 5 peppers
                                      1 quart onions
Cook vegetables separately until tender, all but the onions, peppers, and cucumbers. Mix the following and bring to a boil:
3 tbsp. mustard   2 tbsp. turmeric
3 pints sugar   1 tbsp. salt
1 cup flour   3 pints vinegar
3 pints water
Mix all ingredients and pack into jars. Add syrup to cover and
cold pack 1 hour.

CHOW CHOW

1 pt. green beans   1 pt. carrots
1 pt. yellow beans   1 head cauliflower
1 pt. cucumbers   1 pt. corn
1 pt. lima beans   3 or 4 stalks celery

Cook the above, but not too tender; salt and drain, after chop-
ping them to a uniform size. Chop and salt 1/2 dozen green tomatoes, and 3 red and 3 yellow (large) mangoes. Mix well with the
first ingredients and add to a boiling syrup made from the
following:
3 qts. vinegar   1 tbsp. mustard seed
5 cups sugar   Any other spices you may like
1 tbsp. celery seed
Onions may also be added if desired. Heat, jar and seal.

PICKLED GREEN TOMATOES

5 quart green tomatoes   1 quart vinegar
2 tbsp. salt   2 tbsp. sugar
2 garlic cloves to a quart, sliced in halves.

Mix vinegar, salt and sugar. Heat and add to green tomatoes
and garlic. Bring to a boil and put in jars and seal. Before sealing add 2 dill sprigs or 2 tsp. dill to each quart. The larger
green tomatoes are the best. Can them whole and then slice to
eat in sandwiches.

SWEET PEPPER RELISH

2 oz. celery seeds   1 doz. green peppers
1 doz. sweet red peppers   1 doz. onions
   Grind in food chopper, soak for 10 minutes in boiling water,
then drain. Put the following into a kettle over heat:
1 1/2 pt. vinegar   1/2 tsp. pepper
2 lb. brown sugar   1 tsp. cinnamon
3 tbsp. salt   2 tbsp. mustard seeds

   Add peppers, onions, and celery seeds. Boil for about 10-15
minutes, then jar and seal. Less sugar may be used.

PICKLED PEPPERS

   In a clean cold jar, put in pieces of green peppers (red peppers
get mushy), or hot peppers. Add 1 tablespoon pickling salt. Fill
jar 2/3 full with cold water. Fill to the top with cold white vinegar. Seal jar with screw cap and lid. This is ready to eat after
2 weeks. May be kept indefinitely.

* Spices, garlic, pieces of celery, or dried red pepper can be
added.

CUCUMBER RELISH

Take 4 quart cucumbers, sliced thin but not peeled
6 large onions, sliced
1/2 cup salt
   Mix together and let stand overnight. Next morning, wash in
clear water and drain. Make syrup with:
4 cups sugar   1 qt. vinegar (dilute if too
1 tsp. turmeric   1 tsp. celery seeds strong)
1 tsp. mustard seeds
   Heat syrup and when hot, add cucumbers and onions. Boil together for about 15 minutes. Then make paste with 3 tbsp. flour
and some vinegar. Add to pickles and can while hot.

CORN RELISH

12 ears of corn   1 tsp. mustard seed
1 head of cabbage   1 cup sugar
6 peppers   1/4 cup salt
2 stalks celery   1 pt. vinegar
1 tsp. celery seeds

   Mix and boil for 30 minutes. Jar and seal.

HEINZ RELISH

1/2 pk. green tomatoes	2 or more large onions
8 red peppers	

Put the above through a chopper. Boil for 15 minutes. Remove from stove and salt. Boil for 15 minutes again. Drain through colander. Add the following ingredients:

1 pt. vinegar	2 tbsp. allspice
1 pt. sugar	2 tbsp. whole cloves
2 sticks cinnamon	

Boil rapidly, then add 1 tablespoon celery seeds and 1 teaspoon mustard seeds. Jar and seal.

RIPE TOMATO RELISH

18 firm, ripe tomatoes	1 stalk celery
2 green peppers	2 red peppers
4 medium onions	1/3 cup salt
2 1/2 cups sugar (scant)	1/2 tsp. pepper
1/2 tsp. cloves	2 tsp. cinnamon
2 tbsp. mustard seeds	1 1/2 cups vinegar

Peel tomatoes and chop in small pieces. Grind celery, onions and peppers in food chopper with coarse blade. Combine celery, onions, peppers, tomatoes and salt. Let stand in ice box over-night. Next morning drain well. Mix sugar, spices and vinegar, then add to the tomato mixture. Mix well, then put in sterile jars. Cap. This will keep up to 5 months in the ice box. It is very good on hamburgers, and different kinds of meat and also on fried potatoes.

TOMATO CORN RELISH

12 ears of corn	2 qts. ripe tomatoes
2 bunches celery, cut fine	3 cups white sugar
2 cups vinegar	6 onions, cut fine
1 tbsp. salt	1/4 tsp. red pepper, or less

Cut corn off cobs; peel tomatoes and cut in small pieces. Add the rest and boil for 50 minutes. Put in small jars and seal.

PICKLE CATSUP

1 pt. cut onions	1 small head cauliflower, cut up
4 qt. thinly sliced, peeled	1 bunch celery, diced
pickles	

1 tsp. pepper	2 cups white sugar
1/2 tsp. celery seeds	1 tbsp. salt
1/2 tsp. turmeric	1 tbsp. dry mustard
1 cup vinegar	1 tbsp. flour

Mix. Bring to a boil. Put in jars and seal.

KETCHUP

1 pk. tomatoes	3 cups sugar
4 onions	1 tbsp. mixed pickle spices
3 red peppers	1 tbsp. salt
6 peach leaves	1 tbsp. turmeric
1 cup vinegar	1/4 tsp. pepper

Peel tomatoes and cook until soft. Put through a sieve. Tie pickle spices in bag. Add remaining ingredients to the tomatoes and boil until thick. Remove bag. Put hot into jars or bottles and seal.

STORE-LIKE CATSUP

Mix 1/2 bu. tomatoes and 1/2 cup salt in large crock. Weigh down and let stand 5 days. Each day dip off water. Fifth day re-move white top and put tomatoes through colander. Add 4 cups sugar, 2 cups vinegar, a small amount of pepper, 2 grated onions, and 1 oz. catsup spices tied in a bag. Cook 3/4 hour. Remove bag. Tomatoes may be thickened with Clear Jel if desired. Put in bottles or jars and seal.

TOMATO CATSUP

4 qt. tomatoes, cut fine	3 cups sugar
2 cups vinegar	1/2 tsp. red pepper
2 tbsp. salt	1 tsp. dry mustard
1 tbsp. catsup spice	1 stick cinnamon

Boil 2 hours. Put through a sieve. Thicken with approximately 3 tbsp. cornstarch, moistened with a little vinegar. Boil 10 min-utes and seal in sterilized jars.

HEINZ CATSUP

| 1 pk. tomatoes | 3 large onions |

Boil until soft then drain in bag 2 hours. After draining run through a sieve. Pour juice away. Add to pulp:

4 cups white sugar
3 tsp. salt
1/2 tsp. cloves

1/2 tsp. cinnamon
1/2 tsp. dry mustard
1 pint vinegar

Boil 10 minutes. Bottle and seal.

WINTER KETCHUP

5 qts. tomato juice
1 pt. applesauce
2 cups sugar
2 tbsp. pickling spice

6 onions
1 pt. vinegar
Salt, to taste

Cook onions and put through sieve. Tie pickling spices in a cloth and cook all ingredients together for 1 1/2 hours. Remove pickling spice, then thicken with 1 1/4 cups Clear Jel and cook 15 to 20 minutes. Put in jars or bottles. Dip the tops of the ketchup bottles in melted paraffin to be sure they seal. This ketchup can be made in winter months.

SANDWICH SPREAD

3 to 4 qt. green tomatoes
1 qt. onions

12 large peppers
2 large stalks celery

Grind and add 1 cup salt. Drain overnight in a cloth bag. Press remaining juice out in the morning. Add 1 qt. vinegar and 1 1/2 qt. sugar and boil for 25 or 30 minutes. When cold add 1 qt. mayonnaise (more if desired) and 1/2 small jar mustard (optional).
* 1 qt. = 4 cups

MUSTARD SANDWICH SPREAD

6 green peppers
6 red tomatoes
6 pickles

6 red peppers
6 onions

Grind all together. Add 2 tbsp. salt and let stand 2 hours. Drain well, then mix the following and add to the vegetables:
1/2 cup flour
4 cups sugar

2 tbsp. turmeric
2 cups vinegar

Cook everything together for 15 minutes then add 1 qt. mustard and cook 5 more minutes, stirring all the time to prevent burning. Put into hot jars and seal.

WASHING HINTS

*To wash feather pillows, leave them in the machine only 5 minutes. (Foam pillows should not be put through the washer.) Rinse with plenty of clean water. Squeeze out the extra water, then put the pillow between two bath towels and press down with both hands to blot up the water. Hang on the line in a breezy spot.

*A second-hand wash machine saves a lot of time and work. It need not have a wringer. Use it for rinsing. Add a bit of vinegar to the rinse water if you wish. This does just as well as rinsing twice.

*To remove mildew from fabrics, soak in solution of 1/2 cup vinegar, 1/2 cup liquid bleach to 2 quarts water. Soak 1 or 2 hours or overnight.

*Have your clothespins good and warm before hanging up wash in the winter. This helps keep the hands warm.

*Wear woolen gloves to hang up wash. This keeps your hands from getting so cold.

*After washing a chenille bedspread, drape it over the washline with the topside facing each other. The wind will fluff it up nicely.

*Add a teaspoon of epsom salts to each gallon of water and colored garments will neither fade nor run.

*Instead of buying spray starch use one part liquid starch to two parts water in a spray bottle.

*To keep wash from freezing on the line in winter, wash line off with vinegar.

*Rub vinegar or rubbing alcohol over hands just before hanging out wash when the weather is cold. Dry hands thoroughly before going out. This keeps them from getting so cold.

*Hot water sets stains, so be sure to sponge juice and gravy spots with cold water before washing the fabric in warm suds. Blood stains will also come out if treated this way.

*To remove blood stains dampen the spot with cold water than rub in salt. Let stand about a half hour, then rinse in cold water.

PRESERVES

JELLIES

JAMS

THERE'S NO WORK IN A HOME THAT'S QUITE AS interesting as that which is shared with neighbors. Perhaps that is why there is something special about the making of applebutter. First there is the apple snitzing in the evening when the young folks gather to prepare the apples.

Early the next morning bread dough will be mixed in order to have a special treat with the warm applebutter—fresh bread. A crackling fire is started under the large copper kettle in which sweet cider, sugar and apple snitz are poured. Neighbors take turns pushing the large wooden stirrer back and forth in the kettle to keep the applebutter from burning. Butter is kept handy to throw into the kettle should the applebutter rise to the top.

The excitement of the day comes when the preserves are finished and ready to be canned or put into crocks. It must be dipped out of the kettle in the quickest time. What a rush there is! I never could understand why it is all right to boil the applebutter in a copper kettle, but as soon as it has been boiled down to the right consistency, it has to be removed immediately so it won't "taste like copper."

There's something in applebutter cooking that makes the copper kettle extra nice and bright. When cooking the butter, we children would toss a penny into the boiling preserves. These were pushed back and forth by the stirrer on the bottom of the kettle and helped prevent the applebutter from scorching. The shiny pennies became prized possessions.

STOCKMAN'S APPLE BUTTER

10 gal. fresh cider   8 gal. apple, peeled and cored
20 lbs. sugar

Bring cider to a boil in a copper kettle. Add apples and bring to a boil. Add a lump of butter to keep it from boiling over. After apples are cooked well, add sugar and keep stirring until it thickens. This makes 6 gallons of apple butter. When done, quickly remove from copper kettle.

SIMPLE APPLE BUTTER

4 gal. apples (unpeeled and   1 gal. corn syrup
   cut in quarters)   6 lbs. sugar

Put apples in a heavy kettle or canner with tight-fitting lid. Pour syrup and sugar over apples and set overnight to form juice. Bring to a slow boil and cook for 3 hours. Don't open lid or stir during the entire cooking period. Put through strainer.

CIDER APPLE BUTTER

3 gal. snitz   1/2 gal. light Karo
1 gal. sweet cider   4 lb. sugar

Follow the same directions as Simple Apple Butter.

PEAR BUTTER

Boil 1/2 gallon pears. Then mash as for apple sauce. Add 1 quart white sugar, 1 quart light syrup. Bake in moderate oven, or simmer on top of stove until right consistency. When cooked on stove, extreme care must be taken to avoid scorching. Nutmeg or cinnamon may be added.

GRAPE BUTTER

1 qt. (whole) grapes   2 tbsp. water
1 qt. sugar

Cook 20 minutes, then put through fruit press or colander. Pour in jars. Paraffin on top.

GRAPE MOLASSES

1 pt. white Karo   3 lb. granulated sugar
1 pt. grape juice

Boil a few minutes until the right consistency. Pour into jars and seal. Raspberries, blackberries or elderberries may be used instead of grapes.

WILD GRAPE JELLY

Wash clusters and put in large kettle with only enough water to cover. Bring to boil and boil about 15 minutes. Pour into cloth bag and squeeze out all the juice. Then add as much water as juice. This is now ready for jelly making. **Use 5 cups juice, 7 cups sugar and 1 box Sure-Jell.** Follow the directions on the Sure-Jell box for concord-type grape jelly.

Put the remaining juice in quart cans with 1/2 cup sugar per quart and process it 10 minutes at 10 pounds pressure or 30 minutes in boiling water bath for later use.

STRAWBERRY JAM

1 cup strawberries   2 cups sugar
  (crushed or whole)

Boil for 3 minutes. Remove from heat. Add 1 teaspoon Epsom Salts.

STRAWBERRY PRESERVES

1 qt. berries   2 cups sugar

Boil 5 minutes then add 2 more cups sugar and 2 teaspoons lemon juice and boil 10 minutes longer. Let stand 24 hours. Put in glasses and seal while cold. Seal with paraffin or cover with lid.

FRESH STRAWBERRY JAM

3 cups well crushed berries   6 cups sugar

Mix and let stand 20 minutes. Stir several times.
Combine: 1 pkg. certo crystals, 1 cup water. Boil 1 minute stirring constantly. Mix with berries and stir 2 minutes. Put in jars and cold pack a few minutes to seal jars.
 * Other fruit may be used instead of strawberries.

PEACH AND PINEAPPLE PRESERVES

6 cups sliced peaches   6 cups sugar
2 cups crushed pineapple

Cook 20 minutes then add orange jello (2 small packs).

In early spring jam and jellies may be scarce. This recipe may be the answer to this problem.

PINEAPPLE HONEY

6 lbs. sugar
5 lbs. light corn syrup

1 large can (or quart) of crushed pineapple

Mix well and bring to a boil. There's no need to boil longer. Makes 1 gallon.

PEACH PRESERVES

3 cups peaches
3 oranges

4 1/2 cups sugar

Boil till it sheets from the spoon, 20 to 30 minutes. Remove from heat and add a few chopped maraschino cherries.

PEACH MARMALADE

5 cups sliced peaches
1 small can crushed pineapple

7 cups sugar

Cook together 15 minutes. Add 2 small or 1 large box orange or strawberry jello. Cook until dissolved. Pour into jars. Seal. Paraffin may be used.

PEACH JELLY

Cook peach stones and peelings in enough water to cover, for 10 minutes. Drain. Take the juice and make same as raspberry jelly, using the recipe on the Sure-Jell box.

APRICOT JAM

2 lbs. dried apricots
2 qt. water

8 1/2 cups sugar

Wash apricots. Put through food grinder (coarse). Put with water into a large bowl. Let stand in a cool place 48 hours. Stir occasionally. Put on fire and cook 15 minutes. Add sugar and cook slowly, for 1 hour until thick, stirring frequently.

LEMON BUTTER

1/4 cup lemon juice and grated
   rind of 1 lemon
1 cup sugar

2 eggs, well beaten
1/2 tbsp. butter

Cook in double boiler until it thickens.

RHUBARB JAM

Let stand overnight: 5 cups rhubarb, cut fine
4 cups sugar

In the morning boil 5 minutes, then add 1 small package of strawberry jello. Boil 3 minutes.

* 1 small can pineapple may be added; then add only 4 cups rhubarb instead of 5.

1, 2, 3, 4 RASPBERRY SPREAD

1 cup water   3 cups chopped apples
2 cups red raspberries   (Northern Spy are good)
                                   4 cups white sugar

Cook for 10 minutes. Put in jars. Paraffin.

QUINCE HONEY

1/4 cup clear Karo   2 cups quince (ground)
1 cup water   or 1 cup quince and
3 cups sugar   1 cup apples

Cook approximately 5 minutes.

CHURCH SPREAD

Thoroughly mix:
 1 gal. green label waffle syrup
 1 gal. marshmallow cream

* 4 cups (or more) peanut butter may be added.

* 1 gallon marshmallow cream mixed with grape or any berry preserves is also good.

* Leftover Peanut Butter Spread may be used to make soft peanut butter cookies, omitting the sugar in the recipe.

MAPLE SYRUP FOR CHURCH

4 cups brown sugar   1/4 cup light Karo
2 cups boiling water   2 tsp. maple flavor

Mix first 3 ingredients and bring to a good boil. Remove from heat and add maple flavor. (Double this recipe, plus 1/2 of it, mixed with 5 or 6 pounds of peanut butter and 2 quarts of marshmallow creme will almost fill an 8-quart bowl.)

* When mixing peanut butter and syrup for spread, add a bit of cold water and it will not be so stringy.

CARAMEL SPREAD

2 cups brown sugar	1 cup Karo
2 cups granulated sugar	1 cup water

Put on stove and cook till it is boiling all over the bottom of the kettle. Set off and let cool. When cold add 2 whites of eggs, beaten stiff. Stir together well. Add Maple flavor.

WASHING HINTS

*Grease spots can be removed from most fabrics by a salt solution of mild to medium strength. Spread the fabric on a flat surface and sponge the salt solution freely onto the stained area. Then rub lightly with a soft, dry cloth. If necessary, repeat the procedure.

*To hang coats or dresses on the clothesline to air or drip dry, use two hangers for each article — turn the hooks of the hangers in opposite directions on the line and then place the garment on them. The hangers cannot fall off the line even in a breeze.

*Go easy on fabric softeners. They make clothes soft by lubricating the fabric fibers with an oil-like film. However, this film builds up with continued use and produces a water proofing effect which is undesirable, particularly in baby clothing. (The cheapest way to make clothes softer is to rinse them thoroughly.)

*Some mothers check the time when putting clothes through the washer, allowing so many minutes for each batch. They learn to finish washing sooner in this way.

*Soak handkerchiefs in a pan of cold water into which 1/3 teaspoon of cream of tartar has been dissolved. Wash in the usual way, soak 30 minutes, and rinse. This keeps them snowy white.

*It is well to wash your wash machine occasionally with a solution of pine oil disinfectant in your water, to free it from bacteria.

HOUSEHOLD HINTS

*Do not throw away old generators, but soak them in vinegar overnight. The next day blow them out with an air hose (tire pump). The generator may not be worn out but merely full of dirt.

*To get rid of flies at an upstairs or attic window, set a small, tin can of kerosene on the windowsill. For some reason the flies tumble in.

*Buggy robes are expensive. Make your own by quilting wool material with 2 layers of quilting dacron. A heavy plush may be used on the outside. Plush is slippery so it is best to use such material on the outside and a rough woolen blanket on the inside.

CHEESE

* *Try scalding your milk for cottage cheese in a*
  waterless cooker. The cooker has an insulated base.
  The milk will then require less watching and with
  a low fire is not apt to be overheated.

GENERAL DIRECTIONS FOR CHEESEMAKING

1. Let milk set in cool place overnight to ripen. A commercial starter may be added to hasten ripening. Add about 1 cup to 1 gallon of milk.

2. Next morning warm the milk slowly to 86 degrees.

3. Dissolve cheese color tablet in 1/4 cup water and add to milk. Use 3/4 tablet for 10 gallons milk. Never mix the cheese coloring with the rennet tablet solution.

4. Dissolve the cheese rennet tablet in 1/4 cup cold water. Mix with the milk at 86 degrees. Ice cream junket tablets may also be used, instead of the rennet.

5. Remove the milk from the stove. Stir gently but thoroughly with wooden spoon for 2 minutes.

6. Cover container and let stand by a warm stove for 1 hour or until thick enough. To test, put finger into the milk and bring up like a hook. If the curd breaks clean across finger like jelly it is thick enough.

7. Cut curds into cubes using a long-blade kinfe that extends to the bottom of kettle. Cut 1/2 inch squares, then cut diagonally. A wire bent in a U-shape may be used to cut the curds horizontally, using two ends as handles. Cutting should give a clear whey. A milky whey signifies loss of cassein and fat.

8. Let stand 5 minutes. Return curds to stove, then stir slowly and gently to keep pieces from sticking together while the temperature is slowly raised to 100-102 degrees, and kept there. Then stir only occasionally so pieces won't stick together. Instead of returning the curds to the stove, some of the whey may be taken from the top, strained into a dipper, then brought to a boil. Slowly pour the hot whey back into the curds, stirring the curds all the time. Continue this process until the temperature has risen to 100-102 degrees.

The curds are ready when a handful, squeezed firmly, does not squirt out between the fingers, but almost falls apart when hand is opened. Takes about 1 hour.

9. Pour heated curds into a colander which has been lined with

cheese cloth, organdy, or gauze diaper cloth. Catch whey; it is a healthy drink, or may be used in recipes calling for water, and is also a good tonic for flowers.

10. Gently work salt into the curds — about 1 tablespoon to 2 gallons of milk, or according to taste.

11. Leave curds in cloth, having only 1 thickness over the top, and place in the prepared press — lard press, bucket or cans. Do not use an aluminum container. Place the lid on top of the cheese. Weigh down with 2 bricks, or the equivalent in weight. In the evening turn the cheese and double the weight. Next morning remove the cheese from the press. Keep it in a warm room for 36 to 48 hours. By laying it in the sun by a window for 1/2 day will hasten the aging process.

12. Seal the cheese by brushing it with smoking hot paraffin. Take heed for hot paraffin catches fire like oil. If cheese is not solid, do not seal. Instead of paraffin, vegetable or mineral oil may be rubbed into the cheese to keep from molding. Another method to prevent molding is to mix only half of the salt into the cheese, then rub salt over it every few days. If mold appears, wash the cheese in warm salt water and salt again. Turn every few days.

13. Place cheese in room (cellar) with temperature about 60 degrees and turn every other day for 3 to 6 weeks. If kept longer, turn twice a week. Cheese may be kept several months. The longer it is cured, the sharper it becomes.

* One gallon of curds produces approximately 1 pound of cheese.

* To make hard, dry cheese, press with 25-30 pound weights.

* If mold forms on cheese that's being used, trim it off and use.

* Cheese may be kept longer while using, when placed in a large container. Set a cup with vinegar beside it. Cover container tightly and set in a cool place. Do not set vinegar with cheese while cheese is in the aging process.

* Rennet tablets and coloring may be bought at a drug or grocery store. If not available they may be ordered from:
   In the U.S.A. - Hansen's Laboratory, Inc. Milwaukee 14 Wisconsin 53200
   In Canada - Horan Lally Co. Limited, 26 Kelfield St., Rexdale, Ontario.

EQUIPMENT NEEDED TO MAKE SOLID CHEESE

rennet tablet
yellow food coloring, when yellow cheese is preferred
wooden spoon to stir
sharp knife with long blade
thermometer — a clean weather thermometer is sufficient
to press the cheese, use an old lard press, or 2 canners which
fit together like a double boiler (put water into the upper for
weight), or a lard or jam bucket which can be obtained from res-
taurants. Holes should then be punched from inside out into the
one side of the bucket bottom (about 18) to drain off whey. Set it
on the table with the holes extending over the edge. Place a bucket
beneath to catch the whey. Put lid over the cheese with bricks on
top.

The following cheese is economical and will take the place of
the more expensive Philadelphia Cream Cheese. To make yogurt,
simply buy a small quantity of plain yogurt, stir 3 tablespoons into
1 quart milk that had been slowly warmed to 98 degrees. Keep the
milk in a warm room for 5 or 6 hours. When thickened, the yogurt is ready to use. Keep refrigerated. More yogurt can be
made from this yogurt then by following the above simple
directions.

MARVEL CREAM CHEESE

Make yogurt. Instead of refrigerating the yogurt once it has
formed, pour it into a colander lined with a triple thickness of
cheese cloth, or an old clean gauze diaper will do. Catch the whey
by placing a bowl under the colander. Allow the whey to drip for
one minute, then lift up the four corners of the cheese cloth and
tie them together, then hang the bag at the sink faucet or else-
where and let the whey drip for 6 to 8 hours. It is then ready to
be removed from the bag and stored in the refrigerator. This
cheese is almost identical to Philadelphia Cream Cheese. One
quart of yogurt makes about 6-8 ounces of Marvel Cream Cheese.

CREAM CHEESE

1 qt. light cream of good flavor
1/4 cup fresh sour milk

Mix well in top of double boiler or stainless bowl. Cover and
let stand at room temperature until thick. Skim thin layer off top,

if necessary. Cut in squares; heat over warm water to 110°. Make few strokes across bottom while warming. Handle carefully so cream doesn't get thin and drain off with the whey. Pour into cloth bag. After 15 minutes place bag on rack in ice box with bowl underneath to catch whey. Drain 10 hours or so. Press curd with weight on top of bag, until curd is pasty. **Turn into bowl. With** fork or mixer work in salt to taste (about 3/4 tsp.). Mix thoroughly. Good with crushed pineapple and served on drained pear chunks.

The following two recipes may also be used for Philadelphia Cream Cheese.

BUTTERMILK CHEESE

Let a quart buttermilk set until thick. Pour 1 quart boiling water over it, stirring at the same time. Let set a few minutes. Cheese will go to the bottom. Pour off water. Put cheese in cloth to drain a half day. Add salt, according to taste.

SOFT CHEESE

Select a quantity of very rich milk. Mix with this, 3 to 5 per cent of its bulk of clean well-soured skim milk or this amount of a commercial starter. Add dissolved rennet and set the mixture at 80 degrees fahrenheit. When well thickened, cool down to 60 degrees by placing in a refrigerator or by letting cold water run around the container. Care should be taken not to break the curd. After it has cooled for 24 hours, turn it into a cheesecloth sack and allow to drain for another 24 hours. Add salt to taste. (The presence of fat makes a smooth, soft cheese.) This cheese can be molded into balls or printed in a butter printer and wrapped in oil paper or tinfoil.

Use about 2 ounces of rennet for each 10 pounds of milk.

SMEAR KASE

Take drained dry cheese and add salt, pepper and milk or cream. Mix until smooth, then spread on bread. May be topped with molasses or applebutter.

CROCK CHEESE

Place a gallon of thickened sour milk on stove. Stir constantly and heat (about 102 degrees) until you can press curds of milk together with the hand. Pour the milk into cheese cloth and thor-

oughly press out whey. Put 2 tablespoons butter in a hot skillet.
Melt, then add the curds, 1 teaspoon soda, salt (approx. 1 teaspoon or according to taste). Stir with a potato masher. Cook
until smooth then add cream or milk to thickness desired. Pour
into a bowl and it is ready to serve.

STINK KASE

Put about 5 cups dry curds in dish. Mix in 1 teaspoon soda and
let stand in a warm room until mold has begun to form over the
top. The older it is, the stronger the flavor. Add 1 teaspoon salt
and then proceed with the same directions as the above cheese, by
heating and adding milk or cream.

MUENSTER CHEESE

2 1/2 gallon sour milk- let set till thick like junket.
Scald till it is too hot to hold your hand in, then pour into cheese
cloth. Let hang until curds are dry — overnight or about 12 hours.
Crumble curds and mix 2 heaping teaspoons soda and 1/2 cup
butter into them. Let set for 2 hours then put in the double boiler.
Add 1 cup sour cream and melt. When melted, add another cup of
sour cream and 1 tablespoon salt. Mix well. Pour into a buttered
mold. Let set until completely cold, and slice.

KRAFT CHEESE

5 gal. skimmed milk

Let sour until thick. Then scald on top of stove until hot enough
that it is uncomfortable for the hand, or that you can squeeze the
whey out of the cheese with the hand. Then strain through cloth
and squeeze real dry.
Put through food grinder, to make fine. Cook the following in a
double boiler until smooth. (Approximately 1 hour or little more.)

5 cups dry cheese	1/2 cup butter
1 tsp. soda	1 to 1 1/2 cups cream or milk
2 tsp. salt	

Stir occasionally while cooling.
To make a softer cheese add more milk. Makes approximately
3 quart.

SPREADING CHEESE

2 1/2 gallon skimmed milk. Let milk sour until it is very thick, then heat until it is too hot to hold your hand in, but not boiling. Drain through a coarse cloth bag, putting only half of the milk through at a time, so as to be able to squeeze out all water possible. (If too hot, hold bag under running water a minute to cool). Put in a bowl and crumble. This makes 4 cups or a little more, of crumbs. Let set at room temperature for 2 to 3 days, or longer if a stronger taste is desired.

To 4 cups crumbs, add 2 tsp. soda and mix. Let stand for about 30 minutes then stir in 1 1/2 cups warm water (scant).

Set bowl in a dishpan of boiling water or use double boiler. Heat the mixture to a boiling point, then stir vigorously. Add 1/3 cup butter, and 2 level tsp. salt. Add 1 cup hot water, a little at a time, stirring after each addition. Cook 10 to 12 minutes longer or until crumbs are mostly dissolved. If necessary, put through a strainer. Stir occasionally until cold. Makes approximately 1 1/2 quart cheese.

* Variation- Use milk instead of water with only 1 tsp. soda. 1 cup hot cream may be added.

CHILD CARE HINTS

*The top of empty powder boxes can be pried lose and cornstarch or Sure-Jel put in to powder the baby.

*To save time sprinkle powder on the baby's diapers when you fold them.

*Mark children's stockings and other clothes with the child's age (not initials). When the garment is passed down it will stay with the child nearest that age.

*Take heavy paper or pasteboard and make animal and fruit patterns for children to trace around. Animal cookie cutters may also be used. Plastic caps make nice toys also and may be strung by the little ones.

*When children are slow in getting ready for school or to go out and do chores, give them so much time then set the timer.

*To keep a baby from tumbling out of a too-low spider walker, put a folded envelope (average-sized envelope will do) in the stop catch and tape it fast. The back and front legs may also be tied together to make it higher.

*When emptying a child's training chair put a drop of Pine Sol cleaner into the empty container each time. This will disinfect and deodorize.

*Into a plastic box gather all kinds of small bottles, popbeads, a collapsible drinking cup, a bright string, large buttoms, etc. Give this to the child only when he sits on the training chair, or when braiding a little girl's hair.

*If your baby is bothered with diaper rash, try adding 2/3 cup vinegar to the last rinse water when washing the diapers.

SEWING HINTS

*The plastic bleach or disinfectant jugs may be used for bonnet boards. These are soft and flexible and almost indestructible. They sew easier than bonnet board. First mark the cutting line with a pencil.

*Sew a blanket on top of your worn out fitted sheets. This keeps the blanket in place in bed. Sheets hardly wear out around the edges.

MISCELLANEOUS RECIPES

DRIED FRUIT AND VEGETABLES

CRACKERS

YEAST

PRETZELS

HOMINY

NOODLES

SYRUPS

PLAY DOUGH

PLANT FOOD

SOAP RECIPES

PASTE FOR SCHOOLS

ROASTING SOYBEANS

BUTCHERING SHEEP

HOME REMEDIES

WALL PAPER CLEANER

JAR YEAST (sourdough)

4 medium-sized potatoes
3 pints boiling water
1 cake yeast, dissolved
  in 1/4 cup water

1/2 cup sugar
1/2 cup bread flour
2 tsp. salt

Pare potatoes and boil in 3 **pints boiling water until soft, then** mash potatoes, or put through strainer. Use the hot water mixture to scald the flour, sugar and salt. Let cool, then add yeast. Set aside to rise. There should be 1 quart of this mixture. (Use 1 cup sourdough (jar yeast) for 1 cake yeast.) Always save 2 cups starter from each baking. To this **add the same** amount of water that was used from the jar and store in a cool place for the next baking. This may be done for a long time, but occasionally a fresh starter needs to be made.

JAR YEAST (yogurt culture)

Heat 1 cup milk to lukewarm, then add 1/8 cake of yeast. Cover and set in a warm place until next day — 24 hours. Take half the liquid and pour in 1 cup warm milk. For 7 days add 1/2 cup warm milk to half the liquid. Always keep the yeast milk at a warm place. On the 7th day use all the yeast milk and add 2 cups warm milk. Let set another 24 hours. Makes 3 cups yogurt starter.

TO MAKE YOGURT

Take 3 tablespoons yogurt culture to 1 qt. warm milk. Set in a warm place (about 100 degrees) until it thickens. Do not serve all of the yogurt but let at least 3 tablespoons remain. To this add 1 pint of milk. Set in a warm place until it thickens, and then it is ready to serve. Repeat this process to make more yogurt from yogurt. Eventually it is necessary to buy fresh yogurt again as a starter.

MAKING YOGURT (from yogurt)

The most economical way is to buy a small jar of freshly made yogurt from the healthfood store. Serve all but about 3 tablespoons for a starter. To this add 1 pint milk heated to 100 degrees. Set at a warm place until it thickens. Then it is yogurt again. You can repeat this process for a long time. Yogurt culture may be bought at a healthfood store, but this can spoil if not used within a certain period of time.

NOODLES

6 egg yolks	3 cups flour (approx.)
6 tbsp. water	1 tsp. salt

Beat egg yolks and water a few minutes. Add flour to make dough stiff as can be worked in. Divide in four balls, roll very thin. Lay separately on a cloth to dry. They are ready to cut when they are almost dry and don't stick together.

METHOD FOR QUICK CUTTING NOODLES

Put as many as 12 sheets of noodles on top of each other when they are dry enough to cut. Roll tightly and cut with a sharp butcher knife. After they are cut, lay them out on a table in a warm place, cover with a cloth and let them dry thoroughly. Store in a tight container.

People have different methods of roasting soybeans. Even if they do not quite agree on the method, they all agree that roasted soybeans are delicious as well as nutritious. Here the different ways of preparing them are all merged into one recipe. The reader can decide his own method of roasting them.

HOW TO ROAST SOYBEANS

Wash the beans in cold water and remove debris. Some soak the beans overnight, some 6 hours, others 3 hours and some only 10 minutes in warm water. Drain well by placing them on a towel. Place soybeans in oil that has been preheated to 375-400 degrees. (They may be put into a colander and then set in the oil.) Cook until soybeans begin to crack in half and float to the top and the oil stops bubbling — some keep them in 3 minutes, others 10 minutes, and still others 20 minutes. Watch closely, for soybeans burn easily. Drain and then add salt. (Add more oil if beans cook dry).
* Some prefer to cover the soybeans with water and then freeze, and thaw them before roasting.

OVEN-ROASTED SOYBEANS

Soak washed soybeans overnight. Boil 1 hour in salted water. Spread in shallow pan, and roast in 350° oven until brown. Sprinkle with salt while warm.

GRAHAM CRACKERS

2 cups sugar	2 cups flour
4 cups graham flour (sifted)	1 cup shortening
1 tsp. soda	1 tsp. baking powder
1 tsp. salt	1 cup milk
1 tsp. vanilla	

Mix, roll thin; cut and prick with fork. Bake in oven 350° until nice and brown.

TEETHING COOKIES

Break 2 eggs into a bowl. Stir in one direction until creamy. Add 1 cup sugar. Continue stirring in the same direction. Gradually stir in 2 to 2 1/2 cups sifted flour into mixture and continue stirring until mixture is stiff. Roll out dough with rolling pin, between 2 lightly floured sheets of wax paper, to a thickness of 3/4 inch. Use a drinking glass and a salt shaker to cut out doughnut shaped cookies. Place cookies on a lightly buttered cookie sheet. Let formed cookie stand overnight (10-12) hours. Bake in preheated oven at 325 degrees until lightly brown and hard. This recipe makes approximately 12 durable and relative crumbproof teething biscuits.

HOW TO DRY CORN

Cook corn for 10 minutes as for roasting ears. Cut from cob. To each gallon cut corn add 3/4 cup sweet cream, 1/2 cup white sugar and salt to taste. Pour into flat pans and place into the oven to dry. Stir often so the corn will dry more evenly.

* The cream and sugar may be omitted.
* DON'T FORGET to leave the oven door partly open when using the oven for drying.

CORN MEAL

Dry nice selected ears of field corn or sweet corn in a slow open-door oven for several days, or until the corn shells easily by hand. The cornmeal is tasty when the corn has been slightly browned. Shell, then take to a mill to have it ground. Put into an oblong pan and bake in a slow oven (275°) for a more toasted flavor. Stir occasionally. Place in a tight container when cool.

CORN MUSH

Bring 3 cups of water to a boil. Make a thickening with 1 cup corn meal, 1 teaspoon salt and 1 cup milk. Add to the boiling water. Stir until it has reached the boiling point, then stir occasionally. Cook for 15 to 20 minutes then pour into a deep baking dish. Cool, then slice and fry.

* To clean the mush kettle after the mush has been poured out, put a cup or two of water into the kettle. Add 1 teaspoon soda. Cover, then bring to the boiling point. Set kettle aside, but keep covered until dishwashing time.

DRIED GREEN BEANS

Cook beans for 15 to 30 minutes or until green color disappears. Spread beans in thin layers on pans. Dry in slow oven at 250^0 until dry. Store in tight container for winter use.

HOW TO USE DRIED BEANS

Fry 1/4 lb. bacon. Pour off grease then add 3 cups dried beans, 1 teaspoon salt and water to cover. Cook until beans are soft and most of the water absorbed.

* Pour boiling water over 2 or 3 cups of dried beans. Let set several hours, then drain. Add water to cover and cook for 1 to 1 1/2 hours. The cooked beans may be added to meat and gravy and vegetables as a one dish meal.

Dried pears are a lunch box treat for children (as are other dried fruit), for they are naturally sweet.

DRIED FRUIT

Pears - Take firm pears, peel, then make small snitz. Dry as other fruit.

Peaches - Cut in quarter, unpeeled, then dry. Can also be mashed, spread in a thin layer on pie plates and dried in the oven. This is called "Peach Leather" and is good for snacks.

Prune plums - Cut in half.   Remove seed. Place on dryer.

Apricot - Cut in half; remove seed, and dry.

Plums - These can be dried but if they get too hot, they become mushy.

Apples - Quarter peeled slices, then lay on dryer. When put through the salad master and dried they make a delicious snack or addition to breakfast cereals.

Elderberries - Can be dried in the sun on a warm, sunny day.
Spread thinly on a sugar bag or a brown paper bag
in a warm, dry, sunny place.

DRIED TOMATOES

Pour boiling water over ripe tomatoes. Let stand a few minutes.
Slip skin off then cut in pieces. Put through the food mill. Fill
greased pie pans about 1/2 full, then put in a slow oven. After
they are dried only a thin layer is left. Fold and put in a dry container. When ready to use, add water and cook up again.

GREEN TOMATOES FOR PIE

1 gallon green tomatoes. Wash and trim out stalks. Slice quite
thin. Add 1/2 crock white sugar. Boil until thick. Add 2 lemons,
thinly sliced, about 15 minutes before removing from stove. These
can be kept in crocks, and just used as needed. I usually add water
to make them thinner before putting into the pie shell. Place crust
on top.

PRESERVING ELDERBERRIES

2 gallons elderberries   4 lbs. sugar
1 pint vinegar

Boil until thick. This can be used for pie. Store in crocks.
Plums can also be cooked this way but they need no vinegar for they
are sour. Water should be added before putting plums into pie
crust.

SOFT PRETZELS

1 envelope yeast   Butter as needed
1 tsp. sugar   4 tsp. baking soda
2 tsp. salt   Coarse salt for sprinkling
4 to 5 cups flour

Dissolve yeast in 1/4 cup warm water. Then stir in an additional cup warm water, and sugar. Pour yeast mixture into bowl; add
salt. Beat in flour to make stiff dough. Knead for 10 minutes (or
until dough is elastic). Place in bowl and spread with butter.
Cover. Let rise 45 minutes or until double. Shape in sticks or
twists. Make 1/2 thickness of desired pretzel. Bring 4 cups
water to boil with baking soda. Drop 3 pretzels in at a time. Boil
1 minute or until they float. Remove and drain. Place on buttered

cookie sheets. Sprinkle with coarse salt. Bake at 475° for 12 minutes or until golden brown.

* To make pretzels crisp, lay them on a cookie sheet and place them in a warm oven 200° for 2 hours.

BATTER FOR DEEP FAT FRYING

1 cup flour	1/4 tsp. salt
2 tsp. baking powder	2/3 cup sweet milk
2 eggs	1 tbsp. melted butter

Sift flour and measure. Add salt and baking powder. Sift again. Add beaten egg yolks, milk, and then the beaten egg whites and melted butter. This is good for fish or cooked chicken. Two batches makes enough for 3 fryers.

HOW TO FREEZE EGGS

Stir up eggs as for scrambled eggs. Freeze 2 or 3 eggs in small containers to use later for baking. Eggs can hardly be used in any other way after they are frozen.

CORN COB SYRUP

6 red corn cobs (washed). Boil 1 hour in 3 quarts of water. Strain, then add 3 lb. brown sugar and water enough to make 3 quarts. Boil until consistency of maple syrup.

Be sure to select clean corn cobs, free from mold. Light colored cobs will make a lighter syrup and give a better flavor.

BURNT SUGAR SYRUP

In a heavy skillet that heats uniformly, pour 2 cups granulated sugar. Melt sugar over low heat, stirring constantly with a wooden spoon to prevent scorching. When sugar becomes a clear brown syrup, remove from heat. Slowly stir in 1 cup boiling water. Return to low heat and stir until syrup is smooth again. Cool, pour into a clean pint jar. Cover tightly and store at room temperature. Keeps 6 to 8 weeks. Makes 1 1/3 cups syrup.

HOW TO BUTCHER SHEEP and tan the hide

The sheep should be skinned at once and the meat cooled. In summer time it can be cooled in a clean water trough. Then soak in Tender Quick according to directions on the box. If you use the brine cure, and cut the meat, turn the meat every morning and evening. The shoulders and "hams" I like to leave whole and put in a plastic bag and use the dry cure.

Cut off as much tallow as you can and melt it down. This can be used for soap making or used with a little camphor and glycerin (melted) and put in jars for chapped hands. We always liked it especially well when husking corn.

The skin should have all the meat and tallow removed. This can be done before or after it is stretched out and tacked upside down on the attic floor. It is then rubbed with equal parts of salt and alum. After it is dry I trim it to make a nice shape and wash it and then comb with a coarse comb. It can then be used for a rug or chair back. About one inch long makes the nicest rug. We always like to have the sheep off pasture at least two weeks before butchering.

TANNING HIDE

2 parts salt   1 part salt peter
1 part Boric acid

Apply to inside part of hide. When salt seems to have disappeared in a day or two, apply again and continue this until no water runs from the hide. Then scrape all loose skin from the inside hide. Put olive oil on to soften it.

SHAMPOO

Flake 1 bar Castile soap. Melt soap in 1 pint boiling water, then cool. Put soap mixture into mixing bowl and add 1 egg. Beat with rotary beater. Put in jar. After it is settled, it is ready for use. This shampoo will keep indefinitely.

HOMEMADE BUBBLE BATH

1 cup powdered dertergent (Dreft is recommended)
2 cups epsom salts

Mix together in a large bowl. Combine 6 drops glycerine and about 5 drops food coloring (optional) and stir into the mixture of salts. Sachet may be added to perfume the bubble bath.

BUBBLE PIPE MIXTURE

Mix: 1 part liquid detergent
     1 part glycerine
     5 parts water
   Makes a generous supply

PLAY DOUGH

2 cups flour	1 cup salt
1/2 cup cornstarch	1 tbsp. salad oil
1 tbsp. powdered alum (get at drugstore)	
2 cups water	

Place all ingredients in a saucepan. Stir constantly over low heat until mixture thickens into dough consistency. Remove from heat and let cool until it can be handled. Place on foil, waxpaper or formica top and knead like bread until smooth. Add food coloring if you wish. Store in airtight container or plastic bag. This recipe keeps for months, is safe and non-toxic. Give the children some cookie cutters, old pans, a table knife and watch them work in their world of pretense. The dough will stay pink longer if the children wash their hands well before playing with it!

PASTE for schools or scrapbooks

1 cup flour (winter wheat is best)	1 tbsp. powdered alum
1 cup sugar	30 drops oil of cloves

Mix the dry ingredients well in double boiler. Make into a smooth paste with 3 cups warm water. Add, as you stir the mixture, one quart boiling water. Cook until clear — like cooked starch. Remove from fire and add oil of cloves. The paste will keep indefinitely. Put into small jars.

FINGER PAINT

You need 1/2 cup soap chips, 6 cups water, 1 cup liquid starch. Some dry tempera paint or chalk or food coloring: Dissolve soap chips in a small amount of water till there are no lumps. Then add liquid starch and rest of the water. Color it with the dry tempera or ground up bits of chalk. Food coloring works but it makes a washed out painting. When you use finger paint you wet the smooth paper (shelf paper is best) and put a glob of paint on it for mushing around — great for making wrapping paper or book covers.

PANTRY PLANT FOOD

Stir:	1 tsp. baking powder	1 tsp. salt petre
	1 tsp. epsom salt	1/2 tsp. household ammonia

Mix with 1 gallon lukewarm water. Give this to plants in place of a regular watering every 4 to 6 weeks. This works very well to perk up house plants, especially vines and ivys.

* Pour hot water over empty egg shells and let set until cool, then pour on plants.

RASPBERRY PLANT FOOD

Mix: 1 gallon wood ashes
      1 gallon lime
      a handful of sulphur

Put a handful to each berry stalk once a month in February, March and April and again when they have small berries, and in the fall.

WINDOW CLEANER

Add a dash of ammonia and 1 tablespoon vinegar to a pint of water. Put in spray bottle.

* Cooked starch — made somewhat thinner than directions — may be put into a spray bottle for SPRAY STARCH.

FURNITURE POLISH

Mix: 1 quart warm water
      2 tbsp. vinegar
      2 tbsp. good cooking oil

Wash furniture off with a rag saturated with the polish, then wipe dry with a soft rag.

WALL PAPER CLEANER

Make a paste of 1 cup flour and 1/2 cup cold water. Add 2 tbsp. salt, 2 tbsp. vinegar and 1 tbsp. kerosene. Cook until mixture loops off pan. Stir constantly until cool. When cold enough knead until smooth, then wrap in wax paper until you wish to use it.

AMAZING CLEANER

1 cup ammonia   1/4 cup baking soda
1/2 cup vinegar   1 gallon water

This is for cleaning walls and for taking off extra varnish.

PAINT AND VARNISH REMOVER

Take equal parts of laundry starch and powdered ammonia. Wet with enough water to moisten then pour boiling water over it, enough to make a thick paste. Rub on thickly and let set a few minutes until paint or varnish loosens then scrape off with knife or pieces of broken glass.

PAINT REMOVAL

Dissolve 1 can of lye in 1 quart of water. In another container, stir 4 heaping tablespoons of cornstarch or flour into 2 quarts of water. Pour starch or flour mixture very slowly into lye solution, stirring continously to make a thick paste without lumps. Rubber gloves will protect your hands when removing paint.

Directions: Swab the paste onto the painted or varnished surface in an even thick coat, using an old brush or rag on stick. Cover only a small section at a time as the paste must be removed as soon as it shows signs of drying. When drying begins scrape off with a putty knife, wire brush or steel wool. The paint or varnish is softened by the lye paste and will come off with it. After the finish has been removed from a section, flush it with water and wipe with weak vinegar solution (2 tbsp. vinegar to 1 pt. water) before starting on the next section.

For best results work on a small section at a time, completely removing all traces of lye paste just as soon as the softened paint has been scraped.

* Paint may also be removed by a lye solution of 1 can of lye in 1 gallon of water. For removal, follow the procedure for lye paste.

Lye solution or paste is not recommended on natural-finish floors or furniture as it may cause discoloration. Do not use on oak or other hardwood floors.

PASTE

A first-class paste that will stick on tin, glass or wood surfaces may be made with lye. Use 3 teaspoons of lye to each pound of flour, mixing with cold water and stirring until free from lumps, after which, bring to a boil.

Try to avoid breathing in lye fumes.

STOVE AND OVEN CLEANER

The following cleaner is just as effective as that bought in stores yet costs only a fraction of the price.

Dissolve 2 heaping tablespoons of lye in 1/2 cup of cold water in a glass jar. In another container stir 1 level tablespoon of cornstarch or flour in 1/2 cup of cold water. Pour starch solution slowly into the warm lye solution, stirring continously. This cleaner may be used immediately or stored in a closed glass jar until required.

Directions: Place a newspaper on the floor under the oven or stove door. Spread cleaner on oven or stove surfaces, using a sponge or cloth tied to a stick, or an old paint brush. Leave for one ot two hours or overnight. Wash off with water and wipe with a weak vinegar solution (2 tablespoons to 1 pint of water).

The cleaner may be used on iron, steel and porcelain enamel surfaces. Do not use on painted surfaces or aluminum. Do not allow it to remain on skin or clothing, wash off with water. Rubber gloves are helpful in preventing irritation of the skin.

Try to avoid breathing in lye fumes.

TOILET HAND SOAP

Wash: 5 pounds of strained grease 2 or 3 times by melting; then pour a quart or more of cold water into the grease. Let it harden, then scrape all sediment from the underside of the cake of grease.

Soak: 1 cup of rolled oats in 2 quarts of rain water overnight.

Dissolve: 1 can of lye, or 1 pound of caustic soda in 3 pints of the rolled oats water.

Put: 3 tablespoons borax in 1 cup of the oat water.

Put: 2 tablespoons white sugar in 1 cup of the oat water.
         When all ingredients are cold and dissolved (Lye heats the water), pour borax and sugar water into the lye water. Stir well. Pour all ingredients slowly into the melted grease. Stir for 10 minutes or until mixture is thick like honey.

Add: 1/2 cup of glycerine
         several drams of oil of bergamot, cloves, citronella, or any scent you prefer. Pour into molds. Cut the next day. Let it harden 2 weeks before using.

LAVA SOAP

Add 1 1/2 lbs. of Mione Hand Soap to the above Toilet Soap when removing from heat. Stir occasionally until fairly thick to keep the Mione from settling to the bottom.

COLD SOAP RECIPE

5 pt. cold water	4 tbsp. white sugar
4 tbsp. ammonia	1/2 cup sal soda
1/2 cup borax	2 oz. glycerine
1 oz. oil of sassafras	2 cans lye
1 box Tide (optional)	

Combine all the above ingredients. Let come to the right temperature (lukewarm). (It is heated by the lye.) Then pour this mixture into 10 lbs. melted lard. Be sure and pour the lye mixture into the lard. (Never pour the lard into the lye.) Stir until it is creamy. Let harden, but cut in pieces before it gets too hard. Use a granite or iron kettle to mix it in.

POWDERED LYE SOAP

Dissolve 1/4 cup borax in 5 1/2 pt. cold soft water. Add 4 1/2 pt. grease, melted just enough to pour. Stir, then gradually add one can dry lye, stirring slowly until it forms soap — about 30 minutes (usually less). Let set in warm place till next day.

COLD HOMEMADE SOAP

1 can lye	1/2 cup powdered borax
3 pt. cold water	1/2 cup turpentine
5 1/2 lb. fat	Blueing

Have lye water cold and fat lukewarm before mixing. Stir until it starts to thicken, then add turpentine and borax. Add blueing enough to tint.

GRANULATED SOAP

1 can lye	3 qts. cold water
3/4 cup Borax	4 1/2 lbs. melted fat

Dissolve lye in cold water in crock or granite dishpan, using wooden spoon to stir. When dissolved, add Borax. Slowly add to melted fat, stirring slowly for 10 to 15 minutes. Continue to stir off and on for 24 hours. The soap will be white and granulated. Spread out into pasteboard boxes or other containers and let dry well for at least a month before using. Store in tight containers.

Here is a very good laundry soap that makes suds in hard water.

FLOATING SOAP

2 qts. of grease   1 can of lye

Dissolve lye in 1 quart of cold water. When both are lukewarm, stir lye into the grease. Immediately add 1/2 cup ammonia (fill cup with cold water), and 1 tablespoon borax dissolved in 1/2 cup cold water, and a little laundry blueing to whiten.

"GO BACK" DROPS (stomach remedy for children)

1 oz. glycerine
1 oz. rain water
10 drops aconite tincture
Directions:

3 to 5 drops twice a day for 3 days. Wait 3 days and repeat dose. This remedy can be mixed by your druggist.

PINEX COUGH SYRUP

From the drugstore get 2 1/2 oz. of Pinex; then make a syrup of 2 cups of granulated sugar and 1 cup of hot water. No cooking needed. Corn syrup or honey can be used instead of sugar and water. Put Pinex into a pint bottle and fill up with syrup. This makes a full pint of cough syrup. Very effective and quick acting. Will not spoil.

REMEDY FOR WHOOPING COUGH

Take 1 lemon, slice thin and add 1/2 pt. flax seed and 1 qt. water. Simmer, but do not boil, for 4 hours. Strain while hot and add 2 oz. honey. If there is less than a pt. of mixture add water to make a pt.
Dose - 1 tablespoon 4 times a day and in addition a dose after each severe fit of coughing.

BRONCHIAL SALVE

3 oz. white rosin (optional)   2 Drams oil of Turpentine
3 oz. bees wax   2 Drams oil of cedar
2 oz. camphor pulverize   1 pt. fresh lard

Melt white rosin and bees wax separately. Melt lard; put lard and bees wax in rosin, stir and put the above ingredients in. Stir till cooled off. To use spread on cloth. Warm cloth with salve well before you apply it to chest. Put a warm flannel cloth on top.

NON-BLISTER MUSTARD PLASTER

Beat the white of an egg, add a little flour, then enough dry mustard to make a soft paste, it should not be too thick. Spread this on an old cotton cloth large enough to fold double. Apply several thicknesses of cloth on top to prevent soiling clothing.

FROST BITE REMEDY

1 oz. olive oil   1 oz. peppermint oil
1 oz. turpentine   1 oz. ammonia

Mix and bottle. Apply a small amount to hands when they are frost bitten, and rub in well.

ANOTHER BUTTER METHOD

Take sweet cream (not sour) and bring it to a boil. Then cool it to room temperature (not real cold). Then churn. This butter will not turn rancid nearly as quickly as the butter made with un-heated cream. Also the buttermilk will not taste sour, so to make good buttermilk, add some lemon juice (reconsituted, bottled) about two teaspoons to a cup. This buttermilk is then good to drink or to use in baking.

TO TURN CIDER INTO VINEGAR

Bring the barrel out of the cellar, and set in the hot sun. Re-move the bung and in its place put a glass bottle, inverted to keep out insects, and give the sun a chance to shine in a little. Add a cupful or so of yeast to hasten the process and if wanted extra sharp, add 2 or 3 quarts of sorgum syrup or N.O. molasses. A few weeks in the open air will change it, then it may again be re-moved to the cellar.

WHO ARE THE AMISH?

WHO THEY ARE HISTORICALLY. The Old Order Amish are the most conservative segment of the Mennonite church. They are direct descendants of the Anabaptists, a group which emerged from the Reformation in Switzerland as early as 1525. The Anabaptists felt that Zwingli, Luther, and the other reformers compromised in their stand, and did not go all the way in bringing the church back to a Scriptural foundation. The Anabaptists differed especially with the popular reformers in that they rejected infant baptism, and insisted that the church was to be a voluntary brotherhood of adult believers. They were the first to teach separation of church and state, an idea otherwise unheard of in those days. For three centuries after their origin, the Anabaptists were persecuted relentlessly by both Protestant and Catholic authorities.

The word Amish comes from Jacob Ammann, the name of an influential bishop of the late 1600's and early 1700's.

WHO THEY ARE TODAY. Driven by persecution from their homes in Switzerland, Germany, and Alsace-Loraine, hundreds of Amish emigrated to North America during a period of 150 years, beginning soon after 1720. Today there are Amish congregations in twenty states and one province. There are no really accurate figures, but the Amish number roughly 25,000 baptized members (baptism occurring around 18 years old) in about 450 church districts. The three largest settlements of Amish (listed in order of size) are in Holmes County, Ohio, Lancaster County, Pennsylvania, and Lagrange County, Indiana.

WHO THEY ARE RELIGIOUSLY.

Brotherhood. The Amish believe in a close-knit brotherhood of believers where there is love and mutual concern for all the members. They do not have a literal community of goods, but help each other voluntarily as the need arises.

They feel the church is responsible to care for its own poor, aged and infirm, (1 Tim. 5:4,8) and accordingly do not accept government subsidies, welfare, child bonus, compensation, or pensions. (1 Thess. 4:11,12).

Nonresistance. The Amish believe that the Christian should not take part in any violence, either in war or in self-defense. Taking the words of Jesus seriously, "Whosoever shall smite thee on thy right cheek, turn to him the other also," they have traditionally chosen to suffer loss or injury rather than to protect themselves by physical force. (Matt. 5:38-42, John 18:36, Romans 12:19-21).

Nonconformity. The Amish feel strongly that the Scriptures teach a distinct separation between the church and the world. They believe it is impossible for a church to maintain its beliefs and values if its members associate freely with people who hold different values, or none at all. In view of this, they have not always unquestioningly accepted all the cultural changes that have been introduced as progress. Therefore they are still driving horses and buggies, not because they think the automobile is wicked in itself, but because they believe the trend of life the automobile brings with it is breaking down the family unit and the basic structure of the community. They dress as they have for centuries, because they do not care to be changing all the time to styles designed to achieve more glamor and less modesty.

Authority of Scriptures. The Amish hold the Bible as the final guide in a changing world. Its teachings are accepted in simple faith.
Many practices that seem quaint or old-fashioned to outsiders are based on Bible principles:
1. Amish women wear a covering on their heads in obedience to the Bible where it says, "Every woman that prayeth or prophesieth with her head uncovered dishonoureth her head." (1 Cor. 11:5).
2. Women do not cut their hair. "It is a shame for a woman to be shorn or shaven." (1 Cor. 11:6).
3. No jewelry is worn. (1 Tim. 2:9-10, 1 Peter 3:3-4).
4. Taking an oath under any circumstances is believed to be contrary to Scriptures: "But above all things, my brethren, swear not." (James 5:12, also Matt. 5:33-34).

320

5. Amish will not go to court to defend themselves, even
when sued unjustly. "Now therefore, there is utterly a
fault among you because ye go to law one with another.
Why do ye not rather take wrong? Why do ye not rather
suffer yourselves to be defrauded?" (1 Cor. 6:7).
6. Membership in world companies or secret societies is
objected to on the basis of such verses as 2 Corinthians
6:14-15.
7. Basic doctrines of salvation as held by the Amish church
include the belief that man by nature is sinful (Rom. 3:23),
needs to repent and be baptized (Acts 2:38), accepting by
grace the atonement of Christ on the cross (Eph. 2:8-9,
Rom. 5:8). They teach that redemption goes hand in hand
with discipleship and self-denial (Luke 9:23, Matt. 20:38).

INDEX

322

328